College 101
A First-Year Reader

John D. Lawry
Marymount College Tarrytown

McGraw-Hill College

Boston, Massachusetts Burr Ridge, Illinois Dubuque, Iowa
Madison, Wisconsin New York, New York San Francisco, California
St. Louis, Missouri

McGraw-Hill College

*A Division of The **McGraw·Hill** Companies*

COLLEGE 101: A FIRST-YEAR READER

This book is printed on acid-free paper.

3 4 5 6 7 8 9 0 DOC/DOC   3 2 1 0

ISBN 0-07-303159-3

Editorial director: *Phillip A. Butcher*
Sponsoring editor: *Sarah Moyers*
Developmental editor: *Alexis Walker*
Marketing manager: *Lesley Denton*
Project manager: *Jim Labeots*
Production supervisor: *Michael R. McCormick*
Cover designer: *Matthew Baldwin*
Compositor: *Shepherd, Inc.*
Typeface: *10/12 Palatino*
Printer: *R.R. Donnelley & Sons Company*

Library of Congress Cataloging-in-Publication Data

College 101 : a first-year reader / [compiled by] John D. Lawry.
    p. cm.
    Includes index.
    ISBN 0-07-303159-3 (alk. paper)
    1. College student orientation—United States. 2. College freshmen—United States. 3. Study skills—United States.
I. Lawry, John D.
LB2343.32.C64 1998
    378.1'98—dc21   98-13918
http://www.mhhe.com

About the Author

JOHN D. LAWRY is professor of psychology at Marymount College Tarry-town and author of *Guide to the History of Psychology* (Littlefield, Adams, 1981; reissue, University Press of America, 1991), and *How to Succeed at School; Letters of a Professor to His Daughter* (Sheed & Ward, 1988; new edition, *May You Never Stop Dancing*, St. Mary's Press, 1998). Studying for the Roman Catholic priesthood, he attended St. Charles Borromeo Seminary in Philadelphia, where he majored in the classics and received his B.A., but he fell in love before he reached ordination. Two years at Duquesne University resulted in an M.A. in general psychology and a teaching position at Marymount College Tarrytown in 1965. Because he enjoyed teaching so much, he went back to school to complete his Ph.D. in educational psychology at Fordham University in 1972. He has been teaching at Marymount ever since, with the exception of a sabbatical year as a lecturer with the University of Maryland in their overseas program from 1978 to 1979, where he taught U.S. military personnel and dependents in Japan and Korea. He has one daughter and plays a mean game of tennis.

For Lili, my daughter,
and for all first-year students everywhere,
present, past, and future

Contents

STARTING OUT: THE JOURNAL—THE JOURNEY

Essay

Poem

Section I
CAMPUS CULTURE

Essays

Students and Teachers   57

Essays

Poem

Short Story

Friendship and Romance   89

Essays

Poem

Community   115

Essays

Section II
PERSONAL DEVELOPMENT

Short Story

Poems

Spiritual Quest   235

Essays

CLOSURE

Essay

Letter

To the Instructor

Dear Instructor,

One of the most challenging and uplifting experiences I have had in my twenty-six-year teaching career was teaching a Freshman Seminar/College 101 course for the first time. I wish you a similar experience!

The idea for this anthology came to me shortly after the publication of my book, *How to Succeed at School: Letters of a Professor to His Daughter*. As a result of the research I did for that book along with my growing interest in the "University 101" movement and attendance at several Freshman Year Experience Annual Meetings at the University of South Carolina and elsewhere, I discovered many of the readings that appear in this book. Most of the readings I have used myself with my General Psychology and College 101 classes with desired effect and enthusiastic response from my students.

This book is designed to stand by itself as a textbook but it can also be used with any of the many fine textbooks emphasizing skills currently available for this kind of course (e.g., *Study Skills For Today's College Student* by Jerold W. Apps, McGraw-Hill, 1990). At the end of each reading you will find four or five discussion questions designed to help in getting a good discussion started. I find the class usually needs only one or two such starters and then they are off and running on their own. You will also notice suggestions for journal entries. I have found the keeping of a journal to be an extremely worthwhile experience for my students. It is an excellent way to get to know them and it provides an opportunity for self-exploration and expression. In fact, I begin the book with the reading, "The Journal," which I have found especially helpful in getting students started on keeping their journals.

While keeping in mind the diversity that exists in the contemporary population of freshmen, and their diverse reading abilities, I have tried to select a variety of articles that address the major issues of the freshman experience from a holistic, student-centered perspective. If any of the readings don't work for you or your students, I would like to hear about it. I would also appreciate any suggestions for new readings.

There are many people I could thank but I will save the tree space by restricting myself to the members of Marymount's Faculty Development Committee and the Academic Dean, Lorna Edmundson, for awarding me two annual consecutive course releases to complete this book; the patient and always helpful librarians at Marymount especially the Director, Sr. Virginia McKenna, RSHM; Lesley Denton, my sponsoring editor at McGraw-Hill for believing in this project when other editors said that it was too risky; the following reviewers, at various stages, who made some excellent suggestions: Dan Berman, University of South Carolina; Rennie Brantz, Appalachian State University; Nancy Brown, Lourdes College; Terry Doyle, Ferris State University; Paula Gibson, Cardinal Stritch College; Stephen Hensley, Marshall University; Eric Hibbison, J. Sargeant Reynolds Community College; Patricia Konal, Blackburn College; Nancy McKinley, Lorraine County Community College; Dale Norton, College of the Sequoias; Alicia Pieper, Kent State University; Josef Raab, University of Southern California; Richard Schmonsky, Columbia-Greene Community College; Harriet Spitzer, New York Institute of Technology; Suzanne Tolliver, University of Cincinnati; Carl Wahlstrom, Genesee Community College; M.C. Ware, SUNY Cortland; Jerry Warner, Northern Kentucky University; and John N. Gardner, friend and colleague at the University of South Carolina, who got me interested in "University 101" in the first place and has given me unfailing encouragement from the very beginning of this project.

Good luck and may all of your students survive and thrive in their freshman year.

Your colleague,

John D. Lawry

Postscript to the Second Edition

This second edition incorporates 19 new readings, which represent a 40 percent revision of the original. Though this is more ambitious than originally planned, there have been so many developments on college campuses (and the world) since the first edition was written in the early 90s that such a major revision was necessary. I hope you agree with the results of the difficult process of selecting which readings to keep and which to replace.

I want to thank the eight consultants who wrote lengthy reviews of the original edition and who made many excellent suggestions for its improvement:

Nejla A. Camponeschi, Hartwick College

Carl M. Wahlstrom, Genesee Community College

Maura L. Ivanick, Syracuse University

Alice L. Trupe, Community College of Allegheny County

William Clark Hartel, Marietta College

David Andrews, Keene State College

Earl J. Ginter, The University of Georgia (Athens)

Rebecca Pollard Cole, Northern Arizona University

I am sincerely indebted to them and I trust their suggestions are reflected in the overall quality of this new edition, including the change in subtitle to "A First-Year Reader." I also want to thank all of the faculty who adopted the original edition and who took the time to write about their experiences and to provide suggestions for improvement.

It has been decided not to produce a new *Instructor's Manual* to accompany this edition but there are copies of the original still available, and I would recommend that you obtain one if you are new to *College 101*. The only substantive change I would add to the pedagogical suggestion in the IM is some information about "the process of council" as a classroom strategy. Fortunately, a new book on the subject has been written by Jack Zimmerman and Virginia Coyle, *The Way of Council* (Bramble Books, 1996). I have written a review of this remarkable book for the journal, *About Campus*, in the March/April 1998 issue.

To the Student

Dear Student,

Like most veteran academics I barely remember my freshman year at college. Although this year marks the 26th year I have been teaching at the college level, I only became interested in the freshman experience when my own daughter, Lili, went off to college in 1985. It was then that I developed a new appreciation of just how difficult the first year of college can be. Somehow both Lili and I survived that first year and she graduated "on time" three years later. But I will never forget the struggles as well as the joys. (Lili tells me that I struggled harder than she did!)

My experience as a teacher and a parent has taught me the importance of a holistic (i.e., the physical, emotional, vocational, and spiritual as well as the intellectual) approach to the freshman year. I hope you will find the advice and the wisdom you need in these pages to give you the best start possible toward the rest of your college career and adult life.

I have used these readings in my own College 101 course and others. These readings are intended to provide various points of view for discussion and reflection. They are not offered as ultimate answers or truths to issues. My students are constantly giving me new articles to read and share with the class. I hope you will do the same.

There was a poster hanging in what was then called an alternative school that I read about. It said: "None of us is as smart as all of us." That is the philosophy that I like to bring to my classes and I would like to extend that invitation to you the student reader as well.

And now it is time to begin the journey toward the fulfillment of your dreams about college.

Bon voyage,

John D. Lawry

Starting Out:
The Journal—The Journey

For the majority of my students in College 101, nothing in the requirements for the course causes more initial resistance than the requirement of keeping a journal. "I hate writing." "How can I be personal if you are going to read it?" "I don't have time to keep a journal," etc. And yet, nothing seems to match the journal in its power to teach self-exploration or, as McCarroll says, "to hear my own story and to search for my part in the story of life." Most students acknowledge this at the end of the course and can't wait for me to read their journals. I strongly recommend, therefore, that you consider keeping a journal, whether it is actually required or not.

My experience has taught me that more often than not my women students have kept a diary sometime during childhood and/or adolescence, whereas it is the exceptional male student who has kept one. Therefore, if you are a female reader, you might not have much trouble keeping a freshman journal. If you are a male reader, it may be difficult at first, but I urge you to keep at it. Our culture does not encourage males to be very introspective, and we pay the price for our ignorance.

If we experience our freshman year as something largely unrelated to who we are as persons, then we have effectively restricted the amount of change that we can expect from our college experience. If you find yourself resisting, think of it as writing the story of your life. What could be more interesting?

In addition to McCarroll's description of journal keeping, I have added the poem "The Journey" by Mary Oliver to the second edition. In addition to underlining the semantic connection between the words "journal" and "journey," I feel it captures some of the sentiment that students experience as they begin "to hear [their] own story."

READING 1

The Journal

Tolbert McCarroll

This is an excerpt from Exploring the Inner World *(1974). The author, psychologist Tolbert McCarroll, University of Oregon '53, describes journal keeping and its tremendous potential for cultivating an inner life.*

You are on a voyage of self-exploration. You need a journal, a log to keep a record of the adventure. The journal is not a place for explaining, for asking or answering why. It is not a diary. It is a log.

On this quest the activities recorded are dreams, fantasy, art, experiences, and similar events. The items are recorded in a simple manner with no comment, editing, or analysis. The journal is a record of what is; not what should be.

There are many other kinds of logs. The master on a ship decides what data to collect, what events to record in the ship's log.

Obtain a good sized notebook. Artists' sketch books are inexpensive and ideal in every way. There is usually an embarrassing moment as you look at your new journal. How do you start? We feel the first entry should be very impressive. Do not use the journal to impress yourself, and certainly not posterity. If nothing else works to break the mystique, rip out the first page. The journal is an existential joke book. It is a place to play, to be free and spontaneous. The journal is you—all of you, including the parts that are not introduced into polite society: the immature you, the dreamer, the child. The journal is the place where they all come together without invitation and without rejection. And you own whatever is there.

There is a haiku by Issa that belongs in the front of every journal:

> He who appears
> before you now—is the Toad
> of this Thicket.

Whatever comes, it's my thicket. My journal is many things to me; above all, it is a companion. It helps me gain self-discipline and keeps my experiences alive.

Discipline is important in this quest. Inner messages are not given to the casual dilettante. Am I really trying to hear myself? This is the basic question. A glance through your journal will tell you whether you are only talking about self-exploration or are actually engaged in the process.

Many of the experiences logged in a journal have a short life span. By your writing them down, their duration is prolonged a few precious moments. The act of recording also allows you to retain some of your emotional involvement each time you return to what you have written.

Each experience is a piece in a puzzle. You could try to work a jigsaw puzzle by using one piece and trying to deduce what the entire puzzle looks like, but it would waste considerable time in unproductive speculation. A better use of your energy and a clearer sense of the picture can be obtained by collecting as many pieces as possible. Each new piece gives additional meaning to the ones already collected. The journal is the table upon which to store and play with the pieces collected.

The discipline of growth is demanding. Its rewards are not always immediate. Why do it? That is the difficult question. If a person is not committed to his own growth, there is no reason to undertake this journey. If you are committed, then you explore your inner world simply because it is a necessary part of you.

It is not always easy to be ourselves. The first step is really to hear what is going on with us. The masks we wear for the benefit of others often deceive us as well. It is important that we learn to be ourselves. We do this by stopping the attempt to be somebody else. There is a wise biblical proverb:

"Drink the water of thy own well."

You must drink your own water, be it bitter or sweet. You must be yourself. If you want to change or grow, you have to accept where you are and be who you are.

The wisdom for growth is within us. Once we have learned really to listen to ourselves we can hear suggestions for our next step. Sometimes there is pain. The wild storms of winter are a necessary preliminary for spring's beauty. Just as bodily discomfort can tell us when we have broken nature's rhythm, the pain in the heart can be a beacon showing us the next step on our journey.

It is through the discipline of keeping a journal that I learn to become me. Without this inner journey, I feel incomplete and lonely. I am conscious of all the "oughts" and "shoulds" of my life. This is not enough. I want to hear from that part of me that never changes and feel those parts that change every second. It feels good to be me and the more me I am the less conscious I am of me.

Each of us is a necessary part of a long story. It would have been nice if we had been taught our place in the story when we were young children, but a while back it seems as if everyone forgot the story. So we all grew up wondering about our value and our worth. We search for a place where we can belong. Now when we are older and it is harder, we must learn that our value is in being who we are and that we belong here. It is through my journal that I begin to hear my own story and to search for my part in the story of life.

DISCUSSION QUESTIONS

1. Have you ever kept a diary or journal and, if so, what was your experience in keeping one?
2. McCarroll writes: "Once we have learned really to listen to ourselves we can hear suggestions for our next step." Can you give an example of where that was true for you? Was it true of your decision to come to this college?

3. What do you think McCarroll means by the phrase "committed to your own growth"?
4. Whether a requirement in this course or not, how do (would) you feel about keeping a journal for a course? Do you think it is a good requirement?

SUGGESTIONS FOR JOURNAL ENTRIES

1. Using the haiku by Issa quoted by McCarroll as an inspiration, write a haiku (three lines containing 5, 7, and 5 syllables respectively) for the beginning of your journal.
2. As a result of reading McCarroll's essay, write out your expectations for keeping a journal for this course.

READING 2

The Journey

Mary Oliver

"The Journey" is a poem about the task of growing up and away from our parents—a process that Jung calls "individuation." Mary Oliver (born 1935) is an acclaimed Pulitzer Prize-winning poet who attended Ohio State University and Vassar College. "The Journey" was collected in Dream Work *(1986).*

One day you finally knew   1
what you had to do, and began,
though the voices around you
kept shouting
their bad advice—   2
though the whole house
began to tremble
and you felt the old tug
at your ankles.
"Mend my life!"   3
each voice cried.
But you didn't stop.
You knew what you had to do,
though the wind pried
with its stiff fingers   4
at the very foundations—
though their melancholy
was terrible.
It was already late
enough, and a wild night,   5
and the road full of fallen
branches and stones.
But little by little,
as you left their voices behind,
the stars began to burn   6
through the sheets of clouds,
and there was a new voice,
which you slowly
recognized as your own,
that kept you company   7
as you strode deeper and deeper
into the world,
determined to do
the only thing you could do—
determined to save   8
the only life you could save.

—Mary Oliver

DISCUSSION QUESTIONS

1. Do you agree with Oliver that your life is "the only life you could save"?
2. Why do you think that Oliver used the metaphor of "the old tug at your ankles"? Why "ankles"?
3. Do you see any similarities between the messages of McCarroll and Oliver? What are they?
4. How did your response to Oliver differ from your response to McCarroll? What does it tell you about the difference between prose and poetry?

SUGGESTIONS FOR JOURNAL ENTRIES

1. Look up the derivations for the words "journal" and "journey," and write about the implications of their semantic origins.
2. Write about the first time you began to hear "a new voice, which you slowly recognized as your own."
3. Write a poem about a journey you have taken, literally or figuratively.

Campus Culture

People who go to college are incredible. We go to classes. We read and absorb and are comprehensively tested on heavy amounts of various materials. We sleep very little. Someone is always sick. Someone is always complaining. We become attached to close friends. We smother each other. We lean too much. We think often of the past and want to go back. We know we cannot. We all have separate lives, families, backgrounds, and pasts. We live totally differently from how we used to live. We are frustrated and sometimes want to give up, but we never stop trying. We are forced to think about the future. We are scared and confused. We reach out for things, yet we don't find them. We try to sort out our minds, which are filled with studies, worries, problems, memories, emotions—powerful feelings. We wander the halls looking for happiness. We hurt—a lot. We keep going though, because, above all else, we never stop learning, growing, changing, and, most important, dreaming. Dreams keep us going and they always will. All we can do is thank God that we have something to hold onto, like dreams and each other.

—Ian Schreuder, University of Colorado–Boulder '99

Whether resident or commuter, young adults or older, all students spend some time at their respective colleges outside as well as inside of the classroom. Each campus has its own unique culture and as Ian Schreuder wrote in his first year of college, "We live totally differently from how we used to live." Every year the "freshmen" challenge that culture and are challenged by it. As a result of that subtle interaction, a new culture emerges—often only by degrees, though sometimes the change is dramatic. For example, one day in the 60s the first-year students at Marymount (the college where I teach) decided to wear jeans to class—and that was the end of the so-called dress code.

But there are some things that are experienced universally (or nearly so), like grades and pressures, friends and lovers. The following entries capture some of that universality as it manifests itself on college campuses toward the end of the 20th century. They will provide you with some important information but also ask you to be critical of what goes on at your college by providing you with diverse points of view from other individuals at other institutions.

ACADEMIC CONCERNS

Since most freshmen have been playing the academic game for much of their lives, they usually come to college with a certain hubris about their ability to do college work. It is usually only after first-semester grades that some humility begins to set in. This section will introduce the reader to some of what I call academic concerns. A light sampling should quickly demonstrate that college is a different ballgame from most high schools.

In fact, this section contains what are possibly the most challenging readings in the entire book. Don't be discouraged if you do not understand everything upon the first reading. The reading level of some of these selections may be higher than anything you have read before. That will probably be true of a lot of what you will have to read during your freshman year. Have confidence that you will begin to understand more as you read more. The important thing is to start reading and keep reading!

The first selection is a list. The list was compiled by me from students in an introductory psychology class who were asked to share the one thing they wished someone had told them before coming to college. See if you agree!

The next selection, "On Becoming a Better Student," by yoga teacher Donna Schuster, discusses what it takes to be a serious student of anything and presents tips on what I call college classroom etiquette. Unfortunately, most American high schools no longer teach good classroom etiquette, so I find I have to spell things out. Good classroom manners are the way we honor each other and the enterprise of learning.

Various feminist scholars have documented how the traditional American university has virtually erased women's experience from the curriculum. Their work resulted in the inauguration of women's studies. The challenge that the feminist perspective can sometimes hold for male students is reported by student Sam Sifton of Harvard in his spirited essay, "John of Arc," in which he sets out to "prove that women's studies isn't just for women."

Getting back to reading, Malcom X makes a strong statement on the importance of reading in "Prison Studies," a moving testament to the power of motivation and the human desire to learn and understand.

In the fifth essay, "Why I Write," Joan Didion writes about the excitement of writing and how writing is a great way to find out what you are thinking (another reason for keeping a journal). In the following essay, "In the Laboratory with Agassiz," Samuel Scudder describes how the great nineteenth-century Harvard biologist taught him how to look with the eyes of a scientist.

In the seventh essay, Professor Earl Shorris writes about the uses and power of a liberal education in the hands and hearts of the "restless poor," in the process challenging many of our stereotypes concerning poor people.

In his "Letter to a B Student," Professor Oliphant discusses the soul-searching that teachers experience when assigning grades and cautions students not to interpret a grade as a "measure of who you are."

In the final essay, Ethan Watters reviews the research of Claude Steele of Stanford University and discusses his provocative findings of "stereotype vulnerability" to explain not only the black-white testing gap but also "gender and white-Asian differences" on math tests.

READING 3

What No One Ever Told Them about College (A Survey)

John D. Lawry

This letter is an excerpt from May You Never Stop Dancing *(1998), a book of letters that I wrote to my daughter Lili when she was a first-year college student, describing a survey of mostly first-year students in a general psychology course at a women's college (Marymount College Tarrytown), on what they wished someone had told them before coming to college.*

Dear Lili,

I conducted a survey recently in my general psychology class of 24 students, mostly freshmen. I asked them to "list five things you wish someone had told you about college before coming to Marymount that you had to learn on your own." I thought you might be interested in the results. The responses are ranked in order of frequency of occurrence (the number in parentheses represents the number of students who have that answer; those without a number had one response each) and are stated in summary form or, in some cases, verbatim.

1. Importance of self-discipline (time management, and so on) (9)
2. Money problems (8)
3. Roommate problems—"Don't expect her to be your best friend!" (6)
4. Amount of responsibility (independence) placed on students (5)
5. Amount of work and time required for studying (4)
6. Heterogeneity of student body (moral standards, social class, and so on) (4)
7. Missing Mom's home cooking (3)
8. Diversity of teaching quality (3)
9. Difficulty attached to registration and course selection (3)
10. Great opportunity for growing up (3)
11. Missing family and friends (3)
12. Learning to get along with so many people (2)
13. Too much walking! (2)
14. I love it! (2)
15. Don't be afraid to get involved (2)
16. People care more than I anticipated
17. The amount of cheating
18. Assertiveness works
19. Importance of library skills
20. Getting a husband seems to be more important than getting an education
21. Students are here because of Daddy

22. No surprises!
23. Need for a car at a residential college
24. What to bring!
25. Importance of attending class
26. Importance of note-taking skills
27. Scary not knowing where I am going
28. Immaturity of the other students
29. Time flies!
30. What to do after college?
31. Don't get sick!
32. Be yourself!
33. Too many requirements!
34. Poor social life
35. The food is good!
36. Not enough washing machines
37. Not enough heat!
38. Not enough hot water for showers!
39. Courses are more interesting than high school
40. Get yourself known by faculty and administrators; they are human too!
41. Difficulty of being a commuter at a residential college
42. Teachers are so nice and helpful
43. Theft in the laundry room

So there you have it, Lil. Let me know what you think and what you can identify with. To self-discipline!

Love,

Dad

DISCUSSION QUESTIONS

1. What was the biggest surprise for you in the list?
2. Do you think the list would be much different for a coed campus? How so?
3. According to your experience, what should be on the list and is not?
4. Is there something on the list that you are resentful about? (In other words, the reality of campus life requires that it be there but it should not have to be there.)

SUGGESTIONS FOR JOURNAL ENTRIES

1. Construct your own list of at least five things that you wished someone had told you about college before coming.
2. Write about one or more of the things on the list that taught you something and what you plan to do as a result.

READING 4

On Becoming a Better Student

Donna Farhi Schuster

A certified yoga teacher and student from the San Francisco Bay Area, Donna Schuster tells about the importance of curiosity, discipline, risk-taking, initiative, and enthusiasm for aspiring students of anything, not just yoga. I especially find her "Tips for the Aspiring Student" helpful because it includes practical things like the importance of being on time and letting your teacher know how much you appreciate him or her, things which most students either never learn or learn belatedly. This article originally appeared in Yoga Journal *in September/October 1987.*

A Zen master invited one of his students over to his house for afternoon tea. After a brief discussion the teacher poured tea into the student's cup and continued to pour until the cup was overflowing

Finally the student said, "Master, you must stop pouring; the tea is overflowing—it's not going into the cup."

"That's very observant of you," the teacher replied. "And the same is true with you. If you are to receive any of my teachings, you must first empty out what you have in your mental cup."

As students we expect a great deal from our teachers. We expect them to be enthusiastic. We expect them to be reliable. We may even have expectations that they be endless repositories of skill and knowledge from which we may partake at will.

As a teacher I have come to feel weighted by these expectations and have begun to see that it is really not possible to teach. All the words and theories and techniques are of no use to students who have yet to open themselves with receptivity and to take it upon themselves to practice. So in a sense I have given up trying to "teach," for I've come to believe that the greatest thing I can offer my students is to help them learn how to find themselves through their own investigation.

Many factors come together to make a fine student. Find someone you think is extraordinary, and you will find many, if not all, of the following qualities. People who learn a great deal in what seems like a very short time embody these qualities.

Curiosity   Such people are tremendously curious. The whole world is of interest to them, and they observe what others do not. Nobel Prize-winning physician Albert Szent-Gyorgyi put it well when he said, "Discovery consists of looking at the same thing as everyone else and thinking something different."[1] With this curiosity comes an "investigative spirit"; the learning is not so much the acquisition of information as it is an investigation—a questioning, a turning over of the object of study to see all sides and facets. It is not knowing in the sense of having a rigid opinion, but the ability to look again at another time, in a different light, as Gyorgyi suggests, and to form a new understanding based on that observation.

One way to develop curiosity is to cultivate "disbelief." By disbelieving what we often take for granted, we begin to investigate and explore on our own. In the process, we stop mindlessly parroting our teachers and begin to find how their understanding works in our own experience. Disbelief can be a major step toward creative exploration. In my own classes I encourage students to investigate, to question my instructions in their own practice. "How does this movement affect my body? What happens if I do it another way? How am I reacting to this posture?" The mere act of saying "What if . . .?" opens a completely new dimension of thought. This kind of questioning has led to some of the most exciting inventions of our time.

Discipline   Any discipline—but especially those with great subtlety and complexity, like yoga or t'ai chi—can be a lifelong pursuit. Persistence, consistency, and discipline are required. Without these, our learning is but froth without substance. There are no shortcuts. The fruit of these seemingly dry qualities (which we prefer to admire in others) is the satisfaction of having tasted the fullness of completion, or the thrill of meeting a difficult challenge with success. Perhaps, though, our culture is in need of redefining what it means to study. If we can look at our chosen discipline or craft as an ongoing process rather than as a discrete accomplishment, the potential for learning can be infinite. With this attitude we may find ourselves treating even the most mundane discovery with wide-eyed wonder and joy.

Almost anyone can recognize when another's understanding has true substance. The admiration we bestow on great dancers, musicians, and artists comes from our sense that these people have stepped into the unknown. When we see something extraordinary, we sense the unexpressed third dimension of our own two-dimensional, limited selves. When we take it upon ourselves to step into the unknown, we stop asking our teachers to give our lives meaning and start asking how we ourselves can bring meaning to all aspects of our lives.

Risk-Taking   Why is it, then, that so few people live up to their true potential? Beyond the well-paved roads and secure structures we usually build for ourselves lie demons, unsure footing—and unfelt pleasures. To be a student is to take risks. Yet most education discourages people from venturing far enough to take risks to make mistakes. "Children enter school as question marks and leave as periods," observes educator Neil Postman. What kind of punctuation mark do you represent? Do you find yourself looking for tidy answers that give you a feeling of security? By learning to find the one right answer, we may have relinquished our ability to find other answers and solutions. We learn, then, not to put ourselves into situations where we might fail, because failure has tremendous social stigma. When we try different approaches and do things that have no precedence in our experience, we will surely make mistakes. A creative person uses these "failures" as stepping stones.

Initiative   Can we begin, then, to see that our teachers are guides on our journey, but that the journey itself is our own responsibility? There is nothing quite so satisfying as undergoing a difficult process and after long hard work discovering the true nature of that process. It could be as simple as throwing a perfect pot, or as complex as formulating a new theory of physics. The satisfaction we feel will be directly proportional to the amount of work we do by ourselves to achieve our goal. Successful students do not expect to be spoon-fed, but take their own initiative. Wanting answers from my teacher has often been a way for me to avoid taking the initiative to discover my own answers through my own practice.

Speaking from the other side of the fence, yoga teacher Dona Holleman helps clarify the teacher's role in this relationship when she says: "Helping the pupil must come as a reward for long and persistent work on the part of the pupil. It should be spare and rare. The pupil should do all the work himself, and then the occasional slight help comes as a 'bonus.'"[2]

Looking at our own unexplored terrain helps to strengthen weak areas and to nurture latent talent to fruition. One teacher who profoundly influenced how I learn was the famous Russian ballet teacher Mia Slavenska. After a quick, steely glance at my dance technique, she announced that I could forget everything I had ever learned because it would be of no use to me. Then for one year she demanded that I lift my leg no higher than twelve inches off the floor so that I would learn how to "move from the right place," instead of merely showing off with displays of outward form. When we give up trying to impress the teacher with what we already know and instead humble ourselves to what we do not know, we enter into learning mode. Mia was rarely impressed by anyone and rarely offered praise, but, when she did, you knew you deserved it! She claimed that it took a good eight to ten years to train an excellent dancer, and her prodigies, many of whom entered renowned companies, showed the exceptional brilliance and truth of the combined dedication of teacher and student.

Enthusiasm   To learn, then, is to open oneself. Jim Spira, director of the Institute for Educational Therapy in Berkeley, California, asks his students to prepare themselves to learn in this way: "Drop your prior knowledge . . . [and] attempt to grasp the new framework in its own context. The student complains, 'But I know what is important.' If what you know is important, then it should be there when you finish the course. If you continually 'hold onto it,' then you'll only see what is presented in terms of the old knowledge/framework and never really grow in new ways."

"Drop your self-image . . . [and] become what you are involved with to the fullest. The student says, 'But what I am is important.' I reply, 'Don't get trapped by what you like and dislike.' Being willing to go through each activity as fully as possible will expand your potential well beyond your present limitations."

When I am lucky enough to meet people like Jim Spira, who live life as explorers, I find myself uplifted by their presence. These people, who inspire all of us, seem to have tapped into a limitless supply of enthusiasm. They excite us, they enlighten us, and we want some of whatever it is they have. The Greek word *enthousiasmos* means "infused with the divine."

We often go to classes because we need the enthusiasm of the teacher to bolster us or push us forward, and then we carry that enthusiasm home with us like a fragile package and often watch it diminish until the next class. But eventually we must find a way to stop resisting our own "infusion of the divine." Advanced students of any discipline are constantly finding new ways to connect with the enthusiastic part of themselves that "wants to do." These are the people who will go beyond replication of their teachers or systems to bring fresh new ideas and an iconoclastic vision to fields that have otherwise become jaded and ingrown.

I do not mean to advocate disrespect or casual regard for teachers. They are great gifts to us, but eventually we must become our own person—and the best teachers will help us move in that direction. By devoting yourself to one teacher, you help that teacher learn how best to help you. At the same time, you can develop trust in your teacher and can begin to understand his or her particular vocabulary. Contrary to the belief that more is better, studying simultaneously with many different teachers and packing in one workshop after another may not be the best way to learn. Don't be a teacher or workshop junkie. If you find that you practice little on your own but take many classes and workshops, it may be time to assess how much you are really learning. Only through practice (by yourself) and time can you assimilate new information. Integrate new concepts and ideas into your practice in a meaningful way before stuffing yourself with more information and techniques.

Finally, as we each advance on our own unique journey, let us live each day as beginners. Being "advanced" has its own pitfalls—among them complacency and pushing or forcing. To go deeper may mean to be still, to progress more patiently, or to devote more time to other areas of our lives as yet green and immature. As F. M. Alexander, of the Alexander technique, once said to his students as they strained and labored, "Give up trying too hard, but never give up."[3]

TIPS FOR THE ASPIRING STUDENT

The information that follows is designed as a guide. The author welcomes correspondence from those who can add to it.

- Be attentive. Teachers will usually go out of their way to help a self-motivated and interested student.
- Be seen. If you want the teacher to know that you are serious, sit or stand in the front of the class. Make eye contact and introduce yourself, either before or after class.

- Be on time. Consistent lateness is a sign of disrespect. If you take your teacher's skills so lightly, why should he or she take you seriously? Missing the beginning of class can also be physically dangerous if you have missed explanations and work meant to prepare you for more difficult movements.
- Be consistent. The quality of any class improves when there is a collective commitment to regular attendance. In this way you can gain a cumulative knowledge and progress at a more rapid pace. On a more practical level, your attendance may be your teacher's livelihood.
- Listen with your whole body. We have come to treat words like the background noise of a radio. Plant words in the pertinent area of your body so that information can be "embodied."
- Appreciate constructive criticism. Remember why you're there—to break through restrictive habit patterns and to change. Teachers usually reserve the most scathing criticism for their most promising students!
- Questions can help clarify and enrich both teacher and student if the student's questions are pertinent. If, on the contrary, the student is asking questions because he or she is late or inattentive, the student is being disrespectful to the teacher and fellow classmates and is consequently lowering the quality of the class. Highly personal questions with little relevance to the subject at hand are best asked after class.
- You have the right to disagree—but you do not always have the right to express it. Sometimes it is appropriate to challenge a teacher. It is unethical, however, to argue with a teacher or to badger a teacher in public. If you thoroughly object to what is being taught, you are free to leave and learn elsewhere.
- Let your teacher know how much you appreciate him or her. Teachers need encouragement like everyone else. Giving them feedback when something has proved particularly beneficial or injurious to you can help them improve the quality of their teaching.

NOTES

1. Roger Vaon Oech, *A Whack on the Side of the Head* (New York: Warner, 1983).
2. Dona Holleman, *Centering Down* (Firenze, Italy: Tipografia Giuntina, 1981).
3. Michael Gelb, *Body Learning* (New York: Delilah Books, 1981).

RESOURCES

Richard Feynman, *"Surely You're Joking, Mr. Feynman"—Adventures of a Curious Character* (New York: Bantam Books, 1985).
Hermann Hesse, *Beneath the Wheel* (New York: Noonday Press, 1969).
Jean Houston, *The Possible Human: A Course in Extending Your Physical, Mental, and Creative Abilities* (Los Angeles: Teacher, 1982).

QUESTIONS FOR DISCUSSION

1. What do you think Szent-Gyorgyi meant in the quote: "Discovery consists of looking at the same thing as everyone else and thinking something different"? Can you give an example from your own experience?
2. Think of some achievement in your life which required a lot of discipline. Do you find that same kind of discipline in your academic accomplishments? If not, why not? How might you cultivate such discipline for the rest of your college career?
3. Do you agree with what Schuster says about your right to disagree with a teacher and the limits she suggests? If not, where would you draw the line?
4. To borrow the analogy of Neil Postman, do you feel more like a question mark or a period at this stage of your academic career? Why?
5. Abraham Maslow, the founder of Humanistic Psychology, used to ask his students at Brandeis University who among them aspired to become great. Very few students ever raised their hands. Would you have raised your hand?

SUGGESTIONS FOR JOURNAL ENTRIES

1. Think of some significant accomplishment in your life. Write about the roles that curiosity, discipline, risk-taking, initiative, and enthusiasm had in bringing about that accomplishment. Were there other things that contributed as well? Write about them also.
2. As you embark upon your college career, reflect back to the kind of high school student you were. Write about the traits you would like to keep as a college student as well as those things you would like to change. Do not hesitate to refer specifically to the Schuster essay for ideas.

READING 5

John of Arc

Sam Sifton

Sam Sifton is a Harvard grad (1988) and presently teaches history in a high school in Brooklyn, New York. This essay describes the transformation of stereotypes that he experienced in a women's studies course ("Women and the Victorian Novel") in a class with eighteen women in his senior year.

I took a women's studies course my senior year of college. I was writing my thesis at the time, and "Women and the Victorian Novel" sounded like a breeze. As it turned out, I probably would have had an easier time in medical school.

When the door closed on the first day of class, I found myself alone with eighteen women. That might not sound so bad, but it terrified me. I'd attended an all-boy high school where my contact with women was limited to occasional Friday night dances. More often than you'd think, I'd been told that women are a distraction, especially in the classroom. Sure, I'd had four years of college to rid me of my dark past, but sitting in that seminar I felt very alone. Was I going to be a token for the first time in my life?

Emphatically yes, I thought when the professor introduced the class by asking, "What do we, as women, think of the Victoria novel?" Slumped in a chair in a corner of the room, I wondered whether, if I was quiet, anyone would see me crawl out. "Sam?" the professor asked, as I looked around furtively. "Is everything all right?"

"I'm sorry," I almost said. "I think I have the wrong room. This isn't Gov. 30, is it?"

But I didn't say anything. Instead I just looked at her blankly. And in that instant my fear changed to defiance. "What do we as *women* think?" I asked sarcastically. "How would I know?" Suddenly I found myself on a mission. I'd take the course and prove that women's studies isn't just for women. I'd look at women's roles in Dickens, Gissing, and Eliot, but I'd retain my male perspective and represent my gender honorably. I left that meeting walking tall.

My bravado didn't last. The only feelings I could muster for class discussions were the anger and sarcasm I'd displayed on the first day. I behaved like Stanley Kowalski in *A Streetcar Named Desire*—frightened, antagonistic, defensive. I bristled every time I thought a classmate was implying that a male author had an ulterior motive for casting a woman in a subservient role. "Charles Dickens did *not* endorse a patriarchal system," I snapped once. "He just happened to prefer families with men in charge."

Once the word got out that I was the only man in a women's studies class, I became a minor celebrity. Guys I hardly knew slapped me on the back and congratulated me on my great new scam: "Reduces competition, huh, dude?" The college's weekly paper tracked me down at a party one Saturday night to interview me. "Hey, I'm no Alan Alda," I told them drunkenly, "but women's studies is all right by me." The glares leveled at me in the next class were as disappointed as they were angry.

As the semester progressed, I relaxed. I stopped seeing myself as the last warrior in the citadel of male power and started learning. I found myself reading everything twice just to be able to defend my point of view in discussion. And I listened extra carefully to everyone so I'd feel on solid ground when I expressed my opinions. You know the old saw that says women have to do twice as much as men just to prove themselves? I understand that better now.

I went into women's studies with a lot of preconceptions. I had thought the class would be militantly anti–male. It wasn't. I'd been sure no one would listen to what the guy had to say. They did. And I had thought the whole notion of women's studies was somehow unimportant. It isn't. Women's studies provides a forum for discussions that's unavailable in traditional academia. You don't, for example, learn much about women's politics in Gov. 30.

My thesis probably suffered for all the time I spent examining women's roles in *Little Dorrit* and *The Mill on the Floss*. That's okay. I got to spend three and a half months with eighteen women I came to respect, learning things about myself, about English literature, and about my hero, Charles Dickens. How many guys from *my* high school can say they did that in college?

DISCUSSION QUESTIONS

1. It's not often that a white male is in the minority ("a token") in situations in this country, especially at a place like Harvard. What does this essay teach about the experience of being the minority, irrespective of race and gender?
2. What do you think of women's studies as an academic discipline? Is it necessary? Has this essay changed your opinion?
3. If Sifton's experience in this women's studies course is typical, why do you think so few males take such courses?

SUGGESTIONS FOR JOURNAL ENTRIES

1. Interview several upperclass students of both genders on their attitudes towards women's studies and write about what you find. Were there any surprises?
2. Write about the stereotypes ("preconceptions") that Sifton had before taking the course and why these stereotypes persist in the culture. Do you feel you share in these stereotypes?

Prison Studies

Malcolm X

Malcolm X (1925–1965) was born Malcom Little in Nebraska and became one of the leaders of the black power movement in the sixties. In prison, he became a Black Muslim and two years before his death, converted to orthodox Islam, the apparent cause of his assassination. He wrote the Autobiography of Malcom X *(1965) with the assistance of author, Alex Haley, of* Roots *fame. This essay is an excerpt from the autobiography and describes the author's struggle and determination to teach himself to read and the resultant power and joy he experiences from that achievement.*

Many who today hear me somewhere in person, or on television, or those who read something I've said, will think I went to school far beyond the eighth grade. This impression is due entirely to my prison studies.

It had really begun back in the Charlestown Prison, when Bimbi first made me feel envy of his stock of knowledge. Bimbi had always taken charge of any conversation he was in, and I had tried to emulate him. But every book I picked up had few sentences which didn't contain anywhere from one to nearly all of the words that might as well have been in Chinese. When I just skipped those words, of course, I really ended up with little idea of what the book said. So I had come to the Norfolk Prison Colony still going through only book-reading motions. Pretty soon, I would have quit even these motions, unless I had received the motivation that I did.

I saw that the best thing I could do was to get hold of a dictionary—to study, to learn some words. I was lucky enough to reason also that I should try to improve my penmanship. It was sad. I couldn't even write in a straight line. It was both ideas together that made me request a dictionary along with some tablets and pencils from the Norfolk Prison Colony school.

I spent two days just riffling uncertainly through the dictionary's pages. I'd never realized so many words existed! I didn't know which words I needed to learn. Finally, to start some kind of action, I began copying.

In my slow, painstaking, ragged handwriting, I copied into my tablet everything printed on that first page, down to the punctuation marks.

I believe it took me a day. Then aloud, I read back, to myself, everything I'd written on the tablet. Over and over, aloud, to myself, I read my own handwriting.

I woke up the next morning, thinking about those words—immensely proud to realize that not only had I written so much at one time, but I'd written words that I never knew were in the world. Moreover, with a little effort, I also could remember what many of these words meant. I reviewed the words whose meanings I didn't remember. Funny thing, from the dictionary first page right now, that "aardvark" springs to my mind. The dictionary had a picture of it, a long-tailed long-eared, burrowing African mammal, which lives off termites caught by sticking out its tongue as an anteater does for ants.

I was so fascinated that I went on—I copied the dictionary's next page. And the same experience came when I studied that. With every succeeding page, I also learned of people and places and events from history. Actually the dictionary is like a miniature encyclopedia. Finally the dictionary's *A* section had filled a whole tablet—and I went on into the *B*'s. That was the way I started copying what eventually became the entire dictionary. It went a lot faster after so much practice helped me to pick up handwriting speed. Between what I wrote in my tablet, and writing letters, during the rest of my time in prison I would guess I wrote a million words.

I suppose it was inevitable that as my word-base broadened, I could for the first time pick up a book and read and now begin to understand what the book was saying. Anyone who has read a great deal can imagine the new world that opened. Let me tell you something; from then until I left that prison, in every free moment I had, if I was not reading in the library, I was reading on my bunk. You couldn't have gotten me out of books with a wedge. Between Mr. Muhammad's teachings, my correspondence, my visitors—usually Ella and Reginald—and my reading of books, months passed without my even thinking about being imprisoned. In fact, up to then, I never had been so truly free in my life . . .

As you can imagine, especially in a prison where there was heavy emphasis on rehabilitation, an inmate was smiled upon if he demonstrated an unusually intense interest in books. There was a sizable number of well-read inmates, especially the popular debaters. Some were said by many to be practically walking encyclopedias. They were almost celebrities. No university would ask any student to devour literature as I did when this new world opened to me, of being able to read and *understand*.

I read more in my room than in the library itself. An inmate who was known to read a lot could check out more than the permitted maximum number of books. I preferred reading in the total isolation of my own room.

When I had progressed to really serious reading, every night at about ten p.m. I would be outraged with the "lights out." It always seemed to catch me right in the middle of something engrossing.

Fortunately, right outside my door was a corridor light that cast a glow into my room. The glow was enough to read by, once my eyes adjusted to it. So when "lights out" came, I would sit on the floor where I could continue reading in that glow.

At one-hour intervals the night guard paced past every room. Each time I heard the approaching footsteps, I jumped into bed and feigned sleep. And as soon as the guard passed, I got back out of bed onto the floor area of that light-glow, where I would read for another fifty-eight minutes—until the guard approached again. That went on until three or four every morning. Three or four hours of sleep a night was enough for me. Often in the years in the streets I had slept less than that.

I have often reflected upon the new vistas that reading opened to me. I knew right there in prison that reading had changed forever the course of my life. As I see it today, the ability to read awoke inside me some long dormant craving to be mentally alive. I certainly wasn't seeking any degree, the way a college confers a status symbol upon its students. My homemade education gave me, with every additional book that I read, a little bit more sensitivity to the deafness, dumbness, and blindness that was afflicting the black race in America. Not long ago, an English writer telephoned me from London, asking questions. One was, "What's your alma mater?" I told him, "Books." You will never catch me with a free fifteen minutes in which I'm not studying something I feel might be able to help the black man . . .

Every time I catch a plane I have with me a book that I want to read— and that's a lot of books these days. If I weren't out here every day battling the white man, I could spend the rest of my life reading, just satisfying my curiosity—because you can hardly mention anything I'm not curious about. I don't think anybody ever got more out of going to prison than I did. In fact, prison enabled me to study far more intensively than I would have if my life had gone differently and I had attended some college. I imagine that one of the biggest troubles with colleges is there are too many distractions, too much panty-raiding, fraternities, and boola-boola and all of that. Where else but in prison could I have attacked my ignorance by being able to study intensely sometimes as much as fifteen hours a day?

DISCUSSION QUESTIONS

1. How do you think Malcolm X became so motivated to learn to read and to read so much? Has reading his story been an inspiration to you?
2. Why is it, do you think, that most college students do not share Malcolm X's motivation and commitment to learning?
3. What do you think Malcolm X means by the distinction between reading and understanding? Why is the word, "understand," italicized in the text?
4. What do you think of Malcolm X's critique of college in the last paragraph? Do you agree or disagree and why?

SUGGESTIONS FOR JOURNAL ENTRIES

1. Write about the importance that reading has had on your education up to now and how you expect that to change or remain the same while you are in college.
2. Write an imaginary interview with Malcolm X on reading and its importance in our lives.

Why I Write

Joan Didion

This essay by California-born Joan Didion, University of California, Berkeley '56, describes the excitement of writing and becoming a writer. Didion has written novels such as Play It as It Lays *(1970) and* Democracy *(1984), essays,* The White Album *(1979); and nonfiction,* Salvador *(1983). In this essay, Didion tells us that she writes to find out what she is thinking and "what is going on in these pictures of my mind." The following essay first appeared in 1976 in the* New York Times Book Review.

Of course I stole the title for this talk from George Orwell. One reason I stole it was that I like the sound of the words: *Why I Write.* There you have three short unambiguous words that share a sound, and the sound they share is this:

I

I

I

In many ways writing is the act of saying *I,* of imposing oneself upon other people, of saying *listen to me, see it my way, change your mind.* It's an aggressive, even a hostile act. You can disguise its aggressiveness all you want with veils of subordinate clauses and qualifiers and tentative subjunctives, with ellipses and evasions—with the whole manner of intimating rather than claiming, of alluding rather than stating—but there's no getting around the fact that setting words on paper is the tactic of a secret bully, an invasion, an imposition of the writer's sensibility on the reader's most private space.

I stole the title not only because the words sounded right but because they seemed to sum up, in a no-nonsense way, all I have to tell you. Like many writers I have only this one "subject," this one "area": the act of writing. I can bring you no reports from any other front. I may have other interests: I am "interested," for example, in marine biology, but I don't flatter myself that you would come out to hear me talk about it. I am not a scholar. I am not in the least an intellectual, which is not to say that when I hear the word "intellectual" I reach for my gun, but only to say that I do not think in abstracts. During the years when I was an undergraduate at Berkeley I tried, with a kind of hopeless late-adolescent energy, to buy some temporary visa into the world of ideas, to forge for myself a mind that could deal with the abstract.

In short I tried to think. I failed. My attention veered inexorably back to the specific, to the tangible, to what was generally considered, by everyone I knew then and for that matter have known since, the peripheral. I would try to contemplate the Hegelian dialectic and would find myself concentrating instead on a flowering pear tree outside my window and the particular way the petals fell on my floor. I would try to read linguistic theory and would find myself wondering instead if the lights were on in the bevatron up the hill. When I say that I was wondering if the lights were on in the bevatron you might immediately suspect, if you deal in ideas at all, that I was registering the bevatron as a political symbol, thinking in shorthand about the military-industrial complex and its role in the university community, but you would be wrong. I was only wondering if the lights were on in the bevatron, and how they looked. A physical fact.

I had trouble graduating from Berkeley, not because of this inability to deal with ideas—I was majoring in English, and I could locate the house-and-garden imagery in *The Portrait of a Lady* as well as the next person, "imagery" being by definition the kind of specific that got my attention—but simply because I had neglected to take a course in Milton. For reasons which now sound baroque I needed a degree by the end of that summer, and the English department finally agreed, if I would come down from Sacramento every Friday and talk about the cosmology of *Paradise Lost,* to certify me proficient in Milton. I did this. Some Fridays I took the Greyhound bus, other Fridays I caught the Southern Pacific's City of San Francisco on the last leg of its transcontinental trip. I can no longer tell you whether Milton put the sun or the earth at the center of his universe in *Paradise Lost,* the central question of at least one century and a topic about which I wrote ten thousand words that summer, but I can still recall the exact rancidity of the butter in the City of San Francisco's dining car, and the way the tinted windows on the Greyhound bus cast the oil refineries around Carquinez Straits into a grayed and obscurely sinister light. In short my attention was always on the periphery, and what I would see and taste and touch, on the butter, and the Greyhound bus. During those years I was traveling on what I know to be a very shaky passport, forged papers: I knew that I was no legitimate resident in any world of ideas. I knew I couldn't think. All I knew then was what I couldn't do. All I knew then was what I wasn't, and it took me some years to discover what I was.

Which was a writer.

By which I mean not a "good" writer or a "bad" writer but simply a writer, a person whose most absorbed and passionate hours are spent arranging words on pieces of paper. Had my credentials been in order I would never have become a writer. Had I been blessed with even limited access to my own mind there would have been no reason to write. I write entirely to find out what I'm thinking, what I'm looking at, what I see and what it means. What I want and what I fear. Why did the oil refineries around Carquinez Straits seem sinister to me in the summer of 1956? Why have the night lights in the bevatron burned in my mind for twenty years? *What is going on in these pictures in my mind?*

When I talk about pictures in my mind I am talking, quite specifically, about images that shimmer around the edges. There used to be an illustration in every elementary psychology book showing a cat drawn by a patient in varying stages of schizophrenia. This cat had a shimmer around it. You could see the molecular structure breaking down at the very edges of the cat: the cat became the background and the background the cat, everything interacting, exchanging ions. People on hallucinogens describe the same perception of objects. I'm not a schizophrenic, nor do I take hallucinogens, but certain images do shimmer for me. Look hard enough, and you can't miss the shimmer. It's there. You can't think too much about these pictures that shimmer. You just lie low and let them develop. You stay quiet. You don't talk to many people and you keep your nervous system from shorting out and you try to locate the cat in the shimmer, the grammar in the picture.

Just as I meant "shimmer" literally I mean "grammar" literally. Grammar is a piano I play by ear, since I seem to have been out of school the year the rules were mentioned. All I know about grammar is its infinite power. To shift the structure of a sentence alters the meaning of that sentence, as definitely and inflexibly as the position of a camera alters the meaning of the object photographed. Many people know about camera angles now, but not so many know about sentences. The arrangement of the words matters, and the arrangement you want can be found in the picture in your mind. The picture dictates the arrangement. The picture dictates whether this will be a sentence with or without clauses, a sentence that ends hard or a dying-fall sentence, long or short, active or passive. The picture tells you how to arrange the words and the arrangement of the words tells you, or tells me what's going on in the picture. *Nota bene:*

It tells you.

You don't tell it.

Let me show you what I mean by pictures in the mind. I began *Play It as It Lays* just as I have begun each of my novels, with no notion of "character" or "plot" or even "incident." I had only two pictures in my mind, more about which later, and a technical intention, which was to write a novel so elliptical and fast that it would be over before you noticed it, a novel so fast that it would scarcely exist on the page at all. About the pictures: the first was of white space. Empty space. This was clearly the picture that dictated the narrative intention of the book—a book in which anything that happened would happen off the page, a "white" book to which the reader would have to bring his or her own bad dreams—and yet this picture told me no "story," suggested no situation. The second picture did. This second picture was of something actually witnessed. A young woman with long hair and a short white halter dress walks through the casino at the Riviera in Las Vegas at one in the morning. She crosses the casino alone and picks up a house telephone. I watch her because I have heard her paged, and recognize her name: she is a minor actress I see around Los Angeles from time to time, in places like Jax and once in a gynecologist's office in the Beverly Hills Clinic, but have never met. I know nothing about her. Who is paging her? Why is she here to be paged? How exactly did she come to this? It was precisely this moment in Las Vegas that made *Play It as It Lays* begin to tell itself to me, but the moment appears in the novel only obliquely, in a chapter which begins:

> Maria made a list of things she would never do. She would never: walk through the Sands or Caesar's alone after midnight. She would never: ball at a party, do S-M unless she wanted to, borrow furs from Abe Lipsey, deal. She would never: carry a Yorkshire in Beverly Hills.

That is the beginning of the chapter and that is also the end of the chapter, which may suggest what I meant by "white space."

I recall having a number of pictures in my mind when I began the novel I just finished, *A Book of Common Prayer*. As a matter of fact one of these pictures was of that bevatron I mentioned, although I would be hard put to tell you a story in which nuclear energy figured. Another was a newspaper photograph of a hijacked 707 burning on the desert in the Middle East. Another was the night view from a room in which I once spent a week with paratyphoid, a hotel room on the Colombian coast. My husband and I seemed to be on the Colombian coast representing the United States of America at a film festival (I recall invoking the name "Jack Valenti" a lot, as if its reiteration could make me well), and it was a bad place to have fever, not only because my indisposition offended our hosts but because every night in this hotel the generator failed. The lights went out. The elevator stopped. My husband would go to the event of the evening and make excuses for me and I would stay alone in this hotel room, in the dark. I remember standing at the window trying to call Bogotá (the telephone seemed to work on the same principle as the generator) and watching the night wind come up and wonder what I was doing eleven degrees off the equator with a fever of 103. The view from that window definitely figures in *A Book of Common Prayer*, as does the burning 707, and yet none of these pictures told me the story I needed.

The picture that did, the picture that shimmered and made these other images coalesce, was the Panama airport at 6 a.m. I was in this airport only once, on a plane to Bogotá that stopped for an hour to refuel, but the way it looked that morning remained superimposed on everything I saw until the day I finished *A Book of Common Prayer*. I lived in that airport for several years. I can still feel the hot air when I step off the plane, can see the heat already rising off the tarmac at 6 a.m. I can feel my skirt damp and wrinkled on my legs. I can feel the asphalt stick to my sandals. I remember the big tail of a Pan American plane floating motionless down at the end of the tarmac. I remember the sound of a slot machine in the waiting room. I could tell you that I remember a particular woman in the airport, an American woman, a *norteamericana*, a thin *norteamericana* about forty who wore a big square emerald in lieu of a wedding ring, but there was no such woman there.

I put this woman in the airport later. I made this woman up, just as I later make up a country to put the airport in, and a family to run the country. This woman in the airport is neither catching a plane nor meeting one. She is ordering tea in the airport coffee shop. In fact she is not simply "ordering" tea but insisting that the water be boiled, in front of her, for twenty minutes. Why is this woman in this airport? Why is she going nowhere; where has she been? Where did she get that big emerald? What derangement, or disassociation, makes her believe that her will to see the water boiled can possibly prevail?

> She had been going to one airport or another for four months, one could see it, looking at the visas on her passport. All those airports where Charlotte Douglas's passport had been stamped would have looked alike. Sometimes the

sign on the tower would say "Bienvenidos" and sometimes the sign on the tower would say "Bienvenue," some places were wet and hot and others dry and hot, but at each of these airports the pastel concrete walls would rust and stain and the swamp off the runway would be littered with the fuselages of cannibalized Fairchild F-227's and the water would need boiling.

"I knew why Charlotte went to the airport even if Victor did not."
"I knew about airports."

These lines appear about halfway through *A Book of Common Prayer*, but I wrote them during the second week I worked on the book, long before I had any idea where Charlotte Douglas had been or why she went to airports. Until I wrote these lines I had no character called "Victor" in mind: the necessity for mentioning a name, and the name "Victor," occurred to me as I wrote the sentence. *I knew why Charlotte went to the airport* sounded incomplete. *I knew why Charlotte went to the airport even if Victor did not* carried a little more narrative drive. Most important of all, until I wrote these lines I did not know who "I" was, who was telling the story. I had intended until that moment that the "I" be no more than the voice of the author, a 19th-century omniscient narrator. But there it was:

"I knew why Charlotte went to the airport even if Victor did not."
"I knew about airports."

This "I" was the voice of no author in my house. This "I" was someone who not only knew why Charlotte went to the airport but also knew someone called "Victor." Who was Victor? Who was this narrator? Why was this narrator telling me this story? Let me tell you one thing about why writers write: had I known the answer to any of these questions I would never have needed to write a novel.

DISCUSSION QUESTIONS

1. Do you agree with Didion that writing is "an aggressive, even a hostile act"?
2. What does Didion mean when she says, "Grammar is a piano I play by ear"?
3. Describe an experience where writing helped you to understand what you were thinking.
4. Is prose the only medium to express the "pictures in your mind"? Which is the way you prefer?

SUGGESTIONS FOR JOURNAL ENTRIES

1. Take a "picture in your mind" and write about what is going on there.
2. The next time you have an intense experience, write about it and see whether the writing helps you to understand its meaning.

READING 8

In the Laboratory with Agassiz

Samuel H. Scudder

After graduating from Williams College in 1857, Samuel H. Scudder (1837–1911) had the good fortune to study with one of America's great scientists and teachers, (Swiss-born) Jean Louis R. Agassiz (1807–1873), at Harvard University. This essay, which was published anonymously in Every Saturday *in 1874, describes the "inestimable" lesson in scientific observation that Scudder received from a legendary teacher.*

It was more than fifteen years ago that I entered the laboratory of Professor Agassiz, and told him I had enrolled my name in the scientific school as a student of natural history. He asked me a few questions about my object in coming, my antecedents generally, the mode in which I afterwards proposed to use the knowledge I might acquire, and finally, whether I wished to study any special branch. To the latter I replied that while I wished to be well grounded in all departments of zoology, I purposed to devote myself specially to insects.

"When do you wish to begin?" he asked.

"Now," I replied.

This seemed to please him, and with an energetic "Very well," he reached from a shelf a huge jar of specimens in yellow alcohol. "Take this fish," said he, "and look at it; we call it a Haemulon; by and by I will ask what you have seen."

With that he left me, but in a moment returned with explicit instructions as to the care of the object entrusted to me.

"No man is fit to be a naturalist," said he, "who does not know how to take care of specimens."

I was to keep the fish before me in a tin tray, and occasionally moisten the surface with alcohol from the jar, always taking care to replace the stopper tightly. Those were not the days of ground glass stoppers, and elegantly shaped exhibition jars; all the old students will recall the huge, neckless glass bottles with their leaky, wax-besmeared corks, half eaten by insects and be-grimed with cellar dust. Entomology was a cleaner science than ichthyology, but the example of the professor, who had unhesitantly plunged to the bottom of the jar to produce the fish, was infectious; and though his alcohol had "a very ancient fish-like smell," I really dared not show any aversion within these sacred precincts, and treated the alcohol as though it were pure water. Still I was conscious of a passing feeling of disappointment, for gazing at a fish did not commend itself to an ardent entomologist. My friends at home, too, were annoyed, when they discovered that no amount of eau de cologne would drown the perfume which haunted me like a shadow.

In ten minutes I had seen all that could be seen in that fish, and started in search of the professor, who had however left the museum; and when I returned, after lingering over some of the odd animals stored in the upper apartment, my specimen was dry all over. I dashed the fluid over the fish as if to resuscitate the beast from a fainting-fit, and looked with anxiety for a return of the normal, sloppy appearance. This little excitement over, nothing was to be done but return to a steadfast gaze at my mute companion. Half an hour passed—an hour—another hour; the fish began to look loathsome. I turned it over and around; looked it in the face—ghastly; from behind, beneath, above, sideways, at a three quarters view—just as ghastly. I was in despair; at an early hour I concluded that lunch was necessary; so, with infinite relief, the fish was carefully replaced in the jar, and for an hour I was free.

On my return, I learned that Professor Agassiz had been at the museum, but had gone and would not return for several hours. My fellow students were too busy to be disturbed by continued conversation. Slowly I drew forth that hideous fish, and with a feeling of desperation again looked at it. I might not use a magnifying glass; instruments of all kinds were interdicted. My two hands, my two eyes, and the fish; it seemed a most limited field. I pushed my finger down its throat to feel how sharp the teeth were. I began to count the scales in the different rows until I was convinced that that was nonsense. At last a happy thought struck me—I would draw the fish; and now with surprise I began to discover new features in the creature. Just then the professor returned.

"That is right," said he; "a pencil is one of the best of eyes. I am glad to notice, too, that you keep your specimen wet and your bottle corked."

With these encouraging words, he added, "Well, what is it like?"

He listened attentively to my brief rehearsal of the structure of parts whose names were still unknown to me; the fringed gill-arches and movable operculum; the pores of the head, fleshy lips, and lidless eyes; the lateral line, the spinous fins, and forked tail; the compressed and arched body. When I had finished, he waited as if expecting more, and then, with an air of disappointment, "You have not looked very carefully; why," he continued, more earnestly, "you haven't even seen one of the most conspicuous features of the animal, which is as plainly before your eyes as the fish itself; look again, look again!" and he left me to my misery.

I was piqued; I was mortified. Still more of that wretched fish! But now I set myself to my task with a will, and discovered one new thing after another, until I saw how just the professor's criticism had been. The afternoon passed quickly, and when, toward its close, the professor inquired, "Do you see it yet?"

"No," I replied, "I am certain I do not, but I see how little I saw before."

"That is next best," said he, earnestly, "but I won't hear you now; put away your fish and go home; perhaps you will be ready with a better answer in the morning. I will examine you before you look at the fish."

This was disconcerting; not only must I think of my fish all night, studying, without the object before me, what this unknown but most visible feature might be; but also, without reviewing my new discoveries, I must give an exact account of them the next day. I had a bad memory; so I walked home by the Charles River in a distracted state, with my two perplexities.

The cordial greeting from the professor the next morning was reassuring; here was a man who seemed to be quite as anxious as I, that I should see for myself what he saw.

"Do you perhaps mean," I asked, "that the fish has symmetrical sides with paired organs?"

His thoroughly pleased, "Of course, of course!" repaid the wakeful hours of the previous night. After he had discoursed most happily and enthusiastically—as he always did—upon the importance of this point, I ventured to ask what I should do next.

"Oh, look at your fish!" he said, and left me again to my own devices. In a little more than an hour he returned and heard my new catalogue.

"That is good, that is good!" he repeated; "but that is not all; go on;" and so for three long days he placed that fish before my eyes, forbidding me to look at anything else, or to use any artificial aid. "Look, look, look," was his repeated injunction.

This was the best entomological lesson I ever had—a lesson, whose influence has extended to the details of every subsequent study; a legacy the professor has left to me, as he left it to many others, of inestimable value, which we could not buy, with which we cannot part.

A year afterward, some of us were amusing ourselves with chalking outlandish beasts upon the museum blackboard. We drew prancing starfishes; frogs in mortal combat; hydra-headed worms; stately crawfishes, standing on their tails, bearing aloft umbrellas; and grotesque fishes with gaping mouths and staring eyes. The professor came in shortly after, and was as amused as any, at our experiments. He looked at the fishes.

"Haemulons, every one of them," he said; "Mr. —— drew them." True; and to this day, if I attempt a fish, I can draw nothing but Haemulons.

The fourth day, a second fish of the same group was placed beside the first, and I was bidden to point out the resemblances and differences between the two; another and another followed, until the entire family lay before me, and a whole legion of jars covered the table and surrounding shelves; the odor had become a pleasant perfume; and even now, the sight of an old, six-inch worm-eaten cork brings fragrant memories!

The whole group of Haemulons was thus brought in review; and, whether engaged upon the dissection of the internal organs, the preparation and examination of the bony frame-work, or the description of the various parts, Agassiz' training in the method of observing facts and their orderly arrangement was ever accompanied by the urgent exhortation not to be content with them.

"Facts are stupid things," he would say, "until brought into connection with some general law."

At the end of eight months, it was almost with reluctance that I left these friends and turned to insects; but what I had gained by this outside experience has been of greater value than years of later investigation in my favorite groups.

DISCUSSION QUESTIONS

1. Why do you think that Agassiz gave Scudder a fish rather than an insect to observe?
2. What did Agassiz mean when he said, "Facts are stupid things until brought into connection with some general law"?
3. How would you describe Agassiz as a teacher? Would you have liked him? Why, or why not?
4. What is the significance of this story with regard to the importance of science in the general curriculum?

SUGGESTIONS FOR JOURNAL ENTRIES

1. Reflect on the importance of science in your own education. Write about what science has taught you in the area of observation.
2. Repeat the experience of the essay preferably using a specimen from a science laboratory. Write about the experience remembering Agassiz' words, ". . . a pencil is one of the best of eyes."

READING 9

On the Uses of a Liberal Education
as a Weapon in the Hands
of the Restless Poor

Earl Shorris

Earl Shorris attended the University of Chicago, 1950–53. He is a writer and contributing editor of Harper's Magazine, *where this essay appeared in 1997. This essay makes a case for the practicality and power of a liberal education and the humanities.*

Next month I will publish a book about poverty in America, but not the book I intended. The world took me by surprise—not once, but again and again. The poor themselves led me in directions I could not have imagined, especially the one that came out of a conversation in a maximum-security prison for women that is set, incongruously, in a lush Westchester suburb fifty miles north of New York City.

I had been working on the book for about three years when I went to the Bedford Hills Correctional Facility for the first time. The staff and inmates had developed a program to deal with family violence, and I wanted to see how their ideas fit with what I had learned about poverty.

Numerous forces—hunger, isolation, illness, landlords, police, abuse, neighbors, drugs, criminals, and racism, among many others—exert themselves on the poor at all times and enclose them, making up a "surround of force" from which, it seems, they cannot escape. I had come to understand that this was what kept the poor from being political and that the absence of politics in their lives was what kept them poor. I don't mean "political" in the sense of voting in an election but in the way Thucydides used the word: to mean activity with other people at every level, from the family to the neighborhood to the broader community to the city-state.

By the time I got to Bedford Hills, I had listened to more than six hundred people, some of them over the course of two or three years. Although my method is that of the *bricoleur,* the tinkerer who assembles a thesis of the bric-a-brac he finds in the world, I did not think there would be any more surprises. But I had not counted on what Viniece Walker was to say.

It is considered bad form in prison to speak of a person's crime, and I will follow that precise etiquette here. I can tell you that Viniece Walker came to Bedford Hills when she was twenty years old, a high school dropout who read at the level of a college sophomore, a graduate of crackhouses, the streets of Harlem, and a long alliance with a brutal man. On the surface Viniece has remained as tough as she was on the street. She speaks bluntly, and even though she is HIV positive and the virus has progressed during her time in prison, she still swaggers as she walks down the long prison corridors. While in prison, Niecie, as she is known to her friends, completed her high school requirements and began to pursue a college degree (psychology is the only major offered at Bedford Hills, but Niecie also took a special interest in philosophy). She became a counselor to women with a history of family violence and a comforter to those with AIDS.

Only the deaths of other women cause her to stumble in the midst of her swaggering step, to spend days alone with the remorse that drives her to seek redemption. She goes through life as if she had been imagined by Dostoevsky, but even more complex than his fictions, alive, a person, a fair-skinned and freckled African-American woman, and in prison. It was she who responded to my sudden question, "Why do you think people are poor?"

We had never met before. The conversation around us focused on the abuse of women. Niecie's eyes were perfectly opaque—hostile, prison eyes. Her mouth was set in the beginning of a sneer.

"You got to begin with the children," she said, speaking rapidly, clipping out the street sounds as they came into her speech.

She paused long enough to let the change of direction take effect, then resumed the rapid, rhythmless speech. "You've got to teach the moral life of downtown to the children. And the way you do that, Earl, is by taking them downtown to plays, museums, concerts, lectures, where they can learn the moral life of downtown."

I smiled at her, misunderstanding, thinking I was indulging her. "And then they won't be poor anymore?"

She read every nuance of my response, and answered angrily, "And they won't be poor no more."

"What you mean is—"

"What I mean is what I said—a moral alternative to the street."

She didn't speak of jobs or money. In that, she was like the others I had listened to. No one had spoken of jobs or money. But how could the "moral life of downtown" lead anyone out from the surround of force? How could a museum push poverty away? Who can dress in statues or eat the past? And what of the political life? Had Niecie skipped a step or failed to take a step? The way out of poverty was politics, not the "moral life of downtown." But to enter the public world, to practice the political life, the poor had first to learn to reflect. That was what Niecie meant by the "moral life of downtown." She did not make the error of divorcing ethics from politics. Niecie had simply said, in a kind of shorthand, that no one could step out of the panicking circumstance of poverty directly into the public world.

Although she did not say so, I was sure that when she spoke of the "moral life of downtown" she meant something that had happened to her. With no job and no money, a prisoner, she had undergone a radical transformation. She had followed the same path that led to the invention of politics in ancient Greece. She had learned to reflect. In further conversation it became clear that when she spoke of "the moral life of downtown" she meant the humanities, the study of human constructs and concerns, which has been the source of reflection for the secular world since the Greeks first stepped back from nature to experience wonder at what they beheld. If the political life was the way out of poverty, the humanities provided an entrance to reflection and the political life. The poor did not need anyone to release them; an escape route existed. But to open this avenue to reflection and politics a major distinction between the preparation for the life of the rich and the life of the poor had to be eliminated.

Once Niecie had challenged me with her theory, the comforts of tinkering came to an end; I could no longer make an homage to the happenstance world and rest. To test Niecie's theory, students, faculty, and facilities were required. Quantitative measures would have to be developed; anecdotal information would also be useful. And the ethics of the experiment had to be considered: I resolved to do no harm. There was no need for the course to have a "sink or swim" character; it could aim to keep as many afloat as possible.

When the idea for an experimental course became clear in my mind, I discussed it with Dr. Jaime Inclán, director of the Roberto Clemente Family Guidance Center in lower Manhattan, a facility that provides counseling to poor people, mainly Latinos, in their own language and in their own community. Dr. Inclán offered the center's conference room for a classroom. We would put three metal tables end-to-end to approximate the boat-shaped tables used in discussion sections at the University of Chicago of the Hutchins era,[1] which I used as a model for the course. A card table in the back of the room would hold a coffeemaker and a few cookies. The setting was not elegant, but it would do. And the front wall was covered by a floor-to-ceiling blackboard.

Now the course lacked only students and teachers. With no funds and a budget that grew every time a new idea for the course crossed my mind, I would have to ask the faculty to donate its time and effort. Moreover, when Hutchins said, "The best education for the best is the best education for us all," he meant it: he insisted that full professors teach discussion sections in the college. If the Clemente Course in the Humanities was to follow the same pattern, it would require a faculty with the knowledge and prestige that students might encounter in their first year at Harvard, Yale, Princeton, or Chicago.

I turned first to the novelist Charles Simmons. He had been assistant editor of *The New York Times Book Review* and had taught at Columbia University. He volunteered to teach poetry, beginning with simple poems, Housman, and ending with Latin poetry. Grace Glueck, who writes art news and criticism for the *New York Times,* planned a course that began with cave paintings, and ended in the late twentieth century. Timothy Koranda, who did his graduate work at MIT, had published journal articles on mathematical logic, but he had been away from his field for some years and looked forward to getting back to it. I planned to teach the American history course through documents, beginning with the Magna Carta, moving on to the second of Locke's *Two Treatises of Government,* the Declaration of Independence, and so on through the documents of the Civil War. I would also teach the political philosophy class.

[1]Under the guidance of Robert Maynard Hutchins (1929–1951), the University of Chicago required year-long courses in the humanities, social sciences, and natural sciences for the Bachelor of Arts degree. Hutchins developed the curriculum with the help of Mortimer Adler, among others; the Hutchins courses later influenced Adler's Great Books program.

Since I was a naïf in this endeavor, it did not immediately occur to me that recruiting students would present a problem. I didn't know how many I needed. All I had were criteria for selection:

Age: 18–35.

Household income: Less than 150 percent of the Census Bureau's Official Poverty Threshold (though this was to change slightly).

Educational level: Ability to read a tabloid newspaper.

Educational goals: An expression of intent to complete the course.

Dr. Inclán arranged a meeting of community activists who could help recruit students. Lynette Lauretig of The Door, a program that provides medical and educational services to adolescents, and Angel Roman of the Grand Street Settlement, which offers work and training and GED programs, were both willing to give us access to prospective students. They also pointed out some practical considerations. The course had to provide bus and subway tokens, because fares ranged between three and six dollars per class per student, and the students could not afford sixty or even thirty dollars a month for transportation. We also had to offer dinner or a snack, because the classes were to be held from 6:00 to 7:30 P.M.

The first recruiting session came only a few days later. Nancy Mamis-King, associate executive director of the Neighborhood Youth & Family Services program in the South Bronx, had identified some Clemente Course candidates and had assembled about twenty of her clients and their supervisors in a circle of chairs in a conference room. Everyone in the room was black or Latino, with the exception of one social worker and me.

After I explained the idea of the course, the white social worker was the first to ask a question: "Are you going to teach African history?"

"No. We'll be teaching a section on American history, based on documents, as I said. We want to teach the ideas of history so that—"

"You have to teach African history."

"This is America, so we'll teach American history. If we were in Africa, I would teach African history, and if we were in China, I would teach Chinese history."

"You're indoctrinating people in Western culture."

I tried to get beyond her, "We'll study African art," I said, "as it affects art in America. We'll study American history and literature; you can't do that without studying African-American culture, because culturally all Americans are black as well as white, Native American, Asian, and so on." It was no use; not one of them applied for admission to the course.

A few days later Lynette Lauretig arranged a meeting with some of her staff at The Door. We disagreed about the course. They thought it should be taught at a much lower level. Although I could not change their views, they agreed to assemble a group of Door members who might be interested in the humanities.

On an early evening that same week, about twenty prospective students were scheduled to meet in a classroom at The Door. Most of them came late. Those who arrived first slumped in their chairs, staring at the floor or greeting me with sullen glances. A few ate candy or what appeared to be the remnants of a meal. The students were mostly black and Latino, one was Asian, and five were white; two of the whites were immigrants who had severe problems with English. When I introduced myself, several of the students would not shake my hand, two or three refused even to look at me, one girl giggled, and the last person to volunteer his name, a young man dressed in a Tommy Hilfiger sweatshirt and wearing a cap turned sideways, drawled, "Henry Jones, but they call me Sleepy, because I got these sleepy eyes—"

"In our class, we'll call you Mr. Jones."

He smiled and slid down in his chair so that his back was parallel to the floor.

Before I finished attempting to shake hands with the prospective students, a waiflike Asian girl with her mouth half-full of cake said, "Can we get on with it? I'm bored."

I liked the group immediately.

Having failed in the South Bronx, I resolved to approach these prospective students differently. "You've been cheated," I said. "Rich people learn the humanities; you didn't. The humanities are a foundation for getting along in the world, for thinking, for learning to reflect on the world instead of just reacting to whatever force is turned against you. I think the humanities are one of the ways to become political, and I don't mean political in the sense of voting in an election but in the broad sense." I told them Thucydides' definition of politics.

"Rich people know politics in that sense. They know how to negotiate instead of using force. They know how to use politics to get along, to get power. It doesn't mean that rich people are good and poor people are bad. It simply means that rich people know a more effective method for living in this society.

"Do all rich people, or people who are in the middle, know the humanities? Not a chance. But some do. And it helps. It helps to live better and enjoy life more. Will the humanities make you rich? Yes. Absolutely. But not in terms of money. In terms of life.

"Rich people learn the humanities in private schools and expensive universities. And that's one of the ways in which they learn the political life. I think that is the real difference between the haves and have-nots in this country. If you want real power, legitimate power, the kind that comes from the people and belongs to the people, you must understand politics. The humanities will help.

"Here's how it works: We'll pay your subway fare; take care of your children, if you have them; give you a snack or a sandwich; provide you with books and any other materials you need. But we'll make you think harder, use your mind more fully, than you ever have before. You'll have to read and think about the same kinds of ideas you would encounter in a first-year course at Harvard or Yale or Oxford.

"You'll have to come to class in the snow and the rain and the cold and the dark. No one will coddle you; no one will slow down for you. There will be tests to take, papers to write. And I can't promise you anything but a certificate of completion at the end of the course. I'll be talking to colleges about giving credit for the course, but I can't promise anything. If you come to the Clemente Course, you must do it because you want to study the humanities, because you want a certain kind of life, a richness of mind and spirit. That's all I offer you: philosophy, poetry, art history, logic, rhetoric, and American history.

"Your teachers will all be people of accomplishment in their fields," I said, and I spoke a little about each teacher. "That's the course. October through May, with a two-week break at Christmas. It is generally accepted in America that the liberal arts and the humanities in particular belong to the elites. I think you're the elites."

The young Asian woman said, "What are you getting out of this?"

"This is a demonstration project. I'm writing a book. This will be proof, I hope, of my idea about the humanities. Whether it succeeds or fails will be up to the teachers and you."

All but one of the prospective students applied for admission to the course.

I repeated the new presentation at the Grand Street Settlement and at other places around the city. There were about fifty candidates for the thirty positions in the course. Personal interviews began in early September.

Meanwhile, almost all of my attempts to raise money had failed. Only the novelist Starling Lawrence, who is also editor in chief of W. W. Norton, which had contracted to publish the book; the publishing house itself; and a small, private family foundation supported the experiment. We were far short of our budgeted expenses, but my wife, Sylvia, and I agreed that the cost was still very low, and we decided to go ahead.

Of the fifty prospective students who showed up at the Clemente Center for personal interviews, a few were too rich (a postal supervisor's son, a fellow who claimed his father owned a factory in Nigeria that employed sixty people), and more than a few could not read. Two home-care workers from Local 1199 could not arrange their hours to enable them to take the course. Some of the applicants were too young: a thirteen-year-old and two who had just turned sixteen.

Lucia Medina, a woman with five children who told me that she often answered the door at the single-room occupancy hotel where she lived with a butcher knife in her hand, was the oldest person accepted into the course. Carmen Quiñones, a recovering addict who had spent time in prison, was the next eldest. Both were in their early thirties.

The interviews went on for days.

Abel Lomas[2] shared an apartment and worked part-time wrapping packages at Macy's. His father had abandoned the family when Abel was born. His mother was murdered by his stepfather when Abel was thirteen. With no one to turn to and no place to stay, he lived on the streets, first in Florida, then back in New York City. He used the tiny stipend from his mother's Social Security to keep himself alive.

[2]Not his real name.

After the recruiting session at The Door, I drove up Sixth Avenue from Canal Street with Abel, and we talked about ethics. He had a street tough's delivery, spitting out his ideas in crudely formed sentences of four, five, eight words, strings of blunt declarations, with never a dependent clause to qualify his thoughts. He did not clear his throat with badinage, as timidity teaches us to do, nor did he waste his breath with tact.

"What do you think about drugs?" he asked, the strangely breathless delivery further coarsened by his Dominican accent. "My cousin is a dealer."

"I've seen a lot of people hurt by drugs."

"Your family has nothing to eat. You sell drugs. What's worse? Let your family starve or sell drugs?'

"Starvation and drug addiction are both bad, aren't they?"

"Yes," he said, not "yeah" or "uh-huh" but a precise, almost formal yes."

"So it's a question of the worse of two evils? How shall we decide?"

The question came up near Thirty-fourth Street, where Sixth Avenue remains hellishly traffic-jammed well into the night. Horns honked, people flooded into the streets against the light. Buses and trucks and taxicabs threatened their way from one lane to the next where the overcrowded avenue crosses the equally crowded Broadway. As we passed Herald Square and made our way north again, I said, "There are a couple of ways to look at it. One comes from Immanuel Kant, who said that you should not do anything unless you want it to become a universal law; that is, unless you think it's what everybody should do. So Kant wouldn't agree to selling drugs *or* letting your family starve."

Again he answered with a formal "Yes."

"There's another way to look at it, which is to ask what is the greatest good for the greatest number: in this case, keeping your family from starvation or keeping tens, perhaps hundreds of people from losing their lives to drugs. So which is the greatest good for the greatest number?"

"That's what I think," he said.

"What?"

"You shouldn't sell drugs. You can always get food to eat. Welfare. Something."

"You're a Kantian."

"Yes."

"You know who Kant is?"

"I think so."

We had arrived at Seventy-seventh Street, where he got out of the car to catch the subway before I turned east. As he opened the car door and the light came on, the almost military neatness of him struck me. He had the newly cropped hair of a cadet. His clothes were clean, without a wrinkle. He was an orphan, a street kid, an immaculate urchin. Within a few weeks he would be nineteen years old, the Social Security payments would end, and he would have to move into a shelter.

Some of those who came for interviews were too poor. I did not think that was possible when we began, and I would like not to believe it now, but it was true. There is a point at which the level of forces that surround the poor can become insurmountable, when there is no time or energy left to be anything but poor. Most often I could not recruit such people for the course; when I did, they soon dropped out.

Over the days of interviewing, a class slowly assembled. I could not then imagine who would last the year and who would not. One young woman submitted a neatly typed essay that said, "I was homeless once, then I lived for some time in a shelter. Right now, I have got my own space granted by the Partnership for the Homeless. Right now, I am living alone, with very limited means. Financially I am overwhelmed by debts. I cannot afford all the food I need . . ."

A brother and sister, refugees from Tashkent, lived with their parents in the farthest reaches of Queens, far beyond the end of the subway line. They had no money, and they had been refused admission by every school to which they had applied. I had not intended to accept immigrants or people who had difficulty with the English language, but I took them into the class.

I also took four who had been in prison, three who were homeless, three who were pregnant, one who lived in a drugged dream-state in which she was abused, and one whom I had known for a long time and who was dying of AIDS. As I listened to them, I wondered how the course would affect them. They had no public life, no place; they lived within the surround of force, moving as fast as they could, driven by necessity, without a moment to reflect. Why should they care about fourteenth century Italian painting or truth tables or the death of Socrates?

Between the end of recruiting and the orientation session that would open the course, I made a visit to Bedford Hills to talk with Niecie Walker. It was hot, and the drive up from the city had been unpleasant. I didn't yet know Niecie very well. She didn't trust me, and I didn't know what to make of her. While we talked, she held a huge white pill in her hand. "For AIDS," she said.

"Are you sick?"

"My T-cell count is down. But that's neither here nor there. Tell me about the course, Earl. What are you going to teach?"

"Moral philosophy."

"And what does that include?"

She had turned the visit into an interrogation. I didn't mind. At the end of the conversation I would be going out into "the free world"; if she wanted our meeting to be an interrogation, I was not about to argue. I said, "We'll begin with Plato: the *Apology,* a little of the *Crito,* a few pages of the *Phaedo* so that they'll know what happened to Socrates. Then we'll read Aristotle's *Nicomachean Ethics.* I also want them to read Thucydides, particularly Pericles' Funeral Oration in order to make the connection between ethics and politics, to lead them in the direction I hope the course will take them. Then we'll end with *Antigone,* but read as moral and political philosophy as well as drama."

"There's something missing," she said, leaning back in her chair, taking on an air of superiority.

The drive had been long, the day was hot, the air in the room was dead and damp. "Oh, yeah," I said, "and what's that?"

"Plato's Allegory of the Cave. How can you teach philosophy to poor people without the Allegory of the Cave? The ghetto is the cave. Education is the light. Poor people can understand that."

At the beginning of the orientation at the Clemente Center a week later, each teacher spoke for a minute or two. Dr. Inclán and his research assistant, Patricia Vargas, administered the questionnaire he had devised to measure, as best he could, the role of force and the amount of reflection in the lives of the students. I explained that each class was going to be videotaped as another way of documenting the project. Then I gave out the first assignment: "In preparation for our next meeting, I would like you to read a brief selection from Plato's *Republic:* the Allegory of the Cave."

I tried to guess how many students would return for the first class. I hoped for twenty, expected fifteen, and feared ten. Sylvia, who had agreed to share the administrative tasks of the course, and I prepared coffee and cookies for twenty-five. We had a plastic container filled with subway tokens. Thanks to Starling Lawrence, we had thirty copies of Bernard Knox's *Norton Book of Classical Literature,* which contained all of the texts for the philosophy section except the *Republic* and the *Nicomachean Ethics.*

At six o'clock there were only ten students seated around the long table, but by six-fifteen the number had doubled, and a few minutes later two more straggled in out of the dusk. I had written a time line on the blackboard, showing them the temporal progress of thinking—from the role of myth in Neolithic societies to *The Gilgamesh Epic* and forward to the Old Testament, Confucius, the Greeks, the New Testament, the Koran, the *Epic of Son-Jara,* and ending with Nahuatl and Maya poems, which took us up to the contact between Europe and America, where the history course began. The time line served as context and geography as well as history: no race, no major culture was ignored. "Let's agree," I told them, "that we are all human, whatever our origins. And now let's go into Plato's cave."

I told them that there would be no lectures in the philosophy section of the course; we would use the Socratic method, which is called maieutic dialogue. "'Maieutic' comes from the Greek word for midwifery. I'll take the role of midwife in our dialogue. Now, what do you mean by that? What does a midwife do?"

It was the beginning of a love affair, the first moment of their infatuation with Socrates. Later, Abel Lomas would characterize that moment in his no-nonsense fashion, saying that it was the first time anyone had ever paid attention to their opinions.

Grace Glueck began the art history class in a darkened room lit with slides of the Lascaux caves and next turned the students' attention to Egypt, arranging for them to visit the Metropolitan Museum of Art to see the Temple of Dendur and the Egyptian Galleries. They arrived at the museum on a Friday evening. Darlene Codd brought her two-year-old son. Pearl Lau was late, as usual. One of the students, who had told me how much he was looking forward to the museum visit, didn't show up, which surprised me. Later I learned that he had been arrested for jumping a turnstile in a subway station on his way to the museum and was being held in a prison cell under the Brooklyn criminal courthouse. In the Temple of Dendur, Samantha Smoot asked questions of Felicia Blum, a museum lecturer. Samantha was the student who had burst out with the news, in one of the first sessions of the course, that people in her neighborhood believed it "wasn't no use goin' to school, because the white man wouldn't let you up no matter what." But in a hall where the statuary was of half-human, half-animal female figures, it was Samantha who asked what the glyphs meant, encouraging Felicia Blum to read them aloud, to translate them into English. Toward the end of the evening, Grace led the students out of the halls of antiquities into the Rockefeller Wing, where she told them of the connections of culture and art in Mali, Benin, and the Pacific Islands. When the students had collected their coats and stood together near the entrance to the museum, preparing to leave, Samantha stood apart, a tall, slim young woman, dressed in a deerstalker cap and a dark blue peacoat. She made an exaggerated farewell wave at us and returned to Egypt—her ancient mirror.

Charles Simmons began the poetry class with poems as puzzles and laughs. His plan was to surprise the class, and he did. At first he read the poems aloud to them, interrupting himself with footnotes to bring them along. He showed them poems of love and of seduction, and satiric commentaries on those poems by later poets. "Let us read," the students demanded, but Charles refused. He tantalized them with the opportunity to read poems aloud. A tug-of-war began between him and the students, and the standoff was ended not by Charles directly but by Hector Anderson. When Charles asked if anyone in the class wrote poetry, Hector raised his hand.

"Can you recite one of your poems for us?" Charles said.

Until that moment, Hector had never volunteered a comment, though he had spoken well and intelligently when asked. He preferred to slouch in his chair, dressed in full camouflage gear, wearing a nylon stocking over his hair and eating slices of fresh cantaloupe or honeydew melon.

In response to Charles's question, Hector slid up to a sitting position. "If you turn that camera off," he said. "I don't want anybody using my lyrics." When he was sure the red light of the video camera was off, Hector stood and recited verse after verse of a poem that belonged somewhere in the triangle formed by Ginsberg's *Howl*, the Book of Lamentations, and hip-hop. When Charles and the students finished applauding, they asked Hector to say the poem again, and he did. Later Charles told me, "That kid is the real thing." Hector's discomfort with Sylvia and me turned to ease. He came to our house for a small Christmas party and at other times. We talked on the telephone about a scholarship program and about what steps he should take next in his education. I came to know his parents. As a student, he began quietly, almost secretly, to surpass many of his classmates.

Timothy Koranda was the most professorial of the professors. He arrived precisely on time, wearing a hat of many styles—part fedora, part Borsalino, part Stetson, and at least one-half World War I campaign hat. He taught logic during class hours, filling the blackboard from floor to ceiling, wall to wall, drawing the intersections of sets here and truth tables there and a great square of oppositions in the middle of it all. After class, he walked with students to the subway, chatting about Zen or logic or Heisenberg.

On one of the coldest nights of the winter, he introduced the students to logic problems stated in ordinary language that they could solve by reducing the phrases to symbols. He passed out copies of a problem, two pages long, then wrote out some of the key phrases on the blackboard. "Take this home with you," he said, "and at our next meeting we shall see who has solved it. I shall also attempt to find the answer."

By the time he finished writing out the key phrases, however, David Iskhakov raised his hand. Although they listened attentively, neither David nor his sister Susana spoke often in class. She was shy, and he was embarrassed at his inability to speak perfect English.

"May I go to blackboard?" David said. " And will see if I have found correct answer to zis problem."

Together Tim and David erased the blackboard; then David began covering it with signs and symbols. "If first man is earning this money, and second man is closer to this town . . .," he said, carefully laying out the conditions. After five minutes or so, he said, "And the answer is: B will get first to Cleveland!"

Samantha Smoot shouted, "That's not the answer. The mistake you made is in the first part there, where it says who earns more money."

Tim folded his arms across his chest, happy. "I shall let you all take the problem home," he said.

When Sylvia and I left the Clemente Center that night, a knot of students was gathered outside, huddled against the wind. Snow had begun to fall, a slippery powder on the gray ice that covered all but a narrow space down the center of the sidewalk. Samantha and David stood in the middle of the group, still arguing over the answer to the problem. I leaned in for a moment to catch the character of the argument. It was even more polite than it had been in the classroom, because now they governed themselves.

One Saturday morning in January, David Howell telephoned me at home. "Mr. Shores," he said, anglicizing my name, as many of the students did.

"Mr. Howell," I responded, recognizing his voice.

"How you doin', Mr. Shores?"

"I'm fine. How are you?"

"I had a little problem at work."

Uh-oh, I thought; bad news was coming. David is a big man, generally good-humored but with a quick temper. According to his mother, he had a history of violent behavior. In the classroom he had been one of the best students, a steady man, twenty-four years old, who always did the reading assignments and who often made interesting connections between the humanities and daily life. "What happened?"

"Mr. Shores, there's a woman at my job, she said some things to me and I said some things to her. And she told my supervisor I had said things to her, and he called me in about it. She's forty years old and she don't have no social life, and she's jealous of me."

"And then what happened?" The tone of his voice and the timing of the call did not portend good news.

"Mr. Shores, she made me so mad, I wanted to smack her up against the wall. I tried to talk to some friends to calm myself down a little, but nobody was around."

"And what did you do?" I asked, fearing this was his one telephone call from the city jail.

"Mr. Shores, I asked myself, 'What would Socrates do?'"

David Howell had reasoned that his co-worker's envy was not his problem after all, and he had dropped his rage.

One evening, in the American History section, I was telling the students about Gordon Wood's ideas in *The Radicalism of the American Revolution*. We were talking about the revolt by some intellectuals against classical learning at the turn of the eighteenth century, including Benjamin Franklin's late-life change of heart, when Henry Jones raised his hand.

"If the Founders loved the humanities so much, how come they treated the natives so badly?"

I didn't know how to answer this question. There were confounding explanations to offer about changing attitudes toward Native Americans, vaguely useful references to views of Rousseau and James Fenimore Cooper. For a moment I wondered if I should tell them about Heidegger's Nazi past. Then I saw Abel Lomas's raised hand at the far end of the table, "Mr. Lomas," I said.

Abel said, "That's what Aristotle means by incontinence, when you know what's morally right but you don't do it, because you're overcome by your passions."

The other students nodded. They were all inheritors of wounds caused by the incontinence of educated men; now they had an ally in Aristotle, who had given them a way to analyze the actions of their antagonists.

Those who appreciate ancient history understand the radical character of the humanities. They know that politics did not begin in a perfect world but in a society even more flawed than ours: one that embraced slavery, denied the rights of women, practiced a form of homosexuality that verged on pedophilia, and endured the intrigues and corruption of its leaders. The genius of that society originated in man's re-creation of himself through the recognition of his humanness as expressed in art, literature, rhetoric, philosophy, and the unique notion of freedom. At that moment, the isolation of the private life ended and politics began.

The winners in the game of modern society, and even those whose fortune falls in the middle, have other means to power: they are included at birth. They know this. And they know exactly what to do to protect their place in the economic and social hierarchy. As Allan Bloom, author of the nationally best-selling tract in defense of elitism, *The Closing of the American Mind*, put it, they direct the study of the humanities exclusively at those young people who "have been raised in comfort and with the expectation of ever increasing comfort."

In the last meeting before graduation, the Clemente students answered the same set of questions they'd answered at orientation. Between October and May, students had fallen to AIDS, pregnancy, job opportunities, pernicious anemia, clinical depression, a schizophrenic child, and other forces, but of the thirty students admitted to the course, sixteen had completed it, and fourteen had earned credit from Bard College. Dr. Inclán found that the students' self-esteem and their abilities to divine and solve problems had significantly increased; their use of verbal aggression as a tactic for resolving conflicts had significantly decreased. And they all had notably more appreciation for the concepts of benevolence, spirituality, universalism, and collectivism.

It cost about $2,000 for a student to attend the Clemente Course. Compared with unemployment, welfare, or prison, the humanities are a bargain. But coming into possession of the faculty of reflection and the skills of politics leads to a choice for the poor—and whatever they choose, they will be dangerous: they may use politics to get along in a society based on the game, to escape from the surround of force into a gentler life, to behave as citizens, and nothing more; or they may choose to oppose the game itself. No one can predict the effect of politics, although we all would like to think that wisdom goes our way. That is why the poor are so often mobilized and so rarely politicized. The possibility that they will adopt a moral view other than that of their mentors can never be discounted. And who wants to run that risk?

On the night of the first Clemente Course graduation, the students and their families filled the eighty-five chairs we crammed into the conference room where classes had been held. Robert Martin, associate dean of Bard College, read the graduates' names. David Dinkins, the former mayor of New York City, handed out the diplomas. There were speeches and presentations. The students gave me a plaque on which they had misspelled my name. I offered a few words about each student, congratulated them, and said finally, "This is what I wish for you: May you never be more active than when you are doing nothing . . ." I saw their smiles of recognition at the words of Cato, which I had written on the blackboard early in the course. They could recall again too the moment when we had come to the denouement of Aristotle's brilliantly constructed thriller, the *Nicomachean Ethics*—the idea that in the contemplative life man was most like God. One or two, perhaps more of the students, closed their eyes. In the momentary stillness of the room it was possible to think.

The Clemente Course in the Humanities ended a second year in June 1997. Twenty-eight new students had enrolled; fourteen graduated. Another version of the course will begin this fall in Yucatán, Mexico, using classical Maya literature in Maya.

On May 14, 1997, Viniece Walker came up for parole for the second time. She had served more than ten years of her sentence, and she had been the best of prisoners. In a version of the Clemente Course held at the prison, she had been my teaching assistant. After a brief hearing, her request for parole was denied. She will serve two more years before the parole board will reconsider her case.

A year after graduation, ten of the first sixteen Clemente Course graduates were attending four-year colleges or going to nursing school; four of them had received full scholarships to Bard College. The other graduates were attending community college or working full-time. Except for one: she had been fired from her job in a fast-food restaurant for trying to start a union.

DISCUSSION QUESTIONS

1. Do you agree with the explanation that this essay affords with regard to the causes of poverty in America? Why or why not?
2. Have you or anyone in your family ever experienced what Shorris calls the "surround of force"?
3. Had you ever heard the term "humanities" before coming to college? What did you think it meant when you first heard it?
4. What is the lesson in this essay for first-year college students?

SUGGESTIONS FOR JOURNAL ENTRIES

1. Interview five college classmates (not in this class) and ask them why they think people are poor.
2. Write about an experience in which you had to become "political" in Thucydides' sense, and discuss what you learned from it.

READING 10

Letter to a B Student

Robert Oliphant

This entry is a sensitive and thoughtful letter from Robert Oliphant, Washington & Jefferson '38, English professor at California State University at Northridge, to a student on keeping perspective on grades. It appeared in Liberal Education *in 1986.*

Your final grade for the course is *B*. A respectable grade. Far superior to the "Gentleman's *C*" that served as the norm a couple of generations ago. But in those days *A*'s were rare: only about two out of twenty-five, as I recall. Whatever our norm is, it has shifted upward, with the result that you're probably disappointed at not doing better. I'm certain that nothing I can say will remove that feeling of disappointment, particularly in a climate where grades determine eligibility for graduate school and special programs.

Disappointment. It's the stuff bad dreams are made of: dreams of failure, inadequacy, loss of position and good repute. The essence of success is that there's never enough of it to go round in a zero-sum game where one person's winning must be offset by another's losing, one person's joy offset by another's disappointment. You've grown up in a society where, according to the gospel of Vince Lombardi, winning is not the most important thing—it's the only thing. To lose, to fail, to go under, to go broke—these are deadly sins in a world where prosperity in the present is seen as a sure sign of salvation in the future. In a different society, your disappointment might be something you could shrug away. But not in ours.

My purpose in writing you is to put your disappointment in perspective by considering exactly what your grade means and doesn't mean. I do not propose to argue here that grades are unimportant. Rather, I hope to show you that your grade, taken at face value, is apt to be dangerously misleading, both to you and to others.

As a symbol on your college transcript, your grade simply means that you have successfully completed a specific course of study, doing so at a certain level of proficiency. The level of your proficiency has been determined by your performance of rather conventional tasks: taking tests, writing papers and reports, and so forth. Your performance is generally assumed to correspond to the knowledge you have acquired and will retain. But this assumption, as we both know, is questionable; it may well be that you've actually gotten much more out of the course than your grade indicates—or less. Lacking more precise measurement tools, we must interpret your *B* as a rather fuzzy symbol at best, representing a questionable judgment of your mastery of the subject.

Your grade does not represent a judgment of your basic ability or of your character. Courage, kindness, wisdom, good humor—these are the important characteristics of our species. Unfortunately they are not part of our curriculum.

But they *are* important: crucially so, because they are always in short supply. If you value these characteristics in yourself, you will be valued—and far more so than those whose identities are measured only by little marks on a piece of paper. Your *B* is a price tag on a garment that is quite separate from the living, breathing human being underneath.

The student as performer; the student as human being. The distinction is one we should always keep in mind. I first learned it years ago when I got out of the service and went back to college. There were a lot of us then: older than the norm, in a hurry to get our degrees and move on, impatient with the tests and rituals of academic life. Not an easy group to handle.

One instructor handled us very wisely, it seems to me. On Sunday evenings in particular, he would make a point of stopping in at a local bar frequented by many of the GI-Bill students. There he would sit and drink, joke, and swap stories with men in his class, men who had but recently put away their uniforms and identities: former platoon sergeants, bomber pilots, corporals, captains, lieutenants, commanders, majors—even a lieutenant colonel, as I recall. They enjoyed his company greatly, as he theirs. The next morning he would walk into class and give these same men a test. A hard test. A test on which he usually flunked about half of them.

Oddly enough, the men whom he flunked did not resent it. Nor did they resent him for shifting suddenly from a friendly gear to a coercive one. Rather, they loved him, worked harder and harder at his course as the semester moved along, and ended up with a good grasp of his subject—economics. The technique is still rather difficult for me to explain; but I believe it can be described as one in which a clear distinction was made between the student as classroom performer and the student as human being. A good distinction to make. A distinction that should put your *B* in perspective—and your disappointment.

Perspective. A point of view. The ability to see the big picture—*sub specie aeternitatis,* as our predecessors used to put it. The recognition that human beings, despite differences in class and educational labeling, are fundamentally hewn from the same material and knit together by common bonds of fear and joy, suffering and achievement. Warfare, sickness, disasters public and private—these are the larger coordinates of life. To recognize them, as did Justice Oliver Wendell Holmes as a young man during the Civil War, is to recognize that social labels are basically irrelevant and misleading. It is true that these labels are necessary in the functioning of a complex society as a way of letting us know who should be trusted to do what, with the result that we need to make distinctions on the basis of grades, degrees, rank, and responsibility. But these distinctions should never be taken seriously in human terms, either in the way we look at others or in the way we look at ourselves.

Even in achievement terms, your *B* label does not mean that you are permanently defined as a B achievement person. I'm well aware that *B* students tend to get *B*'s in the courses they take later on, just as *A* students tend to get *A*'s. But academic work is a narrow, neatly defined highway compared to the unmapped rolling country you will encounter after you leave school. What you have learned may help you find your way about at first; later on you will have to shift for yourself, locating goals and opportunities in the same fog that hampers us all as we move toward the future.

The future. Heaven knows what you're going to be doing twenty years from now—or how well you're going to be doing it. On the basis of my experience, I'm very reluctant to make any predictions regarding the subsequent achievement of *B* students. One of my *B* students is now a prominent sportscaster on a local TV station; another is a successful professional writer; a third, I recently discovered, is in Washington running the country. In this connection, may I remind you of a *B*-quality actor with a provincial education who subsequently attained a position of great eminence. Whatever the forces are that produce a Shakespeare or a Reagan, they certainly cannot be charted with exactitude. So I feel you should view your *B* as a small disappointment, not as a permanent tattoo reading, "Born to Lose."

Born to lose. Born to win. I suspect there's a certain amount of consistency in our lives: a consistency that requires the stoic in us to accept the cards heredity and environment deal us, even though we sometimes feel the deck has been stacked in advance. But I've never been able to predict how various hands will be played over a period of years. I've known a number of very bright people who turned out to be nonpracticing geniuses. I've also known a number of people who surprised me greatly by what they did later on: a musician who is now managing director of a great symphony orchestra, an encyclopedia salesman who is now a well-known actor (85 percent recognition level, according to the statistical surveys). Loser or winner, I've never been able to pick them very well, particularly on the basis of achievement or lack of achievement early in life.

Nor am I alone in my clumsiness in making predictions of future success. In *They All Went to College*, Robert Havighurst studied the subsequent careers of a large group of college graduates, concluding that those who "just sat there" in class ended up doing just as well as their academic superiors—with the exception of the rare Phi Beta Kappa varsity athlete. More recently, Christopher Jencks reached the conclusion in *Who Gets Ahead* that academic performance in high school correlated poorly with subsequent economic success, as opposed to personality inventories measuring such intangibles as self-motivation and persistence. The only thing grades do is to predict *other grades*. Beyond that, there's not much point in taking them seriously as indicators of how well you're going to be doing twenty years from now. Motivation, persistence, flexibility of mind, the ability to bounce back from disappointment— these are the great intangibles you need to have going for you. Along with a fair share of good luck to put you in the right place at the right time.

Success as a human being. Success in material things further on down the road. Your *B* neither measures nor predicts matters like these. All that it represents is a small, fallible judgment of your performance in one particular course of study. To interpret it as anything more would be a mistake; to grieve over it would be a harmful distraction from the other tasks that lie before you in a life where final judgments necessarily come at the end, as Solon wisely pointed out to Croesus. Only in academic life are there final examinations and final grades. And as I have tried to show, their value is much less than we like to think. The grades, the prizes, the awards, the scholarships, the fellowships, the grants—we all take them far more seriously than we should, particularly when matched against the unpredictability of what actually lies ahead for us.

I hope that what I've said here assuages your feelings of disappointment. Reviewing it, I suspect that much of my preaching sounds like just another celebration of the American myth of opportunity. As a young person I encountered many such celebrations: Russell Conwell's *Acres of Diamonds*, Elbert Hubbard's *Message to Garcia*, Dale Carnegie's *How to Win Friends and Influence People*. Their sermons were pretty close to mine: conquer your disappointment, be cheerful, dig in and do your best, brighten the corner where you are, work hard, and success will come your way. Pretty trite stuff. Especially during the middle of the Great Depression—a period when it took the economy more than ten years to bring the gross national product back to where it had been in 1929. Today we would call it shucking and jiving: nice to listen to but not something to be taken seriously.

Despite its limitations, our myth of opportunity is still worth taking seriously. It's true that circumstances, education, and native ability often determine what we do with our lives. But it's also true that our society is still reasonably mobile—far more so than is the case in Europe. More important, our myth of opportunity insures that we are psychologically mobile: able to dream of moving up, able to imagine ourselves doing something other than what we're doing. To the European, the gas station attendant is a creature slotted and ticketed for that task in "the station in life to which the Lord has been pleased to call us"—as the Book of Common Prayer put it. To an American, on the other hand, the gas station attendant is a person in motion: stopping over on the way to another job, another life, a business of his or her own, even an advanced degree. While our myth of opportunity may not give us a very accurate picture of how society actually works, it gives us a true picture of ourselves as moving constantly from the present into the future. It's an action picture: more like a film than a static portrait.

The film is not without its drawbacks. Disappointment, failure, self-doubt, regrets over opportunities, missed or misused—these are always the lot of the person in motion, which is why we must never forget the natural human bond that holds us all together and puts each grief into a common store of experience. For those in motion, these griefs are the inevitable consequence of ambition, particularly in a competitive society such as ours.

Many of us today are rather ambivalent about the virtues of a competitive society, particularly one that celebrates material success and celebrity status. In view of these questionable virtues, we have tried to substitute security and reassurance for the loss of self-esteem that comes from not getting an *A*, not getting a promotion, not getting a Mercedes or a Porsche, not getting an appearance on the Johnny Carson show. As a result I am tempted to assuage your disappointment by changing your grade, thereby brightening your life—at least temporarily.

Such a change, I'm afraid, might do far more harm than good in the long run. In my experience, unmerited approval carries with it the risk of seriously distorting a young person's perception of reality: seeing the world as a far more benign place than it actually is, and seeing the self as more able, more competent, than is truly the case. This kind of distortion can be very crippling for the person in motion, giving a false picture of accomplishment that makes the inevitable jolts later on bruising and injurious.

I know your *B* comes as a jolt. Not enough to make you break your stride, I hope. I also hope our perceptions of the course mesh well enough so that the grade seems fair to you. Most of all, I hope that what I've said helps you to understand the limitations of any grade as a measure of who you are and what you can do. It's a symbol, a mark on a piece of paper. Nothing more.

Years ago, our high school principal wrote, as was customary then, a short message to the graduating class for the school yearbook. She was a formidable woman: white-haired, gimlet-eyed, quiet and precise in her manner. Her message to us was: "I believe the class of 1942 will go forward, and as they go forward, achieve."

Not a bad message, I've always felt. Hopeful, encouraging; but qualified just enough to let us know we shouldn't take ourselves too seriously (the "I believe" is certainly less fulsome than "I am sure"). A good way of wishing us all luck in the years to come. May you have your fair share of it as you move along. And may you find strength somewhere to endure whatever disappointments come your way—symbolic and actual.

DISCUSSION QUESTIONS

1. Debate the advantages and disadvantages of having the present grading system in college. Is it the best possible system? What would be better, if any?
2. Do you think that most students and teachers are able to keep clear the distinction between "student as classroom performer and student as human being"? How might teachers help students with this?
3. What do you make of the fact that college grades do not seem to correlate very well with success after graduation?
4. Do you agree with Oliphant about the degree of "mobility" in this country?

SUGGESTIONS FOR JOURNAL ENTRIES

1. Imagine you have just received Oliphant's letter. Write a personal letter in response describing how you feel.
2. Write about an experience you have had where you received a lower grade than you thought you deserved, what you did about it, and what happened as a result.

READING 11

Claude Steele Has Scores to Settle

Ethan Watters

"Claude Steele . . ." is a report by a social science writer on a Stanford professor of social psychology who is researching the effect of "stereotype vulnerability" on the test-taking performance of various groups of college students. This report appeared in The New York Times Magazine *in 1995.*

Gathered here at the Harris School of Public Policy at the University of Chicago on this warm morning is an unusually interdisciplinary group of two dozen academic heavyweights. Hailing from the nation's most elite departments of education, economics, public policy, social psychology and sociology, these scholars have come together to discuss the hot topic of the year. Inspired by last year's controversial book "The Bell Curve," the question today is: Why do African-Americans score significantly worse on standardized tests than whites? As people take their seats around the long wood table, one professor silently reads down the list of presenters, leans to a colleague and asks, "Who's this Claude Steele from Stanford?"

"I don't know," the other says. Looking around the room they locate Steele by name tag. Across the table, Steele, wearing a dark tweed jacket, striped dress shirt and tie, shuffles some papers in preparation for his talk.

"Oh, maybe he's that black essayist," the first professor suggests. "Why would he be presenting here? Some literary angle perhaps?"

Although Steele can't hear the exchange, it would not surprise him that he was mistaken for his estranged brother, the well-known conservative author Shelby Steele. The two are identical twins, right down to their closely trimmed peppered mustaches.

A professor of social psychology, Steele, 49, has a different take than the other scholars presenting today. While they have tried to find an answer to the black-white testing gap by analyzing factors like economic status, family structure and educational opportunities, Steele has looked into the test-taking situation itself and has found new evidence of "a beast" stalking black test takers.

"Our idea," Steele says to the group, "was that whenever black students concentrate on an explicitly scholastic task, they risk confirming their group's negative stereotype. This extra burden, in situations with certain characteristics, can be enough to drag down their performance. We call this burden stereotype vulnerability."

In the first experiment Steel describes, he and Joshua Aronson from the University of Texas gave two groups of black and white Stanford undergraduates a test composed of the most difficult verbal-skills questions from the Graduate Record Exam. Before the test, one group was told that the purpose of the exercise was only to research "psychological factors involved in solving verbal problems," while the other group was told that the exam was "a genuine test of your verbal abilities and limitations."

"This is what we found," Steele says, placing a transparency onto the overhead projector. As the information in the bar charts sinks in, people sit up in their chairs. There are several audible "hmmms," a muffled "wow!" Then a professor at the back of the room asks: "Did you give the groups the same test?"

Steele smiles and says, "Yes." The question speaks to the startling nature of the results. As the graphs indicate, the blacks who thought they were simply solving problems performed as well as the whites (who performed equally in both situations). However, the group of black students who labored under the belief that the test could measure their intellectual potential performed significantly worse than all the other students.

Steele's idea of stereotype vulnerability is not that the student consciously or unconsciously accepts the stereotype (as other social scientists have speculated), but rather, as Steele says, that they have to contend with this whisper of inferiority at the moment when their mental abilities are most taxed. In trying not to give credence to the stereotype, Steele theorizes, the students may redouble their efforts only to work too quickly or inefficiently. The cues that can spark the vulnerability can be subtle—like suggesting the test can measure ability or making students mark down their races before the test begins. While there might be no perceptible bias in a given test or in the test-taking situation, an exam might still be weighted against blacks because the possibility of performing badly has a more devastating meaning.

As Steele goes on to describe his experiments—more than a dozen over the last four years—the audience remains riveted. With his colleague Steve Spencer at Hope College, he has run eight additional experiments showing that stereotype vulnerability can negatively affect women who believe a given math test shows "gender differences." The negative impact of stereotype vulnerability has even appeared in white men who took a difficult math test after being told that Asians tended to outperform whites on that particular exam.

"Have you told anyone about this work?" one professor asks Steele after the conference. "The ramifications are enormous." Janellen Huttenlocher, a professor of psychology at the University of Chicago, says, "I've never heard of him but his work is fascinating." Glenn Loury, an African-American Boston University economist, adds, "He hit a home run." The professor who didn't know who Steele was an hour ago is now whispering to a colleague, "So how did we miss him in our hiring searches?"

A few weeks after the Chicago conference in June, Steele takes the afternoon to further explain his work during a walk in the grassy hills behind his Stanford home. Steele has the patient demeanor of a teacher taking time with a student after class. Handsome and engaging, he is a favorite among the graduate students at the Stanford psychology department.

He began his research on the psychological aspects of race in 1987 while studying the dropout rates of black students at the University of Michigan, where he had just taken a position. This was the year before his brother entered the bitter national debate over race with two essays, one in Harper's and the other in Commentary. Over the next several years, his brother became a prominent commentator and collected his essays into the best-selling book

"The Content of Our Character: A New Vision of Race in America," in which he argued that blacks must stop trying to gain power by claiming victim status.

At Michigan, Steele found a puzzle in the statistics on the performance of black students that drew his interest. According to university data, no matter how well qualified a black student was at a given level, he or she was more likely than an equally qualified white student to fall behind at the next level of achievement. Steele figured that the more well known factors like discrimination, bad schools, broken homes and the poverty and crime that disproportionately damage black communities couldn't fully account for the plight of highly motivated, middle-class African-Americans. "Black students with 1,300 S.A.T. scores were going home from college with 2.4 G.P.A.'s," Steele says. "When I realized that the smartest black students were having these terrible troubles, I figured something else was going on."

After talking with students, Steele decided that the answer was not a lack of a desire to succeed. Nor could he find significant overt or covert racism on the part of the school. He began formulating theories on how the ebbs and flows of anxiety and confidence that all students experience might be exaggerated in black students by the deeper currents in a racially focused society.

As Steele describes it, stereotype vulnerability is a "patient predator" that affects black students not just in testing situations, but in every area of their academic lives. "At each new proving ground the problem can re-emerge," Steele says. "The student who has risen above the stereotype in high school— proving to everyone that he is smart—goes off to college, where a new level of performance is expected."

Eventually, even minor failures—a lapse in grammar while talking to a professor—can discourage. At some point, students may begin to "disidentify" or pull away from the challenge of school.

But Steele doesn't just want to explain away the overall poor showing of black students. "One of the thrills of doing this research," Steele says, "is that I can provide an optimistic take without being political—it's in the results." The results he's referring to are not the ones that demonstrate that stereotype vulnerability exists, but those that show that it disappears with the subtlest of changes. Take away the situational clues that make the setting racially charged (like having to identify race before the exam), and the vulnerability can vanish from the student's performance. If this vulnerability can be consistently kept at bay, Steele says, the downward spiral may never start.

Detractors are hard to find, partly because the research hasn't yet had wide circulation. Steele presented his findings last month in New York at the American Psychological Association's annual meeting. A paper, co-written by Aronson, is being published this fall by the association's Journal of Personality and Social Psychology. A few fellow academics strike a pose of reserved interest. "As with most experimental work, it is hard to judge the magnitude of the effect in real-life testing situations," says Sandra Scarr, the Commonwealth Professor of Psychology at the University of Virginia. "Still, it's novel work." Even Charles Murray, co-author of "The Bell Curve," which argued that blacks were intellectually inferior to other races, is inclined to give it some credence. "I think he probably has hold of something that might be one source of poor academic performance among blacks," Murray says. "The question I have is whether you can extend this theory to tests that exclusively measure cognitive functioning. I doubt he can. I wish him well though. I think it's fascinating stuff."

While Steele's experiments thus far have focused on tests that measure both learning and intelligence—verbal G.R.E. tests for African-Americans and math tests for women—he intends to try his theory on the various I.Q. and cognitive ability tests to which Murray refers.

How Steele and his theories will fare in this national dialogue he's entering remains to be seen. So far, Steele reports that most people he has explained the idea of stereotype vulnerability to have had something of an "aha!" reaction, which is often followed by what he calls the "I knew-it-all-along phenomenon." Stereotype vulnerability is a seductive idea with breathtakingly broad implications.

"I think much of what is mistaken for racial animosity in America today is really stereotype vulnerability," he says. "Imagine a black and a white man meeting for the first time. Because the black person knows the stereotypes of his group, he attempts to deflect those negative traits, finding ways of trying to communicate, in effect, 'Don't think of me as incompetent.' The white, for his part, is busy deflecting the stereotypes of his group: 'Don't think of me as a racist.' Every action becomes loaded with the potential of confirming the stereotype, and you end up with two people struggling with these phantoms they're only half aware of. The discomfort and tension is often mistaken for racial animosity."

The parallel is instructive. The white person who has felt how much energy it takes to communicate the message "I am not the racist person you might think I am" can perhaps also understand how distracting such an effort might be during a standardized test. Following the idea of white vulnerability, he says he can even explain something of the current frustration with racial issues.

"Many whites are just like the black kid in the school situation," Steele says. "When racial issues become frustrating—when there are setbacks—the suspicions about their sincerity re-emerge. If they feel that, in continuing to try, they will only give more evidence to the conclusion that they are really racist, they'll eventually want to withdraw. That is what is happening: the whole thing has become too loaded, and we're seeing whites walking away."

DISCUSSION QUESTIONS

1. Steele seems to be saying that all groups are susceptible to "stereotype vulnerability." Do you agree? Why or why not?
2. Can you think of an example of how "stereotype vulnerability" has affected your own performance?

3. Do you agree with the implication of this report that it is important to talk about these issues (in class), even though difficult?
4. Do you agree with Steele's final conclusion that "the whole (racial) thing has become too loaded"? If so, what can be done to unload it?

SUGGESTIONS FOR JOURNAL ENTRIES

1. Write about an experience of how a "negative stereotype" relating to a group you belong to (based on gender, race, religion, ethnicity, etc.) affected your performance.
2. Experiment with creating for yourself a "positive stereotype" (sometimes called an "affirmation") to overcome some negative one that you may have been exposed to. Write about what happens as you begin to make this shift.

STUDENTS AND TEACHERS

Student-teacher relationships at the college level are a topic that has not been written about very much until recently. Now, it seems that there is a proliferation of articles that address the question of the student-teacher relationship and its impact upon the learning process from both points of view. As the new research on persistence in college shows, one of the best predictors of ultimate success in college is whether a student finds a faculty member who is willing to serve as a mentor or guide. As the readings that follow suggest, teachers can make all the difference in college, especially for first-year students.

As you read through these stories about teachers and by teachers, think about the teachers you have had in grammar school and high school. Was there anyone who made a difference in your life? What were the qualities that this teacher possessed? As you begin the arduous process of selecting courses, inquire about the teachers offering them as you look for a guide to help steer you through the maze of the next four years.

The section begins with the personal stories of two eminent adults and the power of a teacher to teach hate and shame or love and acknowledgment. The first account is by the black comedian Dick Gregory about a primary grade schoolteacher who ridiculed him and his family in front of his classmates and how he turned off school at the age of seven as a result. The second account, by the social scientist/philosopher Jean Houston, describes how a visiting professor at Columbia University acknowledged her brightness and rescued her from a devastating belated sophomore slump.

Michael Kantor in the third essay candidly talks about the sexual attraction that sometimes occurs between teacher and student and how it almost compromised his position as a "lonely" TA (teaching assistant) at UC @ San Diego University.

In the last essay, "Doc" Louis Schmier quotes from one of his student's journals in which she writes about how he helped her to see the folly of marijuana addiction because he cared enough to confront her, and to begin believing in herself.

In the classic poem, "Theme for English B," Langston Hughes writes about the possibility of reciprocal learning between a black student and white professor. Finally, Rebecca Lee, in her short story, "The Banks of the Vistula," narrates how a first-year student learns a hard lesson about plagiarism and telling the truth from a linguistics professor.

Shame

Dick Gregory

Dick Gregory (born 1932) has had many careers in his lifetime, beginning with setting records for the mile and half-mile in track at Southern Illinois University in 1953. From there he went on to become a popular black comedian in the fifties and sixties. During this time, he became political and was active in the civil rights and antiwar movements. He has written many books, the most famous of which are Nigger *(1964) and the controversial* Dick Gregory's Natural Diet for Folks Who Eat: Cookin' with Mother Nature *(1973). The following excerpt comes from a chapter in* Nigger *entitled, "Not Poor, Just Broke," in which he tells of a misguided elementary schoolteacher who taught him hate and shame instead of love and self-confidence.*

I never learned hate at home, or shame. I had to go to school for that. I was about seven years old when I got my first big lesson. I was in love with a little girl named Helene Tucker, a light-complected little girl with pigtails and nice manners. She was always clean and she was smart in school. I think I went to school then mostly to look at her. I brushed my hair and even got me a little old handkerchief. It was a lady's handkerchief, but I didn't want Helene to see me wipe my nose on my hand. The pipes were frozen again, there was no water in the house, but I washed my socks and shirt every night. I'd get a pot, and go over to Mister Ben's grocery store, and stick my pot down into his soda machine. Scoop out some chopped ice. By evening the ice melted to water for washing. I got sick a lot that winter because the fire would go out at night before the clothes were dry. In the morning I'd put them on, wet or dry, because they were the only clothes I had.

Everybody's got a Helene Tucker, a symbol of everything you want. I loved her for her goodness, her cleanness, her popularity. She'd walk down my street and my brothers and sisters would yell. "Here comes Helene," and I'd rub my tennis sneakers on the back of my pants and wish my hair wasn't so nappy and the white folks' shirt fit me better. I'd run out on the street. If I knew my place and didn't come too close, she'd wink at me and say hello. That was a good feeling. Sometimes I'd follow her all the way home, and shovel the snow off her walk and try to make friends with her Momma and her aunts. I'd drop money on her stoop late at night on my way back from shining shoes in the taverns. And she had a Daddy, and he had a good job. He was a paper hanger.

I guess I would have gotten over Helene by summertime, but something happened in that classroom that made her face hang in front of me for the next twenty-two years. When I played the drums in high school it was for Helene and when I broke track records in college it was for Helene and when I started standing behind microphones and heard applause I wished Helene could hear it, too. It wasn't until I was twenty-nine years old and married and making money that I finally got her out of my system. Helene was sitting in that classroom when I learned to be ashamed of myself.

It was on a Thursday. I was sitting in the back of the room, in a seat with a chalk circle drawn around it. The idiot's seat, the troublemaker's seat.

The teacher thought I was stupid. Couldn't spell, couldn't read, couldn't do arithmetic. Just stupid. Teachers were never interested in finding out that you couldn't concentrate because you were so hungry, because you hadn't had any breakfast. All you could think about was noontime, would it ever come? Maybe you could sneak into the cloakroom and steal a bite of some kid's lunch out of a coat pocket. A bite of something. Paste. You can't really make a meal of paste, or put it on bread for a sandwich, but sometimes I'd scoop a few spoonfuls out of the paste jar in the back of the room. Pregnant people get strange tastes. I was pregnant with poverty. Pregnant with dirt and pregnant with smells that made people turn away, pregnant with cold and pregnant with shoes that were never bought for me, pregnant with five other people in my bed and no Daddy in the next room, and pregnant with hunger. Paste doesn't taste too bad when you're hungry.

The teacher thought I was a troublemaker. All she saw from the front of the room was a little black boy who squirmed in his idiot's seat and made noises and poked the kids around him. I guess she couldn't see a kid who made noises because he wanted someone to know he was there.

It was on a Thursday, the day before the Negro payday. The eagle always flew on Friday. The teacher was asking each student how much his father would give to the Community Chest. On Friday night, each kid would get the money from his father, and on Monday he would bring it to the school. I decided I was going to buy me a Daddy right then. I had money in my pocket from shining shoes and selling papers, and whatever Helene Tucker pledged for her Daddy I was going to top it. And I'd hand the money right in. I wasn't going to wait until Monday to buy me a Daddy.

I was shaking, scared to death. The teacher opened her book and started calling out names alphabetically.

"Helene Tucker?"

"My Daddy said he'd give two dollars and fifty cents."

"That's very nice, Helene. Very, very nice indeed."

That made me feel pretty good. It wouldn't take too much to top that. I had almost three dollars in dimes and quarters in my pocket. I stuck my hand in my pocket and held onto the money, waiting for her to call my name. But the teacher closed her book after she called everybody else in the class.

I stood up and raised my hand.

"What is it now?"

"You forgot me."

She turned toward the blackboard. "I don't have time to be playing with you, Richard."

"My Daddy said he'd . . ."

"Sit down, Richard, you're disturbing the class."

"My Daddy said he'd give . . . fifteen dollars."

She turned around and looked mad. "We are collecting this money for you and your kind, Richard Gregory. If your Daddy can give fifteen dollars you have no business being on relief."

"I got it right now, I got it right now, my Daddy gave it to me to turn in today, my Daddy said . . ."

"And furthermore, she said, looking right at me, her nostrils getting big and her lips getting thin and her eyes opening wide, "we know you don't have a Daddy."

Helene Tucker turned around, her eyes full of tears. She felt sorry for me. Then I couldn't see her too well because I was crying, too.

"Sit down, Richard."

And I always thought the teacher kind of liked me. She always picked me to wash the blackboard on Friday, after school. That was a big thrill, it made me feel important. If I didn't wash it, come Monday the school might not function right.

"Where are you going, Richard?"

I walked out of school that day, and for a long time I didn't go back very often. There was shame there.

Now there was shame everywhere. It seemed like the whole world had been inside that classroom, everyone had heard what the teacher had said, everyone had turned around and felt sorry for me. There was shame in going to the Worthy Boys Annual Christmas Dinner for you and your kind, because everybody knew what a worthy boy was. Why couldn't they just call it the Boys Annual Christmas Dinner, why'd they have to give it a name? There was shame in wearing the brown and orange and white plaid mackinaw the welfare gave to three thousand boys. Why'd it have to be the same for everybody so when you walked down the street the people could see you were on relief? It was a nice warm mackinaw and it had a hood, and my Momma beat me and called me a little rat when she found out I stuffed it in the bottom of a pail full of garbage way over on Cottage Street. There was shame in running over to Mister Ben's at the end of the day and asking for his rotten peaches, there was shame in asking Mrs. Simmons for a spoonful of sugar, there was shame in running out to meet the relief truck. I hated that truck, full of food for you and your kind. I ran into the house and hid when it came. And then I started to sneak through alleys, to take the long way home so the people going into White's Eat Shop wouldn't see me. Yeah, the whole world heard the teacher that day, we all know you don't have a Daddy.

It lasted for a while, this kind of numbness. I spent a lot of time feeling sorry for myself. And then one day I met this wino in a restaurant. I'd been out hustling all day, shining shoes, selling newspapers, and I had goo-gobs of money in my pocket. Bought me a bowl of chili for fifteen cents, and a cheeseburger for fifteen cents, and a Pepsi for five cents, and a piece of chocolate cake for ten cents. That was a good meal. I was eating when this old wino came in. I love winos because they never hurt anyone but themselves.

The old wino sat down at the counter and ordered twenty-six cents worth of food. He ate it like he really enjoyed it. When the owner, Mister Williams, asked him to pay the check, the old wino didn't lie or go through his pocket like he suddenly found a hole.

He just said: "Don't have no money."

The owner yelled: "Why in hell you come in here and eat my food if you don't have no money? That food cost me money."

Mister Williams jumped over the counter and knocked the wino off his stool and beat him over the head with a pop bottle. Then he stepped back and watched the wino bleed. Then he kicked him. And he kicked him again.

I looked at the wino with blood all over his face and I went over. "Leave him alone, Mister Williams. I'll pay the twenty-six cents."

The wino got up, slowly, pulling himself up to the stool, then up to the counter, holding on for a minute until his legs stopped shaking so bad. He looked at me with pure hate. "Keep your twenty-six cents. You don't have to pay, not now. I just finished paying for it."

He started to walk out, and he passed me, he reached down and touched my shoulder. "Thanks, sonny, but it's too late now. Why didn't you pay it before?"

I was pretty sick about that. I waited too long to help another man.

DISCUSSION QUESTIONS

1. What does Gregory's story tell you about the sensitivity of young children? Were you or one of your classmates ever ridiculed in school the same way? What did it feel like, whether victim or observer?
2. How do you account for this type of behavior on the part of professional teachers who should know better? Do you think the situation has improved since the thirties and forties? Why or why not?
3. Was there ever a "Helene Tucker, symbol of everything you want," in your life? Why is such a person important in growing up?
4. What is the significance of the story of the old wino at the end of Gregory's account? At first blush, it seems superfluous; but is it?

SUGGESTIONS FOR JOURNAL ENTRIES

1. Whether victim or observer, write about the experience of learning hate and shame from a teacher.
2. Write about an experience of waiting too long to help another person and try to understand why you waited.

READING 13

The Art of Acknowledgment

Jean Houston

This selection is an excerpt from The Possible Human *(1982), "a master course by a master teacher," written by Jean Houston, social scientist and New Age philosopher. In it she describes a belated sophomore slump while at Columbia University and how a visiting professor who cared made all the difference, reminding us that we all have that capacity for caring, student and teacher alike.*

I was eighteen years old and I was the golden girl. A junior in college, I was president of the college drama society, a member of the student senate, winner of two off-Broadway critics' awards for acting and directing, director of the class play, and had just turned down an offer to train for the next Olympics (fencing). In class my mind raced and dazzled, spinning off facile but "wowing" analogies to the kudos of teachers and classmates. Socially, I was on the top of the heap. My advice was sought, my phone rang constantly, and it seemed that nothing could stop me.

I was the envy of all my friends and I was in a state of galloping chutzpah.

The old Greek tragedies warn us that when hubris rises, nemesis falls. I was no exception to this ancient rule. My universe crashed with great suddenness. It began when three members of my immediate family died. Then a friend whom I loved very much died suddenly of a burst appendix while camping alone in the woods. The scenery of the off-Broadway production fell on my head and I was left almost blind for the next four months. My friends and I parted from each other, they out of embarrassment and I because I didn't think I was worthy. My marks went from being rather good to a D-plus average.

I had so lost confidence in my abilities that I couldn't concentrate on anything or see the connections between things. My memory was a shambles, and within a few months I was placed on probation. All my offices were taken away; public elections were called to fill them. I was asked into the advisor's office and told that I would have to leave the college at the end of the spring term since, clearly, I didn't have the "necessary intelligence to do academic work." When I protested that I had had the "necessary intelligence" during my freshman and sophomore years, I was assured with a sympathetic smile that intellectual decline such as this often happened to young women when "they became interested in other things; it's a matter of hormones, my dear."

Where once I had been vocal and high-spirited in the classroom, I now huddled in my oversized camel's-hair coat in the back of classes, trying to be as nonexistent as possible. At lunch I would lock myself in the green room of the college theater, scene of my former triumphs, eating a sandwich in despondent isolation. Every day brought its defeats and disacknowledgments, and after my previous career I was too proud to ask for help. I felt like Job and called out to God, "Where are the boils?" since that was about all I was missing.

These Jobian fulminations led me to take one last course. It was taught by a young Swiss professor of religion, Dr. Jacob Taubes, and was supposed to be a study of selected books of the Old Testament. It turned out to be largely a discussion of the dialectic between St. Paul and Nietzsche.

Taubes was the most brilliant and exciting teacher I had ever experienced, displaying European academic wizardry such as I had never known. Hegel, gnosticism, structuralism, phenomenology, and the intellectual passions of the Sorbonne cracked the ice of my self-noughting and I began to raise a tentative hand from my huddle in the back of the room and ask an occasional hesitant question.

Dr. Taubes would answer with great intensity, and soon I found myself asking more questions. One day I was making my way across campus to the bus, when I heard Dr. Taubes addressing me:

"Miss Houston, let me walk with you. You know, you have a most interesting mind."

"Me? I have a *mind?*"

"Yes, your questions are luminous. Now what do you think is the nature of the transvaluation of values in Paul and Nietzsche?"

I felt my mind fall into its usual painful dullness and stammered, "I d-don't know."

"Of course you do!" he insisted. "You couldn't ask the kinds of questions you do without having an unusual grasp of these issues. Now please, once again, what do you think of the transvaluation of values in Paul and Nietzsche? It is important for my reflections that I have your reactions."

"Well," I said, waking up, "if you put it that way, I think . . ."

I was off and running and haven't shut up since.

Dr. Taubes continued to walk me to the bus throughout that term, always challenging me with intellectually vigorous questions. He attended to me. I existed for him in the "realest" of senses, and because I existed for him I began to exist for myself. Within several weeks my eyesight came back, my spirit bloomed, and I became a fairly serious student, whereas before I had been, at best, a bright show-off.

What I acquired from this whole experience was a tragic sense of life, which balanced my previous enthusiasms. I remain deeply grateful for the attention shown me by Dr. Taubes. He acknowledged me when I most needed it. I was empowered in the midst of personal erosion, and my life has been very different for it. I swore to myself then that whenever I came across someone "going under" or in the throes of disacknowledgment, I would try to reach and acknowledge that person as I had been acknowledged.

I would go so far as to say that the greatest of human potentials is the potential of each one of us to empower and acknowledge the other. We all do this throughout our lives, but rarely do we appreciate the power of the empowering that we give to others. To be acknowledged by another, especially during times of confusion, loss, disorientation, disheartenment, is to be given time and place in the sunshine and is, in the metaphor of psychological reality, the solar stimulus for transformation.

The process of healing and growth is immensely quickened when the sun of another's belief is freely given. This gift can be as simple as "Hot Dog Thou Art!" Or it can be as total as "I know you. You are God in hiding." Or it can be a look that goes straight to the soul and charges it with meaning.

I have been fortunate to have known several of those the world deems "saints": Teilhard de Chardin, Mother Teresa of Calcutta, Clemie, an old black woman in Mississippi. To be looked at by these people is to be gifted with the look that engenders. You feel yourself primed at the depths by such seeing. Something so tremendous and yet so subtle wakes up inside that you are able to release the defeats and denigrations of years. If I were to describe it further, I would have to speak of unconditional love joined to a whimsical regarding of you as the cluttered house that hides the holy one.

Saints, you say, but the miracle is that anybody can do it for anybody! Our greatest genius may be the ability to prime the healing and evolutionary circuits of one another.

It is an art form that has yet to be learned, for it is based on something never before fully recognized—deep psychological reciprocity, the art and science of mutual transformation. And all the gurus and masters, all the prophets, profs, and professionals, can do little for us compared to what we could do for each other if we would but be present to the fullness of each other. For there is no answer to anyone's anguished cry of "Why am I here, why am I at all?" except the reply, "Because I am here, because I am."

DISCUSSION QUESTIONS

1. What does Houston mean when she describes her relationship with Dr. Taubes: "I existed for him in the 'realest' of senses, and because I existed for him I began to exist for myself"?
2. Houston relates that her encounter with Dr. Taubes resulted in a transformation from a "bright show-off" into a "fairly serious student." What do you understand to be the difference?
3. Do you agree with Houston when she says that "the greatest of human potentials is the potential of each one of us to empower and acknowledge the other"? Give an example from your own experience.
4. Houston's definition of a "saint" is somewhat unusual. Have you ever met someone such as she describes? What was it like?

SUGGESTIONS FOR JOURNAL ENTRIES

1. Houston writes that "Our greatest genius may be the ability to prime the healing and evolutionary circuits of one another." Write about an experience where you were able to do that for another.
2. Fr. William McNamara, in his book, *The Art of Being Human* (1962), writes that if we are not becoming "saints," then there is only one alternative, "failures." In light of Houston's revised definition, write about your own personal journey toward "sainthood."

READING 14

Confessions of a Lonely TA

Michael Kantor

Michael Kantor, Cornell '83, received his master of arts in drama from the University of California, San Diego in 1987 and recently produced a PBS documentary on the legendary aviator, Charles Lindbergh. In this essay, he describes some of the traditional temptations of a young male teaching assistant and confesses to a bittersweet lesson from an almost classroom romance.

A year out of college, I left my girlfriend and the East Coast and moved to San Diego to get a master's in drama at the University of California. I didn't know a soul there and I felt extremely unsure of myself—even the ocean seemed to be on the wrong side of the road.

Basically broke, I wheedled a job as a teaching assistant for "American Drama on Film," a popular course attracting 120 students who liked watching movies for credit. I'd never taught before and the prospect terrified me. All I had to guide me was a thin, green handbook for teaching assistants. Full of rules and regulations, it covered everything from roll call to grading, but nowhere did it mention how to convey ideas or make people think.

The morning of the first class, I pictured my students while I was shaving and cut myself in three places. At twenty-four, I felt too young to exert authority. But as it turned out, my youth helped me communicate with my students. Jokes and discussions, occasionally even philosophical debates filled my classes. Some students were genuinely interested in the material, and with these I developed a kind of friendship. The only aspect of the job that I didn't like was office hours—the time I spent sitting in my underground cubicle waiting for people to come by for extra help. No one ever did.

Then Lisa started popping by. She was one of the best students in the class and certainly didn't need my academic advice. She came to hang out. We talked about movies, sexy actors, and the San Diego Chargers. She made me feel like an expert on everything. I began to look forward to office hours. When I was with Lisa I felt as if I'd finally adjusted to California. I thought about asking her out.

Lisa began putting her phone number on assignments, and when she came by there was a certain forwardness about her, a kind of "can-you-handle-this?" attitude. I tried to act cool and not show how interested I was. One afternoon she showed up in a wet suit and said, "Surf's up. Wanna come?" I told her that I'd love to, but I couldn't surf. After she left I cursed myself for not seizing the opportunity to be with her.

That evening I started dialing Lisa's number about ten times. Something stopped me from following through, and it wasn't just because I was nervous. I guess I knew there was something wrong with a teacher dating a student. I decided to see if my little green handbook had anything to say about it. The section on romantic relationships listed three reasons why such liaisons should be strictly avoided: 1) A display of interest from the TA puts the student in the difficult position of fearing repercussions for not reciprocating that interest. 2) It makes the objective evaluation of all students almost impossible. 3) An inevitable loss of respect for the TA occurs.

I tried to rule out each reason as inapplicable to me. Lisa was displaying an interest in me, not the other way around. As for objective evaluation, I always numbered papers and tests, covering students' names to make sure I graded without bias. But the third reason was impossible to dismiss. I knew that if I were a student and found out that my TA and a classmate were involved, no matter how much I had liked him I'd think he was a slimebucket, an oil spill, a tiny dude. I'd be sure he had used his position to seduce her and that without question he'd favor her with a better grade or inside information on the exam.

The idea of my students seeing me as a sleazebag turned my stomach. Their regard for me as a teacher was more important than my desire to go out with Lisa. I decided to wait until the term ended to ask her out.

As soon as I handed in the grades, I called her. We went to a movie. We stayed and watched another and then went out for a drink. Nothing clicked. The desire was gone. Actually, my desire was still there, but hers had vanished along with my grade book. I was disappointed, sad even, but not surprised. No longer her all-knowing TA, I was now just some older guy who couldn't surf.

DISCUSSION QUESTIONS

1. Kantor describes how unprepared young graduate students are frequently thrown into classrooms with little or no guidance and preparation. How much responsibility should the university have in training its TAs? What is the situation at your institution?

2. What do you see as the advantages as well as the disadvantages of having a TA as your instructor? Can you speak from experience?

3. What do you think of the three reasons listed in the TA handbook about why teacher-student liaisons should be strictly avoided? Do you agree? Can you think of other reasons?

4. Kantor says that he eventually became friends with some of the interested students. Have you ever made friends with a teacher? What are your expectations in this regard with your college teachers?

SUGGESTIONS FOR JOURNAL ENTRIES

1. Interview one of your institution's TAs (or new professors) on the issue of teacher-student liaisons and write a report of what you learned from the interview. (You might want to use Kantor's article as a lead into the interview.)

2. Write about how friendship with a teacher made a difference in your life.

The Power of Caring

Louis Schmier

This essay, by my friend Louis Schmier, Adelphi University '62, professor of American history at Valdosta State University (Georgia), was first published on the Internet as a "Random Thought" on December 7, 1995. It was collected in Random Thoughts II: Teaching from the Heart *(1997).*

I had been reading student journals and class evaluations all morning and on into the early afternoon when one stopped me dead in my tracks. I haven't done much since except read it over and over and over. I'd leave the office to get some coffee or walk the halls or chat with someone to break the spell, but every time I returned that journal would draw me like a magnet. Each time I read it, the tears made it as difficult to read as the last time. I've been grasping every word, sometimes touching the page with my fingertips. My office has seemed very warm. How do I share with you how I feel at this very moment? Words like uplifted, fulfilled, satisfied, proud, and humble just seemed hollow, lifeless, and meaningless—maybe even trite. I'm sure there's a turn of a phrase or a catchy word out there for this occasion, but to use it would feel so artificial. I'm really at a loss for words. So I think I should just let you listen to my silence as you read this student's entry:

> In all my 16 years of being a student, I have never run across a teacher who thought and treated me much more than as a piece of black female s--t. But you cared enough about me to give me for the first time what no other teacher did: respect, a chance to say what was on my mind and, above all else, love. You gave me a chance to realize I was capable of succeeding and capable of learning. You gave me confidence that all my other teachers seemed to suck out of me like blood-sucking leeches. You lifted me up when so many others stomped me into the ground. So I want to personally thank you for teaching me so much history, for believing in me and also for teaching me to believe in myself. . . .
>
> Do you know when you did that the most? You probably don't remember. It probably seemed so unimportant. But it was like an event for me. It started when we were discussing a tidbit in class that led to an argument about legalizing marijuana, and I got up and told the class that I smoked to get high and feel good and that there was nothing wrong with it. A few hours later you passed me near the fountain at the library. You stopped and all you said was that you wanted me to think about that smoking was a round trip, you always come back to the low after the high, you always come back to what you're running from. The pain always comes back. But believing in myself is a high like nothing else for getting rid of the hurt. You said it with such concern and sincerity that one of my friends with me called you a soapy sap. I thought it was so jerky too and didn't think about it. Then, a few days later when you were

walking into the Student Union and I asked you to have a picture button made with me, you didn't run away. . . . I don't think you thought much about doing it except having some crazy fun. You probably didn't think it was all that important, but that was serious s--t to me. You don't know how much that picture of us now means to me. After we had it made, I went to my room and looked at that picture and couldn't stop looking and thought that you didn't have to do anything like that. You could have thought that I was a loser like everyone else thought and like I thought. And I started crying, I couldn't stop crying for hours. I realized how unhappy I was and getting high was my way of getting rid of my pain. I see how the pain always came back like you said. I want you to know that I realized I had a problem with drugs, but after I admitted to smoking, a bunch of people came up to me to talk. They didn't yell at me or give me any religious holier than thou crap. They wanted to help and told me about themselves. And some were white! They and especially you made me realize that the life I was living was not my own. I studied, worked, ate, and slept around getting high. I made myself miserable and thought that smoking would make it better. It was just making me more miserable.

I am proud of the fact that I worked hard in this class and learned a lot. I learned to speak my mind without being disrespectful and to listen. I have learned to meet deadlines. I have learned to depend on my triad members. That was the hardest part for me, depending on someone else to come through. But I learned to trust. But you know, the best part of all that was that they trusted and depended on me. One time, I let them down and it was the worst feeling in the world. I cried as I apologized, and they understood and forgave me! Me!!

I want you to know that I don't need weed now to be happy. I haven't had one in four weeks now. I am damn proud of me and you should be of yourself. You're right, succeeding is my natural high. It feels damn good to be a part of something positive.

If anyone gives you any s--t or makes fun of you because of the way you are and how you teach, send them to me. I'll tell them that it doesn't take a whole lot to open a book and teach a lesson in front of a class, but it takes a lot of work, and tenderness to open a mind and educate a soul. I'll show them the power of caring.

I saw her a while ago. We didn't say much. She knew that I had read her journal. We just hugged and wished each other a joyous holiday. I told her that if she ever felt she was faltering, she knew where she could come and get a Tootsie Pop. She promised to come by for a Tootsie Pop anyway. She gave me permission to share her words and feelings in the hope that, as she said, . . . Well, you decide what she said.

That picture button, which I thought until today was cute and which I threw carelessly in my dresser drawer—I went home to rescue it. It now has an honored place among my sacred objects of teaching in my office, as a reminder of the power of caring.

Make it a good day.

DISCUSSION QUESTIONS

1. Is Schmier's "caring" the same as Houston's (Reading 13) "acknowledgment"? How do the readings differ?
2. Have you ever had a "Doc Schmier" in your academic career? Describe him or her and what it was like to be in his or her classroom.
3. Do you think that students are in a position to be able to evaluate their teachers? Defend your answer.
4. How do students, especially first-year students, find out about teachers on your campus? Should a teacher's reputation make a difference in which courses you choose?

SUGGESTIONS FOR JOURNAL ENTRIES

1. Write about a teacher whose teaching enkindled something in you that made a difference in your life.
2. Ask some upperclass students who the best teachers are on campus. Sit in on one of their classes and write about why you think they have such a reputation.

READING 16

Theme for English B

Langston Hughes

James Langston Hughes (1902–1967), Lincoln University '29, a prolific writer of poetry, short stories, plays, novels, and children's books, was for more than thirty years the "dean" of American Black poets. He strove, in his own words, "to explain the Negro condition in America." This is a powerful and much anthologized poem about the differences and similarities between "what is true" for a black student and his white professor. The poem was first published in 1949 in a now defunct magazine, Common Ground; *it was collected in 1951 in* Montage of a Dream Deferred.

The instructor said,

> Go home and write
> a page tonight,
> And let that page come out of you—
> Then, it will be true.

I wonder if it's that simple?

I am a twenty-two, colored, born in Winston-Salem.
I went to school there, then Durham, then here
to this college on the hill above Harlem.
I am the only colored student in my class
The steps from the hill lead down into Harlem,
through a park, then I cross St. Nicholas,
Eighth Avenue, Seventh, and I come to the Y,
the Harlem Branch Y, where I take the elevator
up to my room, sit down, and write this page:

It's not easy to know what is true for you or me
at twenty-two, my age. But I guess I'm what
I feel and see and hear. Harlem, I hear you:
hear you, hear me—we two—you, me, talk on this page.
(I hear New York, too.) Me—who?
Well, I like to eat, sleep, drink, and be in love.
I like to work, read, learn, and understand life.
I like a pipe for a Christmas present,
or records—Bessie, bop, or Bach.
I guess being colored doesn't make me *not* like
the same things other folks like who are other races.
So will my page be colored that I write?
Being me, it will not be white.
But it will be
a part of you, instructor.
You are white—
yet a part of me, as I am a part of you.

That's American.
Sometimes perhaps you don't want to be a part of me.
Nor do I often want to be a part of you.
But we are, that's true!
As I learn from you,
I guess you learn from me—
although you're older—and white—
and somewhat more free.

This is my page for English B.

DISCUSSION QUESTIONS

1. Do you agree with Hughes that "It's not easy to know what is true"?
   Why?
2. What do you think Hughes is saying in these lines?

   But it will be
   a part of you, instructor.
   You are white—
   yet a part of me, as I am a part of you.
   That's American.

3. What would you say was Hughes's perception of his instructor on the
   basis of his poem?
4. Would you have been able to be as candid as Hughes had you received
   the same assignment? Why or why not?

SUGGESTIONS FOR JOURNAL ENTRIES

1. Write your own "Theme for English B" poem.
2. Write about how it feels to read something where race is an issue.

The Banks of the Vistula

Rebecca Lee

Rebecca Lee is a professor of creative writing at the University of North Carolina at Wilmington and is presently working on a novel. This long short story, which was first published in The Atlantic Monthly *in 1997, is concerned with a first-year student's plagiarizing of a paper and her eventual discovery of the importance of telling the truth.*

It was dusk; the campus had turned to velvet. I walked the brick path to Humanities, which loomed there and seemed to incline toward me, as God does toward the sinner in the Book of Psalms. It was late on a Friday afternoon, when the air is fertile, about to split and reveal its warm fruit—that gold nucleus of time, the weekend.

Inside, up the stairs, the door to Stasselova's office was open, and the professor lifted his head. "Oh," he said. "Yes." He coughed, deep in his lungs, and motioned me in. He had requested this visit earlier in the day, following class. His course was titled Speaking in Tongues: Introductory Linguistics. Stasselova was about sixty-five and a big man, his torso an almost perfect square. Behind his balding head the blond architecture of St. Gustav College rose into the cobalt sky. It looked like a rendition of thought itself, rising out of the head in intricate, heartbreaking cornices that became more abstract and complicated as they rose.

I was in my third week of college. I loved every moment of it, every footfall. The students resembled the students I'd known in high school, Scandinavian midwesterners like myself, whose fathers were all pastors or some declension thereof—but the professors thrilled me. Most had come from the East Coast, and seemed fragile and miserable in the Midwest. Occasionally during class you could see hope for us rising in them, and then they would look like great birds flying over an uncertain landscape, asking mysterious questions, trying to lead us somewhere we could not yet go.

I wanted to be noticed by them, to distinguish myself from the ordinary mass of students, and to this end I had plagiarized my first paper for Stasselova's class. This was why, I presumed, he had called me to his office.

The paper, titled "The Common Harvest," was on the desk between us. I had found it in the Kierkegaard Library. It was a chapter in an old green-cloth book that was so small I could palm it. The book had been written in 1945, by a man named Delores Tretsky, and it hadn't been signed out since 1956. I began to leaf through it, and then crouched down to read. I read for a full hour; I thought it beautiful. I had not once in all my life stopped for even a moment to consider grammar, to wonder how it rose out of history like a wing unfurling.

I had intended to write my own paper, to synthesize, as Stasselova had suggested, my own ideas with the author's, but I simply had nothing to contribute.

It seemed even rude to combine this work with my own pale, unemotional ideas. So I lifted a chapter, only occasionally dimming some passages that were too fine, too blinding.

"This is an extraordinary paper," he said. He was holding his coffee cup over it, and I saw that coffee had already spilled on the page to form a small, murky pond.

"Thank you," I said.

"It seems quite sophisticated. You must not have come here straight out of high school."

"I did," I said.

"Oh. Well, good for you."

"Thanks."

"You seem fully immersed in a study of oppression. Any reason for this?"

"Well, I do live in the world."

"Yes, that's right. And you say here—a shocking line—that a language must sometimes be repressed, and replaced, for the larger good. You believe this?"

"Yes."

"You think that the Eastern-bloc countries should be forced to speak, as you say here, the mother tongue?"

Some parts of the paper I had just copied down verbatim, without really understanding, and now I was stuck with them. Now they were my opinions. "Yes," I said.

"You know I am from that region."

"Is that right?"

"From Poland."

"Whereabouts in Poland?" I asked conversationally.

"I was born on the edge of it, in the dark forest land along its northeastern border, before the Soviet Union took it over completely, burning our towns. As children we were forced to speak Russian, even in our homes, even when we said good-night to our mothers as we fell asleep."

This was turning into a little piece of bad luck.

"When did you write this?" he asked.

"Last week."

"It reads like it was written fifty years ago. It reads like Soviet propaganda."

"Oh," I said. "I didn't mean it that way."

"Did somebody help you?"

"Actually, yes. Certainly that's all right?"

"Of course, if done properly. Who was it that helped you, a book or a person?"

"My roommate helped me," I said.

"Your roommate. What is her name?"

"Solveig."

"Solveig what?"

"Solveig Juliusson."

"Is she a linguistics scholar?"

"No, just very bright."

"Maybe I can talk to Solveig myself?"

"Unfortunately, you can't."

"Why not?"

"It's complicated."

"In what way?"

"Well, she's stopped eating. She's very thin. Her parents were worried, so they took her home."

"Where does she live?"

"I don't know."

We both sat silent. Luckily, I had experience lying in my adolescence, and knew it was possible to win even though both parties were aware of the lie. The exercise was not a search for truth but rather a test of exterior reserve.

"I'm sure she'll be returning soon," I said. "I'll have her call you."

Stasselova smiled. "Tell her to eat up," he said, his sarcasm curled inside his concern.

"Okay," I said. I got up and hoisted my bag over my shoulder. As I stood, I could see the upper edge of the sun falling down off the hill on which St. Gustav was built. I'd never seen the sun from this angle before, from above as it fell, as it obviously lit up another part of the world, perhaps even flaming up the sights of Stasselova's precious, oppressed Poland, its dark contested forests and burning cities, its dreamy and violent borders.

My roommate Solveig was permanently tan. She went twice a week to a tanning salon and bleached her hair frequently, so that it looked like radioactive foliage growing out of dark, moody sands. Despite all this she was very beautiful, and sensible.

"Margaret," she said when I came in that evening. "The library telephoned to recall a book. They said it was urgent."

I had thought he might check the library. "Okay," I said. As I rifled through the clothes on my closet floor, I decided it would have to be burned. I would finish the book and then I would burn it. But first there was tonight, and I had that rare thing, a date.

My date was from Stasselova's class. His name was Hans; he was a junior, and his father was a diplomat. He had almost auburn hair that fell to his neckline. He wore, always, long white shirts whose sleeves were just slightly, almost imperceptibly, puffed at the shoulders, like an elegant little joke, and very long, so they hung over his hands. I thought he was articulate, kind. I had in a moment of astonishment asked him out.

The night was soft and warm. We walked through the tiny town, wandered its thin river. We ate burgers. He spoke of Moscow, where he had lived that summer. I had spent my childhood with a vision of Russia in the distance, an anti-America, a sort of fairy-tale intellectual prison. But this was 1987, the beginning of *perestroika*, of *glasnost*, and views of Russia were changing. Television showed a country of rain and difficulty and great humility, and Gorbachev was always bowing to sign something or other, his head bearing a mysterious stain shaped like a continent one could almost but not quite identify. I said to Hans that I wanted to go there myself, though I had never thought of the idea before that moment. He said, "You can if you want." We were in his small iridescent apartment by now. "Or perhaps to Poland," I said, thinking of Stasselova.

"Poland," Hans said. "Yes. What is left of it, after men like Stasselova."

"What do you mean, men like Stasselova?"

"Soviet puppets."

"Yet he is clearly anti-Soviet," I said.

"Now, yes. Everybody is anti-Soviet now." The sign for the one Japanese restaurant in town cast a worldly orange light into the room, carving Hans's body into geometric shapes. He took my hand, and at that moment the whole world seemed to have entered his apartment. I found him intelligent, deliberate, large-hearted. "Now," he said, "is the time to be anti-Soviet."

On Monday afternoon, in class, Hans sat across from me. We were all sitting around a conference table, waiting for Stasselova. Hans smiled. I gave him the peace sign across the table. When I looked back at him, moments later, Hans's hands were casually laid out on the table, palms down. I saw then, for the first time, that his left hand tapered into only three fingers, which were fused together at the top knuckle. The hand looked delicate, surprising. I had not noticed this on our date, and now I wondered if he had purposely kept me from seeing it, or if I had somehow just missed it. For a brief, confused moment, I even wondered if the transformation had occurred between then and now. Hans looked me squarely in the eye, I smiled back.

Stasselova then entered the room. In light of my date with Hans, I had almost forgotten my visit with him the previous Friday. I'd meant to burn the book over the weekend in the darkness at the ravine, though I dreaded this. My mother was a librarian, and I knew that the vision of her daughter burning a book would have been like a sledgehammer to the heart.

Throughout the class Stasselova seemed to be speaking directly to me, still chastising me. His eyes kept resting on me disapprovingly. "The reason for the sentence is to express the verb—a change, a *desire.* But the verb cannot stand alone; it needs to be supported, to be realized by a body, and thus the noun—just as the soul in its trajectory through life needs to be comforted by the body."

The sun's rays slanted in on Stasselova as he veered into very interesting territory. "All things in revolution," he said, "in this way, need protection. For instance, when my country, Poland, was annexed by the Soviet Union, we had the choice of joining what was called Berling's army, the Polish wing of the Russian army, or the independent Home Army. Many considered it anti-Polish to join the Russian army, but I believed, as did my comrades, that more could be done through the system, within the support of the system, than without."

He looked at me. I nodded. I was one of those students who nod a lot. His eyes were like brown velvet under glass. "This is the power of the sentence," he said. "It acts out this drama of control and subversion. The noun always stands for what is, the status quo, and the verb for what might be, the ideal."

Across the table Hans's damaged hand, spindly and nervy, drummed impatiently on the tabletop. I could tell he wanted to speak up. Stasselova turned to him. "That was the decision I made," he said. "Years ago. Right or wrong, I thought it best at the time. I thought we could do more work for the Polish cause from within the Red Army than from outside it."

Hans's face was impassive. He suddenly looked years older—austere, cold, priestly. Stasselova turned then to look at me. This was obviously an issue for him, I thought, and I nodded as he continued to speak. I really did feel supportive. Whatever army he thought was best at the time, that was fine with me.

In the evening I went to the ravine in the elm forest, which lay curled around the hill on which the campus was built. This forest seemed deeply peaceful to me, almost conscious. I didn't know the reason for this at the time—that many elms in a forest can spring from a single tree. In this case a single elm had divided herself into a forest, an individual with a continuous DNA in whose midst one could stand and be held.

The ravine cut through like an old emotional wound. I crouched on its bank and glanced at the book one last time. I flicked open my lighter. The book caught fire instantly. As the flame approached my hand, I arced the book into the murky water. It looked spectacular, a high wing of flame rising from it. Inside, in one of its luminous chapters, I had read that the ability to use language and the ability to tame fire arose from the same warm, shimmering pool of genes, since in nature they did not appear one without the other.

As I made my way out of the woods and into the long silver ditch that lined the highway, I heard about a thousand birds cry, and I craned my neck to see them lighting out from the tips of the elms. They looked like ideas would if released suddenly from the page and given bodies—shocked at how blood actually felt as it ran through the veins, as it sent them wheeling into the west, wings raking, straining against the requirements of such a physical world.

I returned and found Solveig turning in the lamplight. Her hair was piled on her head, so unnaturally blonde it looked ablaze, and her face was bronze. She looked a thousand years old. "Some guy called," she said. "Stasselova or something."

He called again that night at nearly midnight. I thought this unseemly.

"So," he said. "Solveig's back."

"Yes," I said, glancing at her. She was at her mirror, performing some ablution on her face. "She's much better."

"Perhaps the three of us can now meet."

"Oh," I said, "it's too early."

"Too early in what?"

"In her recovery." Solveig wheeled her head around to look at me. I smiled, shrugged.

"I think she'll be okay."

"I'm not so sure."

"Listen," he said. "I'll give you a choice: you can either rewrite the paper in my office, bringing in whatever materials you need, or the three of us can meet and clear this up."

"Fine, we'll meet you."

"You know my hours."

"I do." I hung up and explained to Solveig what had happened—Stasselova's obsession with language and oppression, my plagiarism, the invocation of her name. Solveig nodded and said of course, whatever she could do she would.

When we arrived that Wednesday, the light had almost gone from his office but was still lingering outside the windows, like the light in fairy tales, rich and creepy.

Solveig was brilliant. Just her posture, as she sat in the narrow chair, was enough initially to chasten Stasselova. In her presence men were driven to politeness, to sincerity, to a kind of deep, internal apology. He thanked her, bowing a little at his desk. "Your work has interested me," he said.

"It is not my work, sir. It's Margaret's. We just discussed together some of the ideas."

"Such as?"

"Well, the necessity of a collective language, a mutual tongue."

"And why is that necessary?" Stasselova leaned back and folded his hands across his vast torso.

"To maintain order," she said. And then the sun fell completely, blowing one last blast of light across the Americas before it settled into the Soviet Union, and some of that light, a glittery, barely perceptible dust, settled around Solveig's head. She looked like a dominatrix, an intellectual dominatrix, delivering this brutal news.

"And your history in psycholinguistics?" he said.

"I have only my personal history," she said. "The things that have happened to me." I would not have been surprised if at that declaration the whole university had imploded, turned to liquid, and flowed away. "Besides," she said, "all the research and work was Margaret's. I saw her working on it, night after night."

"Then, Margaret," he turned his gaze on me. "I see you are intimately connected with evolutionary history as well as Soviet ideology. As well, it appears, you've been steeped in a lifetime's study of linguistic psychosocial theory."

"Is it because she's female," Solveig asked, "that she's made to account for every scrap of knowledge?"

"Look," he said after a long silence, "I simply want to know from what cesspool these ideas arose. If you got them from a book, I will be relieved, but if these ideas are still floating around in your bloodlines, in your wretched little towns, I want to know."

I was about to cave in. Better a plagiarist than a fascist from a tainted bloodline.

"I don't really think you should be talking about our bloodlines," Solveig said. "It's probably not appropriate." She enunciated the word "appropriate" in such a way that Stasselova flinched, just slightly. Both he and I stared at her. She really was extraordinarily thin. In a certain light she could look shockingly beautiful, but in another, such as the dim one in Stasselova's office, she could look rather threatening. Her contact lenses were the color of a night sky split by lightning. Her genetic information was almost entirely hidden—the color of her hair and eyes and skin, the shape of her body—and this gave her a psychological advantage of sorts.

Stasselova's lecture on Thursday afternoon was another strange little affair, given as long autumn rays of sun, embroidered by leaves, covered his face and body. He was onto his main obsession again, the verb—specifically, the work of the verb in the sentence, and how it relates to the work of a man in the world.

"The revolution takes place from a position of stability, always. The true revolutionary will find his place within the status quo."

"And this is why you joined the Russian army in attacking your own country?" This was Hans, startling us all.

"I did not attack my own country," Stasselova said. "Never."

"But you watched as the Nazis attacked it in August of 1944, yes? And used that attack for your own purposes?"

"This night I was there, it's true," he said, "on the banks of the Vistula, and I saw Warsaw burn. And I was wearing the fur hat of Russia, yes. But when I attempted to cross the Vistula, in order to help those of my country-men who were escaping, I was brought down—clubbed with a rifle to the back of the head by my commanding officer, a Russian."

"That's interesting, because in accounts of the time you are referred to as an officer yourself—Officer Stasselova, of course."

"Yes. I was a Polish officer though. Certainly you can infer the hierarchy involved?"

"What I can infer . . ." Hans's voice rose, and then Stasselova's joined in, contrapuntally, "What you can infer . . . ," and for a moment the exchange reminded me of those rounds we sang at summer camp. "What you can infer," Stasselova said, drowning out Hans. "is that this was an ambiguous time for those of us who were Polish. You can't judge after the fact. Perhaps you think that I should be dead on those banks, making the willows to grow." Stasselova's eyes were shot with the dying light; he squinted at us and looked out the window momentarily. "You will stand there and think maybe certain men in certain times should not choose their own lives, should not want to live." And then he turned away from Hans. I myself scowled at Hans. So rude!

"And so I did live," Stasselova said finally. "Mostly because I was wearing my Russian hat, made of the fur of ten foxes. It was always Russia that dealt us blows, and it was always Russia that saved us. You see?"

The next day I was with Hans in the woods. We were on our stomachs in a clearing, looking to the east, from where the rain was stalking us through the trees.

"What I want to know," Hans was saying, "is why is he always asking for you to see him?"

"Oh," I said, "he thinks I plagiarized that first paper."

"Did you?"

"Not really."

"Why does he think so?"

"Says it smacks of Soviet propaganda."

"Really? Well, he should know."

"I agree with him—that you're judging him from an irrelevant stance."

"He was found guilty of treason by his own people, not me—by the Committee for Political Responsibility. Why else would he be here, teaching at some Lutheran college in Minnesota? This is a guy who brought martial law down on his own people, and now we sit here in the afternoon and watch him march around in front of us, relating everything he speaks of—*comma splices,* for Christ's sake—to his own innocence."

"Yet all sorts of people were found guilty of all sorts of meaningless things by that committee."

"I bet he thinks you're a real dream—this woman willing to absolve the old exterminator of his sins."

"That's insulting," I said. But I realized how fond I'd grown of this professor in his little office, drinking his bitter coffee, night descending into the musky heart of Humanities.

And then the rain was upon us. We could hear it on the tiny ledges of leaves above us more than feel it. "Let's go," Hans said, grabbing my hand with his left, damaged hand. The way his hand held mine was alluring; his hand had the nimbus of an idea about it, as if the gene that had sprung this hand had a different world in mind, a better world, where hands had more torque when they grasped each other, and people held things differently, like hooks—a world where all objects were shaped something like lanterns, and were passed on and on.

Monday was gray, with long silver streaks of rain. I dragged myself out of the warmth of my bed and put on my rain slicker. At nine forty-five I headed toward Stasselova's office.

"Hello," I said, knocking on the open door. "I'm sorry to disturb you outside your office hours." I was shivering; I felt pathetic.

"Margaret," he said. "Hello. Come in." As I sat down, he said, "You've brought with you the smell of rain."

He poured me coffee in a styrofoam cup. During our last class I had been so moved by his description of that night on the Vistula that I'd decided to confess. But now I was hesitating. "Could I have some of this cream?" I asked, pointing to a little tin cup of it on his windowsill.

"There it is again," he said, as he reached for the cream.

"There is what again?"

"That little verbal tic of yours."

"I didn't know I had one," I said.

"I noticed it first in class," he said. "You say 'this' instead of 'that'; 'this cream,' not 'that cream.' The line people draw between the things they consider *this* and the things they consider *that* is the perimeter of their sphere of intimacy. You see? Everything inside is *this;* everything inside is close, is intimate. Since you pointed at the cream and it is farther from you than I am, 'this' suggests that I am among the things you consider close to you. I'm flattered," he said, and handed me the creamer, which was, like him, sweating. What an idea—that with a few words you could catch another person in a little grammatical clutch, arrange the objects of the world such that they bordered the two of you.

"At any rate," he said. "I'm glad you showed up."

"You are?"

"Yes. I've wanted to ask you something."

"Yes?"

"This spring the college will hold its annual symposium on language and politics. I thought you might present your paper. Usually one of the upperclassmen does this, but I thought your paper might be more appropriate."

"I thought you hated my paper."

"I do."

"Oh."

"So you'll do it?"

"I'll think about it," I said.

He nodded and smiled, as if the matter were settled. The rain was suddenly coming down very hard. It was loud, and we were silent for a few moments, listening. I stared beyond his head out the window, which was blurry with water, so that the turrets of the campus looked like a hallucination, like some shadow world looming back there in his unconscious.

"This rain," he said then, in a quiet, astonished voice, and his word *this* entered me as it was meant to—quietly, with a sharp tip, but then, like an arrowhead, widening and widening, until it included the whole landscape around us.

The rain turned to snow, and winter settled on our campus. The face of nature turned away—beautiful and distracted. After Christmas at home (where I received my report card, a tiny slip of paper that seemed to have flown across the snows to deliver me my A in Stasselova's class) I hunkered down in my dorm for the month of January, and barely emerged. The dorm in which most of us freshman girls lived was the elaborate, dark Agnes Mellby Hall, named after the stern, formidable virgin whose picture hung over the fireplace in our lounge.

As winter crept over us, we retired to Mellby earlier and earlier. Every night that winter, in which most of us were nineteen, was a slumber party in the main sitting room among its ornate furnishings, all of which had the paws of beasts where they touched the floor. There, nightly, we ate heavily, like Romans, but childish foods, popcorn and pizza and ice cream, most of us spiraling downstairs now and then to throw up in the one private bathroom.

On one of those nights I was reading a book in the sitting room when I received a phone call from Solveig, who was down at a house party in town and wanted me to come help her home. She wasn't completely drunk, but calculated that she would be in about forty-five minutes. Her body was like a tract of nature that she understood perfectly—a constellation whose movement across the night sky she could predict, or a gathering storm, or maybe, more accurately, a sparkling stream of elements into which she introduced

alcohol with such careful calibration that her blood flowed exactly as she desired, uphill and down, intersecting precisely, chemically, with time and fer-
tility. Solveig did not stay at the dorm with us much, but rather ran with an
older pack of girls, feminists mostly, who that winter happened to be involved in a series of protests, romantic insurrections, against the president of
the college, who was clearly terrified of them.

About ten minutes before I was to leave, Stasselova appeared in the doorway of the sitting room. I had not seen him in more than a month, since the
last day of class, but he had called a few times. I had not returned his calls, in
the hopes that he would forget about participation in the symposium. But here
he was, wearing a long gray coat over his bulkiness. His head looked huge,
the bones widely spaced, like the architecture of a grand civic building.

The look in his eyes caused me to gaze out across the room and try to see
what he was seeing: perhaps some debauched canvas of absolute female re-
pose, girls lying everywhere in various modes of pajamas and sweats, surrounded by vast quantities of food and books. Some girls—and even I found
this a bit creepy—had stuffed animals that they carried with them to the sitting room at night. I happened to be poised above the fray, straddling a piano
bench, with a book spread in front of me, but almost all the rest were lying on
their backs with their extremities cast about, feet propped on the couch or
stretched up in the air at weird, hyperextended angles. We were Lutherans,
after all, and unlike the more experienced, secular girls across the river, at the
state college, we were losing our innocence right here, among ourselves. It
was being taken from us physically, and we were just relaxing until it fell
away completely.

Stasselova, in spite of all he'd seen in his life, which I'd gleaned from what
he said in class (the corpulent Goering marching through the forest, marking
off Nazi territory, and later Stalin's horses breaking through the same woods,
heralding the swath that would now be Soviet), still managed to look a little
scared as he peered into our sitting room, eventually lifting a hand to wave at
me.

I got up and approached him. "Hey," I said.

"Hello. How are you, Margaret?"

"It's good to see you. Thanks for the A."

"You deserved it. Listen, I have something for you," he said, mildly ges-
turing for us to leave the doorway, because everybody was looking at us.

"Great," I said. "But you know, right now I need to walk downtown to
pick up Solveig at a house party."

"Fine," he said. "I'll walk you."

"Oh. Okay."

I got my jacket, and the two of us stepped into the night. The snow had
arranged itself in curling waves on the Mellby lawn, and stuck in it were hundreds of silver forks, which, in a flood of early-evening testosterone, the freshman boys had placed in the earth, a gesture appropriate to their sexual frustration and also to their faith in the future. Stasselova and I stepped between
then. They looked spooky and lovely, like tiny silver grave sites in the snow.

As we walked across campus, Stasselova produced a golden brochure from his pocket and handed it to me. On the front it said, in emerald-green letters, "9th Annual Symposium on Language and Politics." Inside, under "Keynote Student Speaker," was my name. "Margaret Olafson, 'The Common Harvest.'" I stopped walking. We paused at the top of the stairs that floated down off the campus and into the town. I felt extremely, inordinately proud. Some winter lightning, a couple of great wings of it, flashed in the north. Stasselova looked paternal, grand.

The air at the party was beery and wildish, and the house itself—its many random rooms and slanting floors—seemed the product of a drunken adolescent mind. At first we could not spot Sloveig, so Stasselova and I waited quietly in the hallway until a guy in a baseball cap came lurching toward us, shouting in a friendly way over the music that we could buy plastic glasses for the keg for two dollars apiece. Stasselova paid him and then threaded through the crowd, gracefully for such a large man, to stand in the keg line. I watched him as he patiently stood there, the snowflakes melting on his dark shoulders.

And then Hans was on my arm. "What on earth?" he said. "Why are you here? I thought you hated these parties." He'd been dancing, apparently. He was soaked in sweat, his hair curling up at his neck.

I pointed to Stasselova.

"No kidding," Hans said.

"He showed up at my dorm as I was leaving to get Solveig."

"He came to Mellby?"

"Yes."

"God, look at him. I bet they had a nickname for him, like the Circus Man or something. All those old fascists had cheery nicknames."

Stasselova was now walking toward us. Behind him the picture window revealed a nearly black sky, with pretty crystalline stars around. He looked like a dream one might have in childhood. "He is not a fascist," I said quietly.

"Professor!" Hans raised his glass.

"Hans, yes, how are you? This is a wonderful party," Stasselova said, and it actually was. Sometimes these parties could seem deeply cozy, their wildness and noise an affirmation against the formless white midwestern winter surrounding us.

He handed me a beer. "So," he said rather formally, lifting his glass. "To youth."

"To experience," Hans said, smiling, and lifted his glass.

"To the party." Stasselova looked pleased, his eyes shining from the soft lamplight.

"The Party?" Hans raised an eyebrow.

"This party," Stasselova said forcefully, cheerfully.

"And to the committee," Hans said.

"The committee?"

"The Committee for Political Responsibility."

In one of Stasselova's lectures he had taken great pains to explain to us that language did not describe events, it handled them, as a hand handles an object, and that in this way language made the world happen under its supervision. I could see that Hans had taken this to heart and was making lurching attempts in this direction.

Mercifully, Solveig appeared. Her drunkenness and her dignity had synergized into something quite spectacular, an inner recklessness accompanied by great external restraint. Her hair looked the color of heat—bright white. She was wearing newly cut-off jeans and was absently holding the disassociated pant legs in her hand.

"The professor," she said, when she saw Stasselova. "The professor of oppression."

"Hello, Solveig."

"So you came," she said, as if this had been the plan all along.

"Yes. It's nice to see you again."

"Yes as well," she said. "Why are you here?"

The whole scene looked deeply romantic to me. "To take you home," he said.

"Home?" she said, is if this were the most elegant and promising word in the language. "Yours or mine?"

"Yours, of course. Yours and Margaret's."

"Where is your home again?" she asked. Her eyes were glimmering with complexity, like something that is given to human beings after evolution, as a gift.

"I live downtown," he said.

"No, your real home. Your homeland."

He paused. "I am from Poland," he said finally.

"Then there. Let's go there. I have always wanted to go to Poland."

Stasselova smiled. "Perhaps you would like it there."

"I have always wanted to see Wenceslaus Square."

"Well, that is nearby."

"Excellent. Let us go." And Solveig swung open the front door and walked into the snow in her shorts and T-shirt. I kissed Hans good-bye, and Stasselova and I followed her.

Once outside, Stasselova took off his coat and hung it around Solveig. Underneath his coat he was wearing a dark jacket and a tie. It looked sweet, and made me think that if one kept undressing him, darker and darker suits would be found underneath.

Solveig was walking before us on the narrow sidewalk. Above her, on the hill, hovered Humanities—great, intelligent, alight. She reached into the coat pocket and pulled out, to my astonishment, a fur hat. The hat! The wind lifted, and the trees shook off a little of their silver snow. Humanities leaned over us, interested in its loving but secular way. I felt as sure about everything as those archaeologists who discover a single bone and can then hypothesize the entire animal. Solveig placed the hat on her head and turned to vamp for a moment, opening and closing the coat and raising her arms above her head in an exaggerated gesture of beauty. She looked like some stirring, turning simulacrum of communist and capitalist ideas. As she was doing this, we passed by the president's house. It was an old-fashioned house, with high turrets, and had a bizarre modern wing hanging off one end of it. Solveig studied it for a moment as she walked, and suddenly shouted into the cold night, "Motherf---er!"

Stasselova looked as if he'd been clubbed again in the back of the head, but he kept walking. He pretended that nothing had happened, didn't even turn his head to look at the house, but when I turned to him, I saw his eyes widen and his face stiffen with shock. I said "Oh" quietly, and grabbed his hand for a moment to comfort him, to let him know that everything was under control, that this was Minnesota. Look—the president's house is still as dark as death, the moon is still high, the snow sparkling everywhere.

His hand was extraordinarily big. After Hans's hand, which I'd held for the past few months, Stasselova's more ordinary hand felt strange, almost mutant, its five fingers splayed and independent.

The next night, in the cafeteria, over a grisly neon dish called Festival Rice, I told Hans about the hat. "I saw the hat," I said.

A freshman across the cafeteria stood just then and shouted, in what was a St. Gustav tradition, *I want a standing ovation!* The entire room stood and erupted into wild applause and hooting. Hans and I stood as well, and as we clapped, I leaned over to yell, "He's been telling the truth about that night overlooking Warsaw: I saw the hat he was wearing."

"What does that mean? That means nothing. I have a fur hat."

"No," I said. "It was this big Russian hat. You should have seen it. This big, beautiful Russian hat. Solveig put it on. It saved his life."

Hans didn't even try to object; he just kind of gasped, as if the great gears of logic in his brain could not pass this syllogism through. We were still standing, clapping, applauding. I couldn't help thinking of something Stasselova had said in class: that at rallies for Stalin, when he spoke to crowds over loudspeakers, one could be shot for being the first to stop clapping.

I avoided my paper for the next month or so, until spring crashed in huge warm waves and I finally sought it out, sunk in its darkened drawer. It was a horrible surprise. I was not any more of a scholar, of course, than I had been six months earlier, when I'd plagiarized it, but my eyes had now passed over Marx and a biography of Stalin (microphones lodged in eyeglasses, streams of censors on their way to work, bloody corpses radiating out of Moscow) and the gentle Bonhoeffer. Almost miraculously I had crossed that invisible line beyond which people turn into actual readers, when they start to hear the voice of the writer as clearly as in a conversation. "Language," Tretsky had written, "is essentially a coercive act, and in the case of Eastern Europe it must be used as a tool to garden collective hopes and aspirations."

As I read, with Solveig napping at the other end of the couch, I felt a thick dread forming. Tretsky, with his suggestions of annexations and, worse, of *solutions*, seemed to be reaching right off the page, his long, thin hand grasping me by the shirt. And I could almost hear the wild mazurka, as Stasselova had described it, fading, the cabarets closing down, the music turning into a chant, the bootheels falling, the language fortifying itself, becoming a stronghold—a fixed, unchanging system, as the paper said, a moral framework.

Almost immediately I was on my way to Stasselova's office, but not before my mother called. The golden brochures had gone out in the mail. "Sweetie!" she said. "What's this? Keynote speaker? Your father and I are beside ourselves. Good night!" She always exclaimed "Good night!" at times of great happiness. I could not dissuade her from coming, and as I fled the dorm, into the rare, hybrid air of early April, I was wishing for those bad, indifferent parents who had no real interest in their children's lives.

The earth under my feet as I went to him was very sticky, almost lugubrious, like the earth one sometimes encounters in dreams. Stasselova was there, as always. He seemed pleased to see me.

I sat down and said, "You know, I was thinking that maybe somebody else could take my place at the symposium. As I reread my paper, I realized it isn't really what I meant to say at all."

"Oh," he said. "Of course you can deliver it. I would not abandon you at a moment like this."

"Really, I wouldn't take it as abandonment."

"I would not leave you in the lurch," he said. "I promise."

I felt myself being carried, mysteriously, into the doomed symposium, despite my resolve on the way over to back out at all costs. How could I win an argument against somebody with an early training in propaganda? I had to resort finally to the truth, that rinky-dink little boat in the great sea of persuasion. "See, I didn't really write the paper myself."

"Well, every thinker builds an idea on the backs of those before him—or her, in your case." He smiled at this. His teeth were very square, and humble, with small gaps between them. I could see that Stasselova was no longer after a confession. I was more valuable if I contained these ideas. Probably he's been subconsciously looking for me ever since he'd lain on the muddy banks of the Vistula, Warsaw flaming across the waters. He could see within me all his failed ideals, the ugliness of his former beliefs contained in a benign vessel—a girl!— high on a religious hill in the Midwest. He had found somebody he might oppose, and in this way absolve himself. He smiled. I could feel myself as indispensable in the organization of his psyche. Behind his head, in the sunset, the sun wasn't falling, only receding farther and farther.

The days before the symposium unfurled like the days before a wedding one dreads, both endless and accelerated, the sky filling with springtime events— ravishing sun, great winds, and eccentric green storms that focused everyone's attention skyward. And then the weekend of the symposium was upon us, the Saturday of my speech rising in the east. I awoke early and went to practice my paper on the red steps of Humanities, in whose auditorium my talk was to take place. Solveig was still sleeping, hung over from the night before. I'd been with her for the first part of it, had watched her pursue a man she'd discovered—a graduate student, actually, in town for the symposium. I had thought him a bit of a bore, but I trusted Solveig's judgment. She approached men with stealth and insight, her vision driving into those truer, more isolated stretches of personality.

I had practiced the paper countless times, and revised it, attempting to excise the most offensive lines without gutting the paper entirely and thus disappointing Stasselova. That morning I was still debating over the line "If we could agree on a common language, a single human tongue, perhaps then a single flag might unfurl over the excellent earth, one nation of like and companion souls." Reading it now, I had a faint memory of my earlier enthusiasm for this paper, its surface promise, its murderous innocence. Remembering this, I looked out over the excellent earth, at the town below the hill. And there, as always, was a tiny Gothic graveyard looking peaceful, everything still and settled finally under the gnarled, knotty, nearly human arms of apple trees. There were no apples yet, of course: they were making their way down the bough, still liquid, or whatever they are before birth. At the sight of graves I couldn't help thinking of Tretsky, my ghost-writer, in his dark suit under the earth, delightedly preparing, thanks to me, for his one last gasp.

By noon the auditorium had filled with a crowd of about two hundred, mostly graduate students and professors from around the Midwest, along with Hans and Solveig, who sat together, and, two rows behind them, my long-suffering parents, flushed with pride. I sat alone on a slight stage at the front of the room, staring out at the auditorium, which was named Luther. It had wooden walls and was extremely tall; it seemed humble and a little awkward, in that way the tall can seem. The windows stretched its full height, so that one would see the swell of earth on which Humanities was built, and then, above, all manner of weather, which this afternoon was running to rain. In front of these windows stood the reformed genius of martial law himself, the master of ceremonies, Stasselova. Behind him were maple trees, with small green leaves waving. He had always insisted in class that language as it rises in the mind looks like a tree branching, from finity to infinity. Let every voice cry out! He had once said this, kind of absently, and water had come to his eyes—not exactly tears, just a rising of the body's water into the line of sight.

After he introduced me, I stood in front of the crowd, my larynx rising quite against my will, and delivered my paper. I tried to speak each word as a discrete item, in order to persuade the audience not to synthesize the sentences into meaning. But when I lifted my head to look out at my listeners, I could see they were doing just that. When I got to the part where I said the individual did not exist—citizens were "merely shafts of light lost, redemptively, in the greater light of the state"—I saw Hans bow his head and rake his otherworldly hand through his hair.

". . . And if force is required to forge a singular and mutual grammar, then it is our sacred duty to hasten the birthpangs." Even from this distance I could hear Stasselova's breathing, and the sound of blood running through him like a quiet but rushing stream.

And then my parents. As the speech wore on—"harmony," "force," "flowering," "blood"—I could see that the very elegant parental machinery they had designed over the years, which sought always to translate my deeds into something lovely, light-bearing, full of promise, was spinning a little on its wheels. Only Solveig, that apparatchik of friendship, maintained her confidence in me. Even when she was hung over, her posture suggested a perfect alignment between heaven and earth. She kept nodding, encouraging me.

I waited the entire speech for Stasselova to leap forward and confront me, to reassert his innocence in opposition to me, but he did not, even when I reached the end. He stood and watched as everybody clapped in bewilderment, and a flushed floral insignia rose on his cheeks. I had come to love his wide, excited face, the old circus man. He smiled at me. He was my teacher, and he had wrapped himself, his elaborate historical self, into this package, and stood in front of the high windows, to teach me my little lesson, which turned out to be not about Poland or fascism or war, borderlines or passion or loyalty, but just about the sentence: the importance of, the sweetness of. And I did long for it, to say one true sentence of my own, to leap into the subject, that sturdy vessel traveling upstream through the axonal predicate into what is possible; into the object, which is all possibility; into what little we know of the future, of eternity—the light of which, incidentally, was streaming in on us just then through the high windows. Above Stasselova's head the storm clouds were dispersing, as if frightened by some impending good will, and I could see that the birds were out again, forming into that familiar pointy hieroglyph, as they're told to do from deep within.

DISCUSSION QUESTIONS

1. Were you surprised that Margaret eventually confessed to not having written the paper? What would you have done if you were Margaret? Professor Stasselova?
2. Why do you think plagiarism is so widespread in college? What can be done about it?
3. How do you feel about honor codes? Did you ever attend a school that had one? What effect would it have if your present school had one?
4. What did you learn about student-teacher relationships from this story?

SUGGESTIONS FOR JOURNAL ENTRIES

1. Describe an incident when you cheated or plagiarized and write about what effect it had on you, whether you were caught or not. If you have never cheated, write about how you felt when you discovered (observed) a classmate cheating and what you did about it, if anything.
2. Consider whether the two main characters in this short story illustrate what Langston Hughes (Reading 16) means by different "truths." Write about what you think is the "truth" for Margaret or for Professor Stasselova.

FRIENDSHIP AND ROMANCE

Having just attended an alumnae reunion at the college where I teach, I was struck by the fact that so many former students have remained good friends since graduation from college. It would seem that there is a powerful critical period for bonding that emerges during one's adolescence, and that is why we keep so many friends from high school and college. In the case of college graduates, I think, there is a greater tendency to keep friends from college than from high school.

My definition of a friend is someone who always tells me the truth even though I may not wish to hear it—my daughter is one example. Of course that works both ways. A friend is also someone I can confide in who will listen without judgment, or as the American philosopher, George Santayana, put it, one's friends "are that part of the human race with which one can be human." This bond is so close that Aristotle, the great Greek philosopher, described friendship as a "single soul dwelling in two bodies."

Teaching at a women's college I am often made aware of the difference between female friendship and male friendship. It is only fairly recently that Hollywood has begun to get over its love affair with male buddies like Butch Cassidy and the Sundance Kid. In recent years we have been treated to movies about female friends like *Thelma and Louise* and the circle of women in *How to Make an American Quilt*. Columnist Ellen Goodman pointed out as early as 1979 that such a change in focus reflects a "shift, not just from men to women but from one definition of friendship to another . . . men had buddies, while women had friends. Buddies bonded, but friends loved. Buddies faced adversity, but friends faced each other." I believe that the nature of male friendship has begun to change.

As for "romance," no topic has stimulated more discussion and even protest on college campuses in the 90s than that of sexual politics and other gender issues. *The Village Voice* even characterized it as the "Vietnam of the Nineties." I believe that there is a not-so-quiet revolution going on in how we relate to each other sexually and otherwise, and college campuses are the battleground and laboratory where old mores are dying hard and college communities are struggling to develop new, enlightened policies.

In the first essay, "Training for Real Life," Ellen Goodman humorously describes the coed dorm situation from a mother's standpoint and comes to an interesting and controversial conclusion about its relevance to the modern work world.

In the second essay, "Sleeping with the Enemy," Lynn Darling returns to her alma mater, Harvard, after 20 years to report on the sexual politics of modern campus life. Indeed, Darling discovers that romance has come a long way since *Love Story*. The third essay, by Meghan Daum, "Virtual Love," provides a look at the latest version of romance, à la Internet.

The poem, "After a While," by a precocious and anonymous 12-year-old, is about surviving heartbreak and learning "the subtle difference between holding a hand and chaining a soul," a lesson still worth remembering in the 90s.

READING 18

Training for Real Life

Ellen Goodman

Ellen Goodman is well known as a syndicated columnist and commentator on American manners and foibles, especially in the Boston area where her column originated in the Boston Globe *in 1972. Graduated from Radcliffe College '63, Goodman won a Pulitzer Prize for commentary in 1980. This essay, written in 1987, is a humorous reflection on coed dorms from a mother's perspective with the surprising conclusion that coed living may actually contribute to a more natural working environment later on.*

She went to college last fall carrying two family gifts: a sense of humor and an answering machine. By mid-winter she put together these two weapons in a salvo intended for her elders.

This is what her mother heard: A male voice in the machine stuttered, "Um, uh, you called at a bad time. We're, um, in the shower right now. But we'll be out in a few minutes, so just leave a message."

The unsuspecting caller was not freaked out, as her daughter might put it. She waited for the beep and the giggles to subside and left a return message. After all, the mother said to herself, it was only 10 a.m. The bathroom on her daughter's floor was all female in the morning. It only became coed after noon. Or was it the other way around?

Well, never mind, this dormitory living, 1987. The national fantasy of coed showers and the reality of coed friendships.

What the mother had witnessed when she visited this campus was not a seething caldron of casual sex. It was rather a comfortable atmosphere of casual friendship of young men and women.

In the morning, they lurch past each other, oozing the same unwashed charm they had in their high-school days. Day and night, they walk in and out of each other's room dressed in their finest sweatpants and T-shirts, faces dotted with ritual zit cream. They borrow each other's clothes, cut each other's hair, listen to each other's complaints.

Less has been said about the incest taboo that arises on a floor where people live together like brother and sister, where the family dynamic depends on avoiding the storm and stress of romance and breakup. When the mother was in college in the sixties, a male friend was someone who was shorter than you or maybe your boyfriend's roommate.

Even in the coed schools like hers, where she studied with men, went to class with men, they did not live together in the real daily sense of that word. Women and men had to venture out to meet each other.

As her classmates went into the work world, it took time for them to develop anything like camaraderie. It isn't easy to learn to be buddies late in life. Like learning a new language, it happens most fluently when you're young.

To this day, men and women of her generation who travel together, work together, have to get through the flack of malefemaleness. When the business literature talks about this, it stresses the woeful lack of experience women have as teammates in their college years. Those who never played team sports, they say, have trouble in the corporate huddle.

But maybe the best turf for learning how to work together isn't a playing field, not in competition but in the easy give and take, the naturalness of living together.

Men and women marry one by one, or at least one after another. But we work together in droves. The value of the coed dorm may be in graduating men and women who are natural with each other in the work world.

As for you young man in the recorded shower? The mother cannot resist asking. The daughter laughs at their recorded prank. He lives a couple of doors down the hall, she says, you met him. Oh yes, says the mother, he's your friend.

DISCUSSION QUESTIONS

1. Whether living in a dormitory (coed or otherwise) or at home, discuss the advantages and disadvantages of coed dorm living as you see them. What kind of dorm would be your preference and why?
2. How might your mother have reacted to the recorded prank of her daughter? Do you think the mother in the article is typical? Would it make any difference if it had been her son rather than her daughter?
3. Goodman suggests that your generation is much more comfortable with making friends (platonic) of the opposite sex. Do you agree?
4. What do you think of Goodman's contention that coed-dorm living will contribute to men and women being more natural with each other in the work world?

SUGGESTIONS FOR JOURNAL ENTRIES

1. Assuming you have one, write about what it is like to have a platonic friend and how that friendship differs from the boyfriend/girlfriend kind.
2. Some authorities see coed-dorm living as a solution to the shrinking of the nuclear family in that dorm mates replace the brothers and sisters that many only children never experience. Write either from your experience or in your opinion whether this is realistic.

READING 19

Sleeping with the Enemy

Lynn Darling

Lynn Darling, Harvard '72, is a staff writer for New York Newsday *who decided to return to her alma mater to report on the sexual politics of the 90s for* Esquire *in 1992. What she discovered is that falling in love is risky business.*

It was the naked Amazon that put Larry Sprung over the top. He found himself looking at her as Kate and Allison and Emily lectured at him—once again—about date rape and all the many sins of men. The Amazon looked pretty pleased with herself for a woman who had cut off her own breast, Larry thought. Larry was a senior at Harvard and he'd seen a lot; but to him, the photograph hanging in his friends' living room was a perfect example of what he was up against.

"Have you seen it?" he asks. "It's like the women are saying, 'If you're going to act like an a--hole, then we're going to act like a--holes.' This may be endearing from your perspective, but from mine, it's extremely threatening."

In fact, it did sound a bit endearing from my perspective. It reminded me of the sort of passionate melodrama in which my Harvard friends and I dressed ourselves twenty years ago. But I could see his point. A few weeks before, I had walked through Harvard Yard for the first time since my graduation and found it imbued with all the youthful high spirits of a frontline field hospital braced for the next round of casualties.

TOP 10 QUESTIONS ASKED ABOUT AIDS, read a poster tacked to a small kiosk bristling with flyers. No. 3. CAN I GET AIDS FROM A VIRGIN? Next to it was a flyer from Response, "a confidential peer-counseling group" prepared to discuss issues "surrounding relationships, harassment, sexual abuse, and rape." Response, it turned out, was only one of seven peer-counseling groups on campus; the others deal with issues that range from sexual orientation to eating disorders.

In the last few days, I had been startled by how quickly the talk could turn to violence when the subject of sex or even romance came up. Some of the students I had talked to—even those with no personal experience with sexual catastrophe—seemed to have an almost morbid fascination with the threat of abuse.

Of course, college is a kind of theater, and late adolescence a highly self-dramatizing time of life, one given to fervid extremes. It had been so twenty years ago as well, when an old boyfriend wrote an article for *The Harvard Crimson* explaining why he hadn't killed himself in protest for the Vietnam War. But at least then, such extremity didn't preclude love. How did you fall in love now, I wondered, how did you permit yourself those first extravagant expeditions into sex?

Forget sex, Larry said.

"It's a total f---ing mess. Everything has become so analyzed," he said. How were you meant to flirt, he wanted to know, when everything had to be spelled out? There was no room left for mystery. "In bed, you just don't know what's going on. Sex is so politicized now. But the problem is, good sex is not politically correct." Larry is into transcendental meditation. He believes in the union of opposites, in the passively active and actively passive. He suspects these notions can be applied quite creatively to sex. "But there's this insistence on some superficial equality in bed," he said. "And that's a real chill factor when it comes to totally letting go."

Larry Sprung doesn't look like a target for the sexual wrath heating up so many campuses now. In fact, he is a laid-back, progressive kind of guy, good-looking in a sensitive, nonthreatening way, exhibiting none of the politically in-correct height and muscularity that some of the women at Harvard call buff. And he is very sympathetic to women's issues. It's just that he's tired of being treated like the enemy, personally responsible for the horrors that men visit on women.

"Women are so angry," he said. "But they can only discuss this stuff with men who aren't creeps, because the creeps aren't going to listen to them."

And these women were just friends. When it came to something more inti-mate than that, well, Larry had about given up on the idea of falling in love at Harvard. Desire was a decidedly irrational thing, he had found, mocking his own best intentions. Logic, for instance, hadn't got him safely past the ques-tion of Eleanor Stafford.

Eleanor was beautiful, she was funny, she was smart. "Once she sat down in the dining hall and asked me about TM," he said. "I asked her why she was interested, and she said, 'I'm incredibly nervous and freaked-out all the time.' I thought, *Now, this is a woman who talks straight.*"

As it turned out, Eleanor Stafford was not unaware of Larry Sprung. There was definitely something about him that appealed to her, she said. Un-fortunately it was too late.

Eleanor, too, had given up on the idea of love. In fact, she had just written her declaration of independence on the subject. It was called "Love, Friendship, and My Crazy Daddy," and it would appear in the next issue of the feminist journal *The Rag.* In it she advised women to forget "that oozy oozy love feeling. . . . Before you buy into the myth of romantic love, think carefully. About your mobility. Your autonomy. Your self-respect. And your safety, emo-tional and physical. Take care of your friends and let them take care of you."

Eleanor was exhilarated and tense. After her article was published, she was pretty sure no man would dare to approach her. She had burned her bridges, and she was getting high from the smell of the smoke.

Actually, it wasn't an Amazon. It was a postmastectomy patient, and the display of the intricately tattooed scar on her chest was meant to convey a to-tally joyous acceptance of her body. Allison Mnookin and Emily Cousins find it interesting that Larry remembered the picture as an Amazon brandishing her self-mutilation. But while to me this is one of those odd little psychological glitches into which we all stumble from time to time, it is, to Allison and

Emily, a perfect example of the barricades of misperception and mistrust that separate men and women.

"I can see where it's hard for Larry," Allison says when I mention his exasperation over their date-rape discussions. "When you're talking about date rape and sex, many women are talking from the position of being potential victims, and if men speak from the position of being potentially falsely accused, then how do we ever talk? How do we ever get together when we're starting from such totally different fears?"

I don't know the answer to that question. I have been thinking, I suddenly realize, about a black-lace bra.

The woman wore it under a sheer white blouse, a blouse just transparent enough to make it clear that this was a conscious decision, not a matter of getting dressed in the dark. She was standing in front of me in a cafeteria line my freshman year at Harvard in 1968, and she was in the middle of a wonderfully arcane, wonderfully intellectual discussion with a male colleague, a fellow graduate student.

I was enthralled, made dizzy by the possibilities the black bra implied. Here was a whole new world, where you could be simultaneously really smart and frankly sexy, where looking like a slut carried with it some sort of intellectual imprimatur. Maybe I was, at that moment, a skinny, skittish kid wrapped tight in my middleclass hang-ups, but I could change.

And I did. Before long, the beautiful wardrobe of tasteful dresses my mother had made for me became six inches shorter before giving way entirely to a battered black sweater and a single pair of blue jeans held together with some rusting safety pins. The thrill of the first cocktail disappeared in a river of jug wine and a bonfire of drugs. And the stiff rituals of the Saturday night date splintered under the heel of the freewheeling feminist persona with which I strode forward to meet the world.

Sex was a part of that persona. It was a political statement, a rejection of the path permitted to us, a revolutionary act. Not revolutionary like a Weatherwoman, maybe, who, it was said, walked right up to a man in a roomful of other people and engaged in sex on the spot. But revolutionary just the same, in a world where the Pill was still illegal in Massachusetts for unmarried women.

Parietal hours, which limited the amount of time men and women could be in each other's rooms, ended the first semester of my sophomore year, and that spring, the first Radcliffe students moved into Harvard houses. It was as if the university had given women permission to engage in the same coming-of-age rituals that male students took for granted. We were pioneers, we told ourselves, forging a path for the next generation of women.

And now that generation was here at Harvard. Now men and women live together in the same dormitories from the beginning of their first year. Together they attend workshops on date rape and AIDS. They do not do this over sherry, because the university no longer serves alcohol to undergraduates. Students still go to the Bureau of Study Counsel to talk about what's causing them to flunk economics, but now the terrors can include a recently surfaced memory of childhood sexual abuse. They become peer counselors and listen compassionately to the callers' recurring nightmares about the friend or the father who hurt them.

A recent survey elicited the fact that 32 percent of the undergraduate women had reported "unwanted and inappropriate sexual attention from a peer." Three cases of alleged sexual assault and two cases of other physical violence were under investigation by the end of the fall semester. Several years ago, an unofficial fraternity came under attack after a string of drunken episodes culminated in a sexual assault on a young woman.

Not surprisingly, so harsh an atmosphere tends to color the perspective from which students consider the possible conclusions to a Saturday night date. "Because you know [date rape] can happen with men who are your good friends, all men are enemies, even the nice ones," said one senior. "I don't see how you can make the decision to go back to somebody's room."

Not everyone at Harvard is losing sleep over these issues. The jocks in Kirkland House are still complaining about how unattractive Harvard girls are, while the preppies in Eliot are quite sure they wouldn't respect a girl who slept with them on the first date, although now they do worry about what could happen if, the next morning, she was sorry she had.

But my friends had been the kind who would lose sleep over these issues, and so I had gone looking for me and mine, the students who reminded me of my own long-ago circle: high-strung, neurotic, lefty romantics, trembling a little on the limbs they'd gone out on.

I found them in Dunster House, home to radicals, counterculture messiahs, and bourgeois wannabes when I was here and now a haven for the crunchy-granola faction and the latest incarnations of the Left.

Intense and blazingly articulate, Kate Frucher is, with Eleanor, co-president of the ardently feminist Radcliffe Union of Students, and she shares a warm warren of rooms in Dunster with Emily Cousins and Allison Mnookin, two other roommates, and a constant stream of friends. Emily is tall and thin, a soft-spoken religion major. Allison, dark-eyed, thoughtful, is a law professor's daughter who did a classic Harvard about-face, turning from a freewheeling, preppy-driven social life her first year to the close community she found in women's studies.

They reminded me—in their fast-talking intensity and the sudden way anger dissolved into laughter and in the contradictions into which head and heart were constantly tumbling them—of the women I met here, and of the ardent discussions we had on the hopelessly corrupt nature of the world one moment and on the healthiest way to lose our virginity the next (should we or shouldn't we be in love?).

Except, of course, that that's not what Kate and Emily and Allison talk about. For one thing, they all took care of their virginity in high school. And for another, the landscape against which their discussions take place is so much darker, so much more imperiled.

For them, sex is a terrain where fear threatens to overwhelm curiosity; a place they approach with an exquisite appreciation of their own vulnerability.

"There's a lot of risk associated with sex," Allison said. "Pregnancy and reputation and violence. Look at Anita Hill and the Willie Smith trial—that has a lot of repercussions for me; the only thing we had to hold onto was the judicial system, and now we don't even have that."

Listening to them, I admire their clear eyes and hard heads and think that maybe they are safe from some of the cliffs over which we danced in our naiveté. But they've lost something too, and they recognize that.

Last year Allison took a seminar on pornography and one of the guest speakers was Susie Bright, the editor of a lesbian sex journal. Bright told the class that once she had been asked to appear at a college event carrying a NO MEANS NO sign. I'd rather carry one that said YES MEANS YES, she said, and her comment made a big impression.

"I started thinking about that," Allison said. "I know all the ways to say no, and all the reasons, but I don't know how to say yes." There have been times, she says, when she's removed a man's hand from her breast for perhaps the fifth time, thinking that maybe she didn't want to be removing that hand at all. "I'll be thinking, *Maybe this is what I want, this is what I want for me*," she said. "And then I think, *It's not totally okay for me, I shouldn't be wanting this, because it means I'm a slut, because I don't know him.* And yet all you really want to say is hell, yes."

Lately, these quandaries have been more theoretical than practical, they ruefully acknowledge. "We have deconstructed all these issues, but now we don't know how to relate to each other, especially men," says Kate. They have many close male friendships, but rarely do these turn to romance. It is hard to find a man who has evolved enough. "You put people through the feminist sieve," says Emily, "Because these issues become a part of who you are. It's a politics so personal that political differences really matter. After a while you just can't compromise it anymore."

Which is why the women of Dunster House were very much impressed with Eleanor Stafford's forthcoming piece. It would lay to rest the idea that romantic love was possible in this debased day and age, when words have failed and feelings faltered.

Which, of course, it did, in acceptably vehement terms. Unfortunately, a small problem had developed.

It began the night of the Angela Davis lecture. The lecture was a very big deal among the women Larry Sprung was closest to, and so, of course, he was there. He didn't think much of Davis or the way she polarized everything into a world of good guys and bad guys. He was pretty bored, in fact. But at dinner afterward, the evening began to improve.

Eleanor Stafford was there and suddenly something sparked between them.

She was ablaze that night, she remembers; she was "totally harsh and hysterical," strutting her carefully constructed public persona, loud and strident, and cracking crass jokes, and she could tell Larry found it all very attractive. She was used to that by now, to the way men were attracted to the feminist ice princess, but she wasn't prepared for how attracted she was to Larry, as they stayed up late into the night talking, talking, talking, getting smashed on tequila and wine. By the end of the night, it was clear to both of them that they were going to fool around.

Things happened very fast after that. Two weeks later, they were not only lovers, they had even met each other's parents over the Christmas break. On the other hand, both of them were also wondering whether the relationship wasn't completely doomed.

The issue was love. Larry hadn't ever been in love before. The way he understood it, love was a sledgehammer that came down on your head, bringing with it a total loss of reason. He had friends who had been in love: It looked to be the most dangerous experience they had ever had. The way Larry saw it, you enjoyed a certain psychological stability until you were about nineteen, and then this thing happened to you and you were never the same. Larry was twenty-one and he was ready.

He was aware of the risks. Few of his friends had any happily-ever-after stories to report. In high school, his parents had been among the only adults he knew who weren't divorced. Still, he had to be in love; what else was there? Larry was very ambivalent about the life that faced him after graduation. He was a lawyer's son from Brooklyn—launched with all with all the usual privileges, and yet most of his friends were "totally f---ing lost." He couldn't deal with graduate school; he didn't want to think about job interviews. You couldn't change the world; you couldn't even find an affordable apartment. You could fall in love, though. You could do that much.

But Eleanor knew that love was a ditch.

Eleanor had come a long way from her first year at Harvard, which she spent in an airtight domesticity, . . . talking baby talk with a guy named Miguel. In her sophomore year, she had become fascinated with the feminists of Adams House, the hip nexus of all that was radical, artistic, and cutting edge.

Eleanor had already endorsed feminism's principles, and she was not unacquainted with sexism personally: When she was elected president of the student council at Choate, the preppy, conservative boys demanded a recount. But the feminist fatales of Adams House added another dimension—they were beautiful, they were feared and admired, and they wore these incredibly revealing clothes. They were the most charismatic figures in Adams House, and they could have any man who interested them. Eleanor wanted their power; she wanted to bury forever the private self she so despised—sweet, vulnerable, and needy—under a tough enamel of self-sufficiency and contempt.

She joined RUS and plunged back into her old prep-school overachiever mode. She organized a festival of women in the arts. She helped coordinate the annual "Take Back the Night" rally. She raised her voice in the chorus of indignation over Final clubs, Harvard's long-entrenched, all-male, elitist sanctums. She stayed up until 4:00 in the morning discussing feminist theory, then crawled back home to Miguel. Crawled back, that is, until Miguel decided to retaliate by partying, flirting his brains out, and finally, not coming home at all. That was when Eleanor dropped out of school for a semester and began her angry phase.

Eleanor began to write a lot of rape poetry. She chopped off her long light-brown hair. Her looks had always been a problem; it was hard to take a little Wasp from Woodbury, Connecticut, seriously in culturally diverse Harvard. Eleanor felt she had to work doubly hard at being obnoxious and loud.

She set about liberating herself from her old notions of love. Eventually she embarked on a relationship with a twenty-three-year-old housemate that involved sex but no exclusiveness, no jealousy, and no romance. *Ooh, am I strong*, thought Eleanor; all her friends were so impressed.

But the relationship was boring and Eleanor was confused.

Maybe this is the best I can hope for, she decided. *I'm not in danger, and in this stage of development that's really all I can hope for.* She was completely miserable, but then maybe the next three generations of women had to be miserable if things were ever going to improve. Eleanor had decided she was willing to make that sacrifice.

And now look at me, she thought. *Look at what is happening to me.* Already the change had begun, the reemergence of that soft and needy, vulnerable self.

"Look at you!" Larry had marveled. "You've not only gotten rid of your irony, you have no defense mechanisms at all! You hate your public persona; you don't even like being funny." He loved it. But Eleanor was terrified. She had spent a year and a half constructing this persona and now it was lying in shards at her feet.

So Larry and Eleanor talked and talked. They had intense intellectual conversations. It would be better, Eleanor argued, if she and Larry were simply very good friends who had sex occasionally.

So that was how they left it. But then the sex wasn't as good and the air between them grew thin and cold.

Still, Eleanor held fast. *Maybe there are men out there who would like me strong and unromantic*, she thought. *Maybe he's a sexist pig, and he's manipulating me because he's a sexist pig.*

And then she had a terrible thought: *Oh, my God, I've lost my sweetness! I'm a barren woman! I'm a monster!*

Make no mistake, university officials say, the concern over sexual violence is real and well founded. But in talking to students, it's also clear that the fear and the heightened awareness of danger are also a conduit for other fears and other dreams. For the young women, violence becomes a metaphor for their own confusion over what is permitted and what is not. For the young men, concern over these issues has become a way of expressing a tenderness toward women that is otherwise stymied, a way to give vent to a white-knight's protectiveness that might otherwise invite mockery and scorn.

"I think young women now are very confused," says Janet Viggiani, Harvard's assistant dean for coeducation, co-chair of the college's date-rape task force, and the senior tutor in Adams House. "They don't always know where to place themselves. They don't have many models for how to be strong females and feminine. Many of their models are victim models—passive, weak, endangered."

In Adams House in particular, I was told, one found a very confusing sexual landscape, one in which there are "lots of unclear boundaries" between gay and straight: Straight women who are publicly very physical with their gay male friends, for instance. I kept hearing stories of extravagant, erotically ambiguous, women-only parties that became almost mythic in the telling. It was as if physical intimacy was best expressed within a context in which no romantic assumptions were made.

Otherwise, it seems, it's just too difficult. Love is a leap of faith; and risk isn't a much-admired quality among the young these days. Love yearns for an obliteration of opposites, and in a university beset by a stern insistence on differences, such a step can look a little suspicious. Love is a kind of language, and language, I was told, is subversive. "It's just easier to spend time with people you don't have to explain yourself to," said more than one student.

"How do you find the language?" Emily had asked. "How do you start a revolution in a relationship?"

That's a question we didn't ask. We asked different ones, though they were equally grandiloquent, equally Gothic, much more naive. I found them again, in the crumbling pages of the *Crimson*, in a bound volume so old it was held together by a shoestring.

We lived self-consciously in what we liked to think was the teeth of the apocalypse. "More and more, America feels like Prague during the occupation," wrote James K. Glassman in the fall of 1968. "The frustration does not go away. The outrage is not clean. The vision of victory is no longer there. Look at where we are. We are in Paris and in Prague and in Chicago and we are nowhere. Perhaps we are nowhere at Columbia. This had been a summer of despair. . . . All our goals and our ideals and everything we are fighting for—those things are still there, but now really, for the first time, the fight looks impossible."

"There is an unspeakable sadness all over the place," wrote Frank Rich a year later, in 1969. "It isn't something you can talk about directly. You just feel it. Every morning when you wake up and every night when you go to bed. It is an American sadness."

I had not remembered how gorgeously miserable we were. What I remembered, besides the friends I had made, was a loopy pursuit of an ecstatic dailiness, a belief as one *Crimson* writer put it that we could become "beautiful and human and together," the ardent conviction that as America crumbled around us, we would found the new Jerusalem and defy the corrupt culture that had spawned us. Look out, the *Crimson* warned, "people are actively trying to keep you from becoming one with the universe."

The kids I talked to are not trying to become one with the universe. They were eight years old when Ronald Reagan became President, and they came to college without the casual arrogance and the innate confidence with which we proposed to turn our backs on our cultural and economic birthrights. We were longing to escape the claustrophobia of our stable affluence; they are the cynical survivors of divorce and two-career families, and they have no traditions of permanence to shield them. They are experts on the dark side, on hedging bets and lowering expectations, too familiar with sadness to glamorize it.

"All our parents were experimenting with roles of who was who and who was going to do what, and the kids got neglected in the process," observed Marc Grant, a friend of Larry's. "I always thought parents are supposed to learn stuff and pass that stuff on to their kids, but if parents can't figure out their own life and what makes them happy, then what's the point? It was scary. There was nobody."

So perhaps that is why they retreat to the few things that are permanent about them—the color of their skin, the culture they came from, the gender they belong to. At times Harvard looks like a darkling plain, lit by the light of a thousand different campfires. There are organizations in which to be black or Native American or South Asian; you can belong to one of the new underground fraternities or to a new group called Queer and Catholic. Sometimes it can be difficult to choose, to decide how, as one student put it, to hierarchize your identity: Are you black first or gay first or female first?

"There's this urge to have some self-defining experience," says Rebecca Walkowitz, the outgoing president of the *Crimson*. "There was almost a rapture about the Persian Gulf war. This will be it, we thought, for both sides. But the moment passed quickly. So people return to the questions of identity and sex. Is someone's identity a matter of how I perceive them or of how they perceive themselves? Who has the right to decide?"

The women of Dunster House say the women of my generation were naive about the complexities that faced them. I agree. Our own new vision was not only ephemeral, it left a lot of debris when it broke up on the rocks of its own contradictions. And the society we were rebelling against has come to be coated in the popular culture with a nostalgia that would have left us speechless. But still I was sorry that no one at Harvard was hearing voices, angry, ecstatic, self-proclaiming, and propelled into the future: It's not a bad way to be young. But I was wrong. Someone was.

Sandi DuBowski looked pale and bleary-eyed the morning I went to see him, having been up most of the night postering the campus in advance of his organization's upcoming dance. Sandi is co-chair of the Bi-Gay-Lesbian Student Association, the group that has provoked the most hostility and the most admiration on campus.

This was Sandi's senior year at Harvard, and it had been a gratifying first semester. When a new ultraconservative magazine, *Peninsula*, devoted an entire issue to denouncing homosexuality, Sandi organized an emotional rally in which two professors came out of the closet and a raft of administration officials were present to support gay rights on campus. Even the issue of how much official university aid and comfort ROTC should receive revolved around gay rights: Should Harvard lend recognition to an institution that discriminates against homosexuals?

GET OUT OF BED AND DANCE, read one of the posters Sandi had put up. It depicted two naked men entwined in a haven of rumpled sheets. The posters were fairly demure by the standards of BGLSA, which has tried deliberately and successfully to be shocking, confrontational, and provocative. It is the only group on campus talking about sex in an open, celebratory sort of way, and while it makes some intensely uncomfortable, its joyous radicalizing of sex has also prompted a kind of wistful envy among others.

Sandi realized he was gay his first year at Harvard, but the only person he told then was a counselor back at his old high school in New York. "Miss Hicks, I'm gay," Sandi said. "You know, in the Native American tradition, Sandi, gays are spiritual leaders," Miss Hicks said. This was interesting, but not terribly helpful, and Sandi kept his secret to himself for most of the year. He had one roommate, after all, who had made it very clear what he would do if he ever found "a faggot in my face," and he liked his other roommate too much to jeopardize their friendship.

That summer Sandi went to San Francisco. "I remember going up this huge hill when I was about to reach the Castro, and it was like nirvana was coming." He came back to Harvard for his sophomore year, on fire but still a virgin. But then he met a student, the one he calls St. Charlie the Radiant. "I sat on his couch for two and a half hours and then I said, 'I can't sit here another minute without jumping your bones.' It sounds so tacky but that's what I said."

Charlie was kind and gentle and soon Sandi's "mind and body and soul just fused together where before they had been so separate. Before, I had not had a body. And now, it was one big pleasure point."

Before long, Sandi's parents were worried that their only son was obsessed with his homosexuality. "I wanted to mark my body in some way so that everybody would know who I was." He grew his sideburns and cut his hair short, he wore combat boots and multicolored headbands and sleek vests and harlequin tights. "I wanted to break up the silences, so things could never go back the way they were," he remembers.

Sandi slept with a lot of men that summer; he even slept with men he knew had AIDS. It was a political statement. "Society is constantly policing gay sexuality," he said. "There's this constant chastisement. Even now I have straight friends who say to me, 'Oh, Sandi, I hope you're having safe sex.' What gives them permission to say that? I don't think that's something they're saying to their straight friends."

To Sandi, the point was and has always been community, a place "where you could live a life of ideas and values and show your dissatisfaction with everything wrong with society." And now he's found it, in a community that bears, in its fierce eroticism and its self-conscious exultation in its outsider status, a haunting resemblance to the one I remember. That's not so surprising, I suppose. If the prospect of friends dying in an irrational war in a faraway country can provoke a defiant dance around the fire, then how much more so can the dying and the grief in which Sandi came of age?

It is reading period, a bleak time, when a thick, dry fear coats the tongue and brings the body bolt upright after the few hours allotted to sleep. Two weeks between the end of classes and the beginning of finals in which to complete an entire semester's worth of work.

Eleanor Stafford has to read the Bible this weekend. The entire Bible, Old and New Testament. But that is not the thing that is keeping her awake at night. That is not the thing that has her staring wide-eyed with anxiety as she attempts to explain the thing that has happened to her.

Eleanor is in love.

"It's so confusing, it's so incredibly confusing," she says, shaking her head and clutching at her shorn hair, the hair Larry would like her to grow long again.

They had almost broken up and that really was what did it, realizing that she was going to lose him. And now here they are, sighing as they look into each other's eyes. That oozy feeling she thought she'd never have again—well, she was up to her eyes in oozy feeling.

"But is that good?" Eleanor wants to know. "Now we're totally cute and talking in baby voices."

Eleanor is worried. "We used to have these fierce intellectual discussions and now we sit around cooking dinner together. I'm worried that he won't think I'm smart anymore."

Larry isn't worried. Maybe, he said to her, when you're this intimate and this intense, it's not important to talk. Words, he said, are symbolic representations of things that aren't there, and if it's all there, maybe you don't need them. Besides, he says, if they were talking all the time, they wouldn't need their friends anymore. So perhaps it's just as well.

But there is another problem. Sometimes Larry puts his arm around her in public. "It means I have to deal with the fact that I'm in a relationship," she says, "and that means I'm going to have to lose a lot of power. Men were terrified of me. I loved that. Now I realize I'm going to have to give all that up."

Already there had been some raised eyebrows among her own ranks. "I think I got the prize but some women don't think Larry's affirming enough." Others were amused. "I'd always been the harshest one, and now a lot of them can't keep the smiles off their faces."

And now she began to hear all the old, weird voices, the ancient cross-generational voodoo, the unliberated voices that whispered that Larry would be leaving in the spring, and what about the future, what about marriage, what about being alone again, what in heaven was she talking about?

It was so hard, thought Eleanor. It was so hard to find your voice and your anger and the strength to do battle against the great male misogynist world order that sought to do you in. That, after all, was the reality she faced.

That was the reality, all right, but she was beginning to think it wasn't the whole story. *Maybe we were wrong,* she thought. *Maybe it is possible to be happy.*

DISCUSSION QUESTIONS

1. Were you surprised by the ending? What do you think is Darling's message in the final paragraph?
2. Do you agree with Larry that "sex is a total mess?" Why or why not?

3. How do the sexual politics on your campus today differ from Harvard in 1992?
4. Do you agree with Susie Bright that we need to start learning how to say yes as well as no?
5. How do you think this report would have differed if written by a male alumnus of the class of 1972?

SUGGESTIONS FOR JOURNAL ENTRIES

1. Write about the first time you fell in love and how you feel about falling in love now.
2. Interview one upperclass student of each sex on their perceptions of campus sexual politics and write about any gender differences that you detect.

READING 20

Virtual Love

Meghan Daum

Meghan Daum, Vassar '92 is a nonfiction writer who has published quite extensively in such publications as The New Yorker, The New York Times Book Review, *and* GQ. *In this essay, which appeared in* The New Yorker *in 1997, Daum attempts to answer the question, "Is dating better in cyberspace?"*

It was last November; fall was drifting away into an intolerable chill. I was at the end of my twenty-sixth year, and was living in New York City, trying to support myself as a writer, and taking part in the kind of urban life that might be construed as glamorous were it to appear in a memoir in the distant future. At the time, however, my days felt more like a grind than like an adventure: hours of work strung between the motions of waking up, getting the mail, watching TV with my roommates, and going to bed. One morning, I logged on to my America Online account to find a message under the heading "is this the real meghan daum?" It came from someone with the screen name PFSlider. The body of the message consisted of five sentences, written entirely in lower-case letters, of perfectly turned flattery: something about PFSlider's admiration of some newspaper and magazine articles I had published over the last year and a half, something about his resulting infatuation with me, and something about his being a sportswriter in California.

I was engaged for the thirty seconds that it took me to read the message and fashion a reply. Though it felt strange to be in the position of confirming that I was indeed "the real meghan daum," I managed to say, "Yes, it's me. Thank you for writing." I clicked the "Send Now" icon, shot my words into the void, and forgot about PFSlider until the next day, when I received another message, this one headed "eureka."

"wow, it is you," he wrote, still in lower case. He chronicled the various conditions under which he'd read my few-and-far-between articles—a boardwalk in Laguna Beach, the spring-training pressroom for a baseball team that he covered for a Los Angeles newspaper. He confessed to having a crush on me. He referred to me as "princess daum." He said he wanted to have lunch with me during one of his two annual trips to New York.

The letter was outrageous and endearingly pathetic, possibly the practical joke of a friend trying to rouse me out of a temporary writer's block. But the kindness pouring forth from my computer screen was bizarrely exhilarating, and I logged off and thought about it for a few hours before writing back to express how flattered and "touched"—this was probably the first time I had ever used that word in earnest—I was by his message.

I am not what most people would call a computer person. I have no interest in chat rooms, newsgroups, or most Web sites. I derive a palpable thrill from sticking a letter in the United States mail. But I have a constant low-grade fear of the telephone, and I often call people with the intention of getting their answering machines. There is something about the live voice that I have come to find unnervingly organic, as volatile as live television. E-mail provides a useful antidote for my particular communication anxieties. Though I generally send and receive only a few messages a week, I take comfort in their silence and their boundaries.

PFSlider and I tossed a few innocuous, smart-assed notes back and forth over the week following his first message. Let's say his name was Pete. He was twenty-nine, and single. I revealed very little about myself, relying instead on the ironic commentary and forced witticisms that are the conceit of so many E-mail messages. But I quickly developed an oblique affection for PFSlider. I was excited when there was a message from him, mildly depressed when there wasn't. After a few weeks, he gave me his phone number. I did not give him mine, but he looked it up and called me one Friday night. I was home. I picked up the phone. His voice was jarring, yet not unpleasant. He held up more than his end of the conversation for an hour, and when he asked permission to call me again I granted it, as though we were of an earlier era.

Pete—I could never wrap my mind around his name, privately thinking of him as PFSlider, "E-mail guy," or even "baseball boy"—began phoning me two or three times a week. He asked if he could meet me, and I said that that would be O.K. Christmas was a few weeks away, and he told me that he would be coming back East to see his family. From there, he would take a short flight to New York and have lunch with me.

"It is my off-season mission to meet you," he said.

"There will probably be a snowstorm," I said.

"I'll take a team of sled dogs," he answered.

We talked about our work and our families, about baseball and Bill Clinton and Howard Stern and sex, about his hatred for Los Angeles and how much he wanted a new job. Sometimes we'd find each other logged on simultaneously and type back and forth for hours.

I had previously considered cybercommunication an oxymoron, a fast road to the breakdown of humanity. But, curiously, the Internet—at least in the limited form in which I was using it—felt anything but dehumanizing. My interaction with PFSlider seemed more authentic than much of what I experienced in the daylight realm of living beings. I was certainly putting more energy into the relationship than I had put into many others. I also was giving Pete attention that was by definition undivided, and relishing the safety of the distance between us by opting to be truthful instead of doling out the white lies that have become the staple of real life. The outside world—the place where I walked around avoiding people I didn't want to deal with, peppering my casual conversations with half-truths, and applying my motto "Let the machine take it" to almost any scenario—was sliding into the periphery of my mind.

For me, time on-line with Pete was far superior to the phone. There were no background noises, no interruptions from "call waiting," no long-distance charges. Through typos and misspellings, he flirted maniacally. "I have an absurd crush on you," he said. "If I like you in person, you must promise to marry me." I was coy and conceited, telling him to get a life, baiting him into complimenting me further, teasing him in a way I would never have dared to do in person, or even on the phone. I would stay up until 3 A.M. typing with him, smiling at the screen, getting so giddy that when I quit I couldn't fall asleep. I was having difficulty recalling what I used to do at night. It was as if he and I lived together in our own quiet space—a space made all the more intimate because of our conscious decision to block everyone else out. My phone was tied up for hours at a time. No one in the real world could reach me, and I didn't really care.

Since my last serious relationship, I'd had the requisite number of false starts and five-night stands, dates that I wasn't sure were dates, and emphatically casual affairs that buckled under their own inertia. With PFSlider, on the other hand, I may not have known my suitor, but, for the first time in my life, I knew the deal: I was a desired person, the object of a blind man's gaze. He called not only when he said he would call but unexpectedly, just to say hello. He was protected by the shield of the Internet; his guard was not merely down but nonexistent. He let his phone bill grow to towering proportions. He told me that he thought about me all the time, though we both knew that the "me" in his mind consisted largely of himself. He talked about me to his friends, and admitted it. He arranged his holiday schedule around our impending date. He managed to charm me with sports analogies. He didn't hesitate. He was unblinking and unapologetic, all nerviness and balls to the wall.

And so PFSlider became my everyday life. All the tangible stuff fell away. My body did not exist. I had no skin, no hair, no bones. All desire had converted itself into a cerebral current that reached nothing but by frontal lobe. There was no outdoors, no social life, no weather. There was only the computer screen and the phone, my chair, and maybe a glass of water. Most mornings, I would wake up to find a message from PFSlider, composed in Pacific time while I slept in the wee hours. "I had a date last night," he wrote. "And I am not ashamed to say it was doomed from the start because I couldn't stop thinking about you."

I fired back a message slapping his hand. "We must be careful where we tread," I said. This was true but not sincere. I wanted it, all of it. I wanted unfettered affention, soul-mating, true romance. In the weeks that had elapsed since I picked up "is this the real meghan daum?" the real me had undergone some kind of meltdown—a systemic rejection of all the savvy and independence I had worn for years, like a grownup Girl Scout badge.

Pete knew nothing of my scattered, juvenile self, and I did my best to keep it that way. Even though I was heading into my late twenties, I was still a child, ignorant of dance steps and health insurance, a prisoner of credit-card debt and student loans and the nagging feeling that I didn't want anyone to find me until I had pulled myself into some semblance of an adult. The fact that Pete had literally seemed to discover me, as if by turning over a rock, lent us an aura of fate which I actually took half-seriously. Though skepticism seemed like the obvious choice in this strange situation, I discarded it precisely because it was the obvious choice, because I wanted a more interesting narrative than cynicism would ever allow. I was a true believer in the urban dream: the dream of years of struggle, of getting a break, of making it. Like most of my friends, I wanted someone to love me, but I wasn't supposed to need it. To admit to loneliness was to smack the face of progress, to betray the times in which we lived. But PFSlider derailed me. He gave me all of what I'd never even realized I wanted.

My addiction to PFSlider's messages indicated a monstrous narcissism, but it also revealed a subtler desire, which I didn't fully understand at the time. My need to experience an old-fashioned kind of courtship was stronger than I had ever imagined. And the fact that technology was providing an avenue for such archaic discourse was a paradox that both fascinated and repelled me. Our relationship had an epistolary quality that put our communication closer to the eighteenth century than to the impending millennium. Thanks to the computer, I was involved in a well defined courtship, a neat little space in which he and I were both safe to express the panic and the fascination of our mutual affection. Our interaction was refreshingly orderly, noble in its vigor, dignified despite its shamelessness. It was far removed from the randomness of real-life relationships. We had an intimacy that seemed custom-made for our strange, lonely times. It seemed custom-made for me.

The day of our date, a week before Christmas, was frigid and sunny. Pete was sitting at the bar of the restaurant when I arrived. We shook hands. For a split second, he leaned toward me with his chin, as if to kiss me. He was shorter than I had pictured, though he was not short. He struck me as clean cut. He had very nice hands. He wore a very nice shirt. We were seated at a very nice table. I scanned the restaurant for people I knew, saw none, and couldn't decide how I felt about that.

He talked, and I heard nothing he said. I stared at his profile and tried to figure out whether I liked him. He seemed to be saying nothing in particular, but he went on forever. Later, we went to the Museum of Natural History and watched a science film about storm chasers. We walked around looking for the dinosaurs, and he talked so much that I wanted to cry. Outside, walking along Central Park West at dusk, through the leaves, past the yellow cabs and the splendid lights of Manhattan at Christmas, he grabbed my hand to kiss me and I didn't let him. I felt as if my brain had been stuffed with cotton. Then, for some reason, I invited him back to my apartment. I gave him a few beers and finally let him kiss me on the lumpy futon in my bedroom. The radiator clanked. The phone rang and the machine picked up. A car alarm blared outside. A key turned in the door as one of my roommates came home. I had no sensation at all—only a clear conviction that I wanted Pete out of my apartment. I wanted to hand him his coat, close the door behind him, and fight the ensuing emptiness by turning on the computer and taking comfort in PFSlider.

When Pete finally did leave, I berated myself from every angle: for not kissing him on Central Park West, for letting him kiss me at all, for not liking him, for wanting to like him more than I had wanted anything in such a long time. I was horrified by the realization that I had invested so heavily in a made-up character—a character in whose creation I'd had a greater hand than even Pete himself. How could I, a person so self-congratulatingly reasonable, have been sucked into a scenario that was more akin to a television talk show than to the relatively full and sophisticated life I was so convinced I led? How could I have received a fan letter and allowed it to go this far?

The next day, a huge bouquet of FTD flowers arrived from him. No one had ever sent me flowers before. I forgave him. As human beings with actual flesh and hand gestures and Gap clothing, Pete and I were utterly incompatible, but I decided to pretend otherwise. He returned home and we fell back into the computer and the phone, and I continued to keep the real world safely away from the desk that held them. Instead of blaming him for my disappointment, I blamed the earth itself, the invasion of roommates and ringing phones into the immaculate communication that PFSlider and I had created.

When I pictured him in the weeks that followed, I saw the image of a plane lifting off over an overcast city. PFSlider was otherworldly, more a concept than a person. His romance lay in the notion of flight, the physics of gravity defiance. So when he offered to send me a plane ticket to spend the weekend with him in Los Angeles I took it as an extension of our blissful remoteness, a three-dimensional E-mail message lasting an entire weekend.

The temperature on the runway at J. F. K. was seven degrees Fahrenheit. Our DC-10 sat for three hours waiting for deicing. Finally, it took off over the frozen city, and the ground below shrank into a drawing of itself. Phone calls were made, laptop computers were plopped onto tray tables. The recirculating air dried out my contact lenses. I watched movies without the sound and told myself that they were probably better that way. Something about the plastic interior of the fuselage and the plastic forks and the din of the air and the engines was soothing and strangely sexy.

Then we descended into LAX. We hit the tarmac, and the seat-belt signs blinked off. I hadn't moved my body in eight hours, and now I was walking through the tunnel to the gate, my clothes wrinkled, my hair matted, my hands shaking. When I saw Pete in the terminal, his face seemed to me just as blank and easy to miss as it had the first time I'd met him. He kissed me chastely. On the way out to the parking lot, he told me that he was being seriously considered for a job in New York. He was flying back there next week. If he got the job, he'd be moving within the month. I looked at him in astonishment. Something silent and invisible seemed to fall on us. Outside, the wind was warm, and the Avis and Hertz buses ambled alongside the curb of Terminal 5. The palm trees shook, and the air seemed as heavy and palpable as Pete's hand, which held mine for a few seconds before dropping it to get his car keys out of his pocket. He stood before me, all flesh and preoccupation, and for this I could not forgive him.

Gone were the computer, the erotic darkness of the telephone, the clean, single dimension of Pete's voice at 1 A.M. It was nighttime, yet the combination of sight and sound was blinding. It scared me. It turned me off. We went to a restaurant and ate outside on the sidewalk. We strained for conversation, and I tried not to care that we had to. We drove to his apartment and stood under the ceiling light not really looking at each other. Something was happening that we needed to snap out of. Any moment now, I thought. Any moment and we'll be all right. These moments were crowded with elements, with carpet fibres and automobiles and the smells of everything that had a smell. It was all wrong. The physical world had invaded our space.

For three days, we crawled along the ground and tried to pull ourselves up. We talked about things that I can no longer remember. We read the Los Angeles *Times* over breakfast. We drove north past Santa Barbara to tour the wine country. I felt like an object that could not be lifted, something that secretly weighed more than the world itself. Everything and everyone around us seemed imbued with a California lightness. I stomped around the countryside, an idiot New Yorker in my clunky shoes and black leather jacket. Not until I studied myself in the bathroom mirror of a highway rest stop did I fully realize the preposterousness of my uniform. I was dressed for war, I was dressed for my regular life.

That night, in a tiny town called Solvang, we ate an expensive dinner. We checked into a Marriott and watched television. Pete talked at me and through me and past me. I tried to listen. I tried to talk. But I bored myself and irritated him. Our conversation was a needle that could not be threaded. Still, we played nice. We tried to care, and pretended to keep trying long after we had given up. In the car on the way home, he told me that I was cynical, and I didn't have the presence of mind to ask him just how many cynics he had met who would travel three thousand miles to see someone they barely knew.

Pete drove me to the airport at 7 A.M. so I could make my eight-o'clock flight home. He kissed me goodbye—another chaste peck that I recognized from countless dinner parties and dud dates. He said that he'd call me in a few days when he got to New York for his job interview, which we had discussed only in passing and with no reference to the fact that New York was where I happened to live. I returned home to frozen January. A few days later, he came to New York, and we didn't see each other. He called me from the plane taking him back to Los Angeles to tell me, through the static, that he had got the job. He was moving to my city.

PFSlider was dead. There would be no meeting him in distant hotel lobbies during the baseball season. There would be no more phone calls or E-mail messages. In a single moment, Pete had completed his journey out of our mating dance and officially stepped into the regular world—the world that gnawed at me daily, the world that fostered those five-night stands, the world where romance could not be sustained, because so many of us simply did not know how to do it. Instead, we were all chitchat and leather jackets, bold proclaimers of all that we did not need. But what struck me most about this affair was the unpredictable nature of our demise. Unlike most cyber-romances, which seem to come fully equipped with the inevitable set of misrepresentations and false expectations, PFSlider and I had played it fairly straight. Neither of us had lied. We'd done the best we could. Our affair had died from natural causes rather than virtual ones.

Within a two-week period after I returned from Los Angeles, at least seven people confessed to me the vagaries of their own E-mail affairs. This topic arose, unprompted, in the course of normal conversation. I heard most of these stories in the close confines of smoky bars and crowded restaurants, and we all shook our heads in bewilderment as we told our tales, our eyes focused on some point in the distance. Four of these people had met their correspondents, by traveling from New Haven to Baltimore, from New York to Montana, from Texas to Virginia, and from New York to Johannesburg. These were normal people, writers and lawyers and scientists. They were all smart, attractive, and more than a little sheepish about admitting just how deeply they had been sucked in. Mostly, it was the courtship ritual that had seduced us. E-mail had become an electronic epistle, a yearned-for rule book. It allowed us to do what was necessary to experience love. The Internet was not responsible for our remote fragmented lives. The problem was life itself.

The story of PFSlider still makes me sad, not so much because we no longer have anything to do with each other but because it forces me to see the limits and the perils of daily life with more clarity than I used to. After I realized that our relationship would never transcend the screen and the phone—that, in fact, our face-to-face knowledge of each other had permanently contaminated the screen and the phone—I hit the pavement again, went through the motions of everyday life, said hello and goodbye to people in the regular way. If Pete and I had met at a party, we probably wouldn't have spoken to each other for more than ten minutes, and that would have made life easier but also less interesting. At the same time, it terrifies me to admit to a firsthand understanding of the way the heart and the ego are snarled and entwined like diseased trees that have folded in on each other. Our need to worship somehow fuses with our need to be worshipped. It upsets me still further to see how inaccessibility can make this entanglement so much more intoxicating. But I'm also thankful that I was forced to unpack the raw truth of my need and stare at it for a while. It was a dare I wouldn't have taken in three dimensions.

The last time I saw Pete, he was in New York, three thousand miles away from what had been his home, and a million miles away from PFSlider. In a final gesture of decency, in what I later realized was the most ordinary kind of closure, he took me out to dinner. As the few remaining traces of affection turned into embarrassed regret, we talked about nothing. He paid the bill. He drove me home in a rental car that felt as arbitrary and impersonal as what we now were to each other.

Pete had known how to get me where I lived until he came to where I lived: then he became as unmysterious as anyone next door. The world had proved to be too cluttered and too fast for us, too polluted to allow the thing we'd attempted through technology ever to grow in the earth. PFSlider and I had joined the angry and exhausted living. Even if we met on the street, we wouldn't recognize each other, our particular version of intimacy now obscured by the branches and bodies and falling debris that make up the physical world.

DISCUSSION QUESTIONS

1. Do you see any similarities between the author and Eleanor in the previous Darling report (Reading 19)? What are they?
2. Why do you think the author agreed to spend the weekend with Pete in L. A. after such a disastrous first date? What would you have done?
3. What lesson do you think Daum is trying to communicate in this essay about finding love?
4. Have you ever had an Internet romance or know someone who has? What happened?

SUGGESTIONS FOR JOURNAL ENTRIES

1. Write about what you think are the advantages and disadvantages of a long-distance romance while in college.
2. Daum writes that the failure of romance with Pete helped her "see the limits and perils of daily life with more clarity" than she used to. Write what you have learned from the failure of romance.

After a While

Anonymous

This extraordinarily mature poem about coping with the end of a love affair was written by an anonymous twelve-year old Dutch girl who is confined to a wheelchair.

After a while
you learn the subtle difference between holding a hand
and chaining a soul.

And you learn that love doesn't always mean security.
You learn that kisses aren't contracts, and
presents aren't promises.

And you learn to accept your defeats
with your head up and eyes straight.
With the grace of a woman—
not the grief of a child.

And you learn to build all your roads on today.
Because tomorrow's ground is too uncertain
for plans, as futures have a way of
falling down in mid-flight.

After a while
you learn that even sunshine burns
if you ask too much.
So plant your own garden and decorate
your own soul—
instead of waiting for someone to bring you flowers.

And you learn that *you can* endure
and that you are strong, and
really do have worth.

. . . And you learn. You learn with every heartache,
with every good-bye—
                  You learn . . .

DISCUSSION QUESTIONS

1. What is your reaction to learning that the poem was written by a twelve-year-old girl confined to a wheelchair? What does the poem tell you about her?
2. What do you think is the overall message of the poem?

3. What do you think the author means by "So plant your own garden and decorate your own soul"?
4. Could the poem as easily have been addressed to men? Why or why not?

SUGGESTIONS FOR JOURNAL ENTRIES

1. Write about the feelings this poem evokes in you.
2. Write a poem about "breaking up" based upon your own experience.

COMMUNITY

Several years ago, M. Scott Peck, author of *The Road Less Traveled*, wrote *A World Waiting to Be Born: Rediscovering Civility* (1993). In it, Peck shows how loneliness and existential boredom are the result of our cultural value system with its emphasis on excessive individualism or narcissism. This makes community building difficult, even at a college or university where it should flourish. Peck says it should flourish because young people are not yet co-opted into the who has the most toys game and thus are still available, even disposed, to community building.

To quote Peck, "In community no one gives a hoot about how much money you make or what your title might be. What people get admired and appreciated for in community are their soft skills: their sense of humor and timing, their ability to listen, their courage and honesty, their capacity for empathy—the kind of 'things' that adolescents often possess in spades."

I suspect that some colleges are successful in building community among their faculty, administration, and students, but I believe they are in the minority. Large enrollments, high percentages of commuters and students working long hours off-campus are all factors that militate against community. And yet it can happen, as the three authors in this section testify.

In the first essay, "A Magic Circle of Adult Students," Elvira Franco writes movingly of what it is like to return to school older than 40 and to discover a sea of over-40 classmates who magically become a circle of dear friends. There was a time when over-40 students were assumed to be employees of the institutions by their younger peers; not anymore.

The second essay is the journey of a woman from young mother unable to read well enough to share bedtime stories with her children to student leader at the University of Nevada, Las Vegas, thanks to the support of her husband and children, her neighborhood community, and her fellow students.

The third essay is written by cyberspace guru Howard Rheingold on the evolution of cyberhood ("The Virtual Community") as neighborhood and how computer networking can help bring community back to the center of modern (campus) life. Though not an Internet buff myself, I believe Rheingold is telling us something important about the difference in how your generation and mine relate.

READING 22

A Magic Circle of Adult Students

Elvira Franco

Elvira Franco received her masters of social work degree from New York University in 1989. She has written about her experience of returning to school as a mature woman and discovering other mothers and grandmothers ("late-bloomers") among her classmates who became a critical support group.

Older than forty and starting from scratch: I thought I was a unique item, but as soon as I peeked out of my shell I found a sea of women in similar positions.

The little child in us has grown mature and middle-aged, almost to our surprise. We share a fear that sits in the back of the mind like a spider ready to pounce: but we've also developed determination, almost like a religion.

We know we have friends; at least, I know my friends are with me, if not always, at least most of the time. And most of the time I need them, and they me. We reach over the phone lines for that word of comfort, the encouragement we need to go on when our own store of willpower has become depleted.

Returning to school, I found my friends were my best fans. In spite of their own insecurities, they never failed to offer me the cheering I often needed to rewrite a paper one more time or to stay up one last half-hour to re-read a difficult chapter.

After classes we would go to a diner, a bunch of over-forty classmates. Working together on a project that we felt strongly about ignited a part of us we did not know existed. While we were quite far from orthopedic shoes, bifocals were prominent. Underneath the artful makeup, we would measure the wrinkles on each other's cheeks across the table, almost as if these lines could form a cord to link us.

It was a good time. For years, in a locked-up corner of our minds, we had held the unspoken fear that we might actually be brain-dead. We were finally giving ourselves permission to celebrate our minds.

For some, it was a return to the carefree years of college. For others, a first-time discovery that learning can be both fun and exhilarating. Besides the intellectual surprises, we found joy in each other's company, and we delved in this new-found camaraderie with an intensity we did not know we could achieve outside of love and pregnancies. We were, and are, proud of our ages. The only woman in the group who was under thirty struck most of us as brash, angry, and frankly, quite inappropriate. We were probably insensitive to her needs, but somehow we failed to find out how she felt in our midst and were almost relieved when she found excuses for not joining our study sessions.

We ended up treating her almost like a daughter, and doing for her what most of us had been doing for our own daughters: that is, picking up the slack. The hidden bonus was that now we could continue to do things our way, which, we all knew, was the best anyway. Things were smoother when she was not around: the rest of us would always agree, and even our disagreements were somehow smooth and enjoyable.

We had, in fact, created a sort of bubble around us, a magic circle that follows us still and says we are bright, successful, caring, ambitious, and finally, ready to change the world. We will not do it, as we might have been ready to do at twenty, pushing and fighting and abrading.

We will do it instead at a slower pace, because, along the way, we have learned lessons both small and big: for example, that the world is in no hurry to be changed and that we will have a better shot at it after a good night's sleep. We may not complete our plans by tomorrow, or even by the end of the week, because the details of our lives may interfere, such as a child home from college, or a neighbor's emergency.

Our goals may not even be achieved exactly as originally planned, and that is fine, too, because time has also brought us a sense of flexibility and an appreciation for the serendipitous properties of practically any action. The end product could turn out to be infinitely more complex, and in its way more perfect, more multifaceted and rich, than what we had first envisioned. The process is in itself an achievement.

They call us "late bloomers," they call us "returnees." We are sought by schools, thanks to the sheer numbers we represent, not to mention the life experience and the common sense that even the least bright among us brings to the classroom. We feel flattered and surprised, and our ego is bolstered by the realization that we are indeed quite capable.

There are fears, too, ("Will it all make sense at some point?" "What if I'll never be able to get a decent job?") but they are kept for only a few pairs of ears, where we know we will find support and understanding.

Graduation comes: the last papers have been handed in with trepidation, the test booklets carrying in their pages the very essence of our knowledge closed for the last time. Goodbyes, with promises and some tears, even a photograph to keep as souvenir. We've made it: watch out world, here come the mothers and the grandmothers, ready to push, cajole, smile and negotiate to achieve those goals we did not have a chance to effect the first time around.

We may just be beginning to feel a few arthritic pangs in our toes and fingers, but with our hair neatly streaked and some expensive dental work, we know we still look good. We know we are still strong, smart, vital, and, most especially, ready to work. This time around we will make a big difference. We know, because, for sure, we already are different.

DISCUSSION QUESTIONS

1. Students of non-traditional ages are growing in numbers on most college campuses. Irrespective of your own age, how does it feel to be in a classroom with people of diverse ages?

2. Many eighteen-year-old students complain that it is not fair having to compete for grades with older students who have more life experience. What do you think of that argument?
3. There appeared to be a conflict between the older women and the woman under thirty. How would you have felt had you been the younger woman (or man assuming the opposite gender)?
4. What would you feel if your mother informed you that she was returning to school and would be attending classes at the same school you are attending?

SUGGESTIONS FOR JOURNAL ENTRIES

1. Interview an older student about his/her experience of being a "late-bloomer" at your institution and write about how it is similar and different from Franco's account.
2. Share the article with your mother and write about what she has to say about the idea of older women returning to school.

READING 23

Touching Lives

Rosalee Romano

Rosalee Romano, Mojave Community College '93, writes movingly about her journey from young mother unable to read well enough to share bedtime stories with her five children to student leader at the University of Nevada, Las Vegas. This essay was first published in About Campus *in 1996.*

I have worn several labels that acclaimed me a leader, but those labels did not make me a leader. Leadership is not a position nor a label but the act of touching others' lives, making a true difference for someone else. My development as a leader has been a long and ongoing process, with considerable support and guidance from others. My story is the story of those who have touched me.

As a young divorced mother, I was frustrated by the fact that I could not read a simple bedtime story to my children. I knew there were people who could not read, but I never considered myself one of them. After all, I knew my ABCs and could sound out simple words. Rather than realizing I had a reading problem, I just felt stupid. How could I ask my children to work hard in school, to learn to read, when I could not show them how? Fortunately, I was blessed to have a person come into my life who believed in me and my abilities, my husband Tom.

Tom worked with me for long hours to help me develop skills needed for reading. My skills developed slowly, but with each success, greater confidence grew. Reading opened a whole new world for me. New, exciting ideas and concepts were all around me and available for the first time. An explosion of self-esteem came with my newly learned and blossoming reading skills. I wanted to give my children the same chance to learn, so they could feel the joy I felt. I did not know then that it would be my children who would give to me, touching my life in the most profound of ways.

My life, like that of most folks, has not been simple. We were a low-income family, struggling every day to pay the bills and have enough to eat. My parents helped out whenever they could. Their help was especially generous during the Christmas of 1989, when they gave their five grandchildren a large number of presents. Their act of love was only exceeded by the children's unselfish act of caring.

After opening their gifts on Christmas morning, the children started to rewrap all but a few of their new possessions. When I asked what they were doing, they told me there were several children down at the welfare hotel that were not getting anything for Christmas. My children explained that they wanted to share with those who didn't have as much. I was greatly moved and a little ashamed; I had never thought to share with anyone who had less. Moreover, my children did it so innocently, asking nothing in return, not even thanks. Their reward was a feeling of self-worth, the ability to hold their heads up high. I was in awe and realized that the greatest reward of giving is in achieving that inner sense of value.

My children's act of innocent caring resulted not only in a merrier Christmas but in my first opportunity to lead. The following year, with the help of my husband, mother-in-law, and some caring women in our community, I started the Needles, California, Christmas Joy Toy Drive. I served as the toy drive president for four years; however, the drive folded the year I left to attend the University of Nevada, Las Vegas. In retrospect, I realized that I had not been the leader of the toy drive, only an organizer. A leader would have encouraged and empowered fellow workers to develop their potential so that they, too, could lead. I had not helped others assume leadership, and therefore, no one stepped forward to lead when I left.

However, I have jumped ahead in my story, so let me return to the time when I was discovering the excitement of learning. Tom and I realized that our children had in their futures opportunities we never had. I became focused on the children doing well in school, but felt I could not ask something of them that neither Tom nor I had achieved. Neither of us had graduated from high school, so first we committed ourselves to achieving that goal, to demonstrate to our children the importance of education. Tom took the GED immediately and passed with flying colors. I, however, had a lot to learn before I could achieve my goal.

My GED studies proceeded slowly as I worked my way through a study book, unaware that my life was again about to be blessed. The local newspaper asked me to take a part-time job as a photographer and captions writer. I believed that I could do this job and have fun at it—photography was my hobby, and I had improved my reading and writing skills. The job did turn out to be fun, but I could not do it on my own. Tom checked my spelling, punctuation, and grammar. The editor liked my approach to writing but recognized my need for further training, so he sent me to Mojave Community College (MCC) to take an English class. In the summer of 1991, at thirty-two years of age, I found myself back in school. I also discovered I loved every minute of it. My college career had begun.

The exposure I had received through the toy drive and my newspaper job had made me well known in my little town. Townspeople would stop me at the store, in church, or on the street to see how I was doing. There were those who anonymously paid for my tuition and books. There were those at the MCC Success Center who spent hours with me, explaining a concept or tutoring me in math. Always encouraging me and believing in my unproved abilities, they assisted me in the development of new skills, which emerged daily. My life was profoundly affected by those who wished nothing but to see me succeed. These individuals became significant leaders in shaping my life. I found myself wanting with all my heart to positively contribute to others' lives as they had to mine.

In the spring of my first year at MCC, I was elected secretary of the student government. I was also serving as public relations secretary for Phi Theta Kappa, the community college academic honor society. Both roles required hours of investment from me—and from Tom. My English skills were improving, but they were not yet at the level my positions demanded. Then during the next year, Tom slowly pulled back from helping me. I was scared by the realization that I would be on my own, but he helped me realize that I could do it. Tom had taught me to read, had been my partner in writing for the newspaper, had guided and coached me in managing the toy drive, and was now demonstrating that a time comes when the teacher must pull back and give the student room to take wing.

My official leadership positions at MCC allowed me to observe others in similar roles, and I came to realize that people choose leadership positions for a variety of reasons. At college, some sought financial gain from scholarships while others longed for the power they believed accompanied their positions. Those who chose leadership positions for these reasons became easily discouraged and frustrated. There were, however, other leaders who did not vie for control. They stood back, contributing and assisting as needed. These were the ones who made the difference between the success and failure of a project. They seemed to infuse confidence and purpose in those with whom they worked. I came to understand that these were the true leaders. These were the students who made a difference in the lives around them, including mine. They helped plant in my heart the seeds of leadership.

I graduated with honors in December 1993, two and a half years after taking that English class for the newspaper. I had graduated, but I could not stop there. I loved everything about school, the challenges, the new information, and all the possibilities. I was no longer doing this just for my children or for my family's future; I was also doing it for me. I could not go back: I needed to go on—to grow and most of all to learn. The children, Tom, and I had many talks about the pros and cons involved and how we would need to work together. In the end, we all agreed that I would apply to the University of Nevada, Las Vegas (UNLV), the closest university but still a three-hour drive. Acceptance to UNLV meant I would be home only three days each week. Tom and the oldest children would cook, clean, and maintain the family.

Spring of 1994 was my first experience of being away from home. Even at thirty-four, I experienced many of the same feelings as younger students. I had, however, my own unique set of adjustments. I needed to come to terms with leaving my family, and it was living in the residence halls that gave me the support and encouragement to find a resolution to my feelings. I could only justify not being at home for my children by committing myself to making a difference in the lives of those around me, in my community, and among my fellow students. My children, on Christmas day five years before, had made a difference and, I believe, started me on my journey of leadership. Now I would honor them by making a difference for someone else.

My leadership roles at UNLV have been varied but tied together with this common thread. Just as I have been encouraged, supported, guided, helped, given new opportunities, cared for, and cared about, I attempt to do the same. There are many ways one may take the role of leader. The role that best represents my leadership is that of servant. The role of a student leader is just that, an opportunity to serve other students and to enhance the campus experience for everyone. My belief that my efforts as a leader may make a difference is a source of great reward to me. Other accomplishments in life pale in comparison. Although getting good grades and earning a good wage are rewarding, they are also temporary. I have found that the best prize is the knowledge that I have made a lasting imprint on someone, no matter how small, and that they may be the better for it. My husband describes me as having a servant's heart, saying that this is my underlying drive. I think that may be true, but this does not mean I am completely unselfish. My wish to assist people is not based solely on what that assistance does for them but also on the sense of purpose and worth it brings to my life.

I can read a bedtime story to my children now, but my children's needs have grown beyond that simple pleasure. My goals have also grown beyond the desire to be a good role model for my children. My journey continues, and I do not know exactly where it will take me. I struggle to balance my family with my education. At one moment, I find myself questioning my commitment. At another moment, I am absolutely sure that I am headed in the right direction. Regardless of the pressure I feel at any particular moment, I try to keep a picture in my mind—of Christmas morning and my children rewrapping their presents. I know that my journey has purpose; I do make a difference in the lives I touch.

DISCUSSION QUESTIONS

1. This is a story of the making of a student leader. What did you learn from Romano's story about leadership?
2. What does Romano mean when she writes that "the greatest reward of giving is in achieving that inner sense of value"? Can you think of an example of how that has been true in your life?
3. Rosalee's marriage to Tom appears to be quite remarkable. What seems to be their secret?

SUGGESTIONS FOR JOURNAL ENTRIES

1. Write about a time when you made a difference in the life of someone you touched, or when someone touched you.
2. Walker Percy, the author, shared Romano's sentiments about grades when he wrote that "You can get all As and still flunk life." Write about what this means to you and whether you agree or disagree.

The Virtual Community

Howard Rheingold

This essay by science fiction novelist and cyberspace guru Howard Rheingold, Reed College '68, is from The Virtual Community: Homesteading on the Electronic Frontier *(1993). In it Rheingold tries to make a case for how the "cyberhood" may be replacing the neighborhood bar and more.*

In the summer of 1986, my then 2-year-old daughter picked up a tick. There was this blood-bloated *thing* sucking on our baby's scalp, and we weren't quite sure how to go about getting it off. My wife, Judy, called the pediatrician. It was 11 o'clock in the evening. I logged onto the WELL, the big Bay Area infonet, and contacted the Parenting conference (a conference is an on-line conversation about a specific subject). I got my answer on-line within minutes from a fellow with the improbable but genuine name of Flash Gordon, M. D. I had removed the tick by the time Judy got the callback from the pediatrician's office.

What amazed me wasn't just the speed with which we obtained precisely the information we needed to know, right when we needed to know it. It was also the immense inner sense of security that comes with discovering that real people—most of them parents, some of them nurses, doctors, and midwives—are available, around the clock, if you need them. There is a magic protective circle around the atmosphere of the Parenting conference. We're talking about our sons and daughters in this forum, not about our computers or our opinions about philosophy, and many of us feel that this tacit understanding sanctifies the virtual space.

The atmosphere of this particular conference—the attitudes people exhibit to each other in the tone of what they say in public—is part of what continues to attract me. People who never have much to contribute in political debate, technical argument, or intellectual gamesmanship turn out to have a lot to say about raising children. People you knew as fierce, even nasty, intellectual opponents in other contexts give you emotional support on a deeper level, parent to parent, within the boundaries of this small but warmly human corner of cyberspace.

In most cases, people who talk about a shared interest don't disclose enough about themselves as whole individuals on-line to inspire real trust in others. But in the case of the subcommunity called the Parenting conference, a few dozen of us, scattered across the country, few of whom rarely if ever saw the others face to face, have a few years of minor crises to knit us together and prepare us for serious business when it comes our way. Another several dozen read the conference regularly but contribute only when they have something important to add. Hundreds more read the conference every week without comment, except when something extraordinary happens.

Jay Allison and his family live in Massachusetts. He and his wife are public-radio producers. I've never met them face to face, although I feel I know something powerful and intimate about the Allisons and have strong emotional ties to them. What follows are some of Jay's postings on the WELL:

"Woods Hole. Midnight. I am sitting in the dark of my daughter's room. Her monitor lights blink at me. The lights used to blink too brightly so I covered them with bits of bandage adhesive and now they flash faintly underneath, a persistent red and green, Lillie's heart and lungs.

"Above the monitor is her portable suction unit. In the glow of the flashlight I'm writing by, it looks like the plastic guts of a science-class human model, the tubes coiled around the power supply, the reservoir, the pump.

"Tina is upstairs trying to get some sleep. A baby monitor links our bedroom to Lillie's. It links our sleep to Lillie's too, and because our souls are linked to hers, we do not sleep well.

"I am naked. My stomach is full of beer. The flashlight rests on it, and the beam rises and falls with my breath. My daughter breathes through a white plastic tube inserted into a hole in her throat. She's 14 months old."

Sitting in front of our computers with our hearts racing and tears in our eyes, in Tokyo and Sacramento and Austin, we read about Lillie's croup, her tracheostomy, the days and nights at Massachusetts General Hospital, and now the vigil over Lillie's breathing and the watchful attention to the mechanical apparatus that kept her alive. It went on for days. Weeks. Lillie recovered, and relieved our anxieties about her vocal capabilities after all that time with a hole in her throat by saying the most extraordinary things, duly reported on-line by Jay.

Later, writing in *Whole Earth Review*, Jay described the experience:

"Before this time, my computer screen had never been a place to go for solace. Far from it. But there it was. Those nights sitting up late with my daughter, I'd go to my computer, dial up the WELL, and ramble. I wrote about what was happening that night or that year. I didn't know anyone I was "talking" to. I had never laid eyes on them. At 3:00 a.m. my "real" friends were asleep, so I turned to this foreign, invisible community for support. The WELL was always awake.

"Any difficulty is harder to bear in isolation. There is nothing to measure against, to lean against. Typing out my journal entries into the computer and over the phone lines, I found fellowship and comfort in this unlikely medium."

Many people are alarmed by the very idea of a virtual community, fearing that it is another step in the wrong direction, substituting more technological ersatz for yet another natural resource or human freedom. These critics often voice their sadness at what people have been reduced to doing in a civilization that worships technology, decrying the circumstances that led some people into such pathetically disconnected lives that they prefer to find their companions on the other side of a computer screen. There is a seed of truth in this fear, for communities at some point require more than words on a screen if they are to be other than ersatz.

Yet some people—many who don't do well in spontaneous spoken inter-action turn out to have valuable contributions to make in a conversation in which they have time to think about what to say. These people, who might constitute a significant proportion of the population, can find written commu-nication more authentic than the face-to-face kind. Who is to say that this pref-erence for informal written text is somehow less authentically human than opting for audible speech? Those who critique computer-mediated communi-cation because some people use it obsessively hit an important target, but miss a great deal more when they don't take into consideration people who use the medium for genuine human interaction. Those who find virtual communities cold places point at the limits of the technology, its most dangerous pitfalls, and we need to pay attention to those boundaries. But these critiques don't tell us how the Allisons, my own family, and many others could have found the community of support and information we found in the WELL when we needed it. And those of us who do find communion in cyberspace might do well to pay attention to the way the medium we love can be abused.

Although dramatic incidents are what bring people together and stick in their memories, most of what goes on in the Parenting conference and most virtual communities is informal conversation and downright chitchat. The model of the WELL and other social clusters in cyberspace as "places" emerges naturally whenever people who use this medium discuss its nature. In 1987, Stewart Brand quoted me in his book *The Media Lab* about what tempted me to log onto the WELL as often as I did: "There's always another mind there. It's like having the corner bar, complete with old buddies and de-lightful newcomers and new tools waiting to take home and fresh graffiti and letters, except instead of putting on my coat, shutting down the computer and walking down to the corner, I just invoke my telecom program and there they are. It's a place."

I've changed my mind about a lot of aspects of the WELL over the years, but the sense of place is still as strong as ever. As Ray Oldenburg proposes in his 1989 book *The Great Good Place,* there are three essential places in people's lives: the place we live, the place we work, and the place we gather for con-viviality. Although the casual conversation that takes place in cafés, beauty shops, pubs, and town squares is universally considered to be trivial, idle talk, Oldenburg makes the case that such places are where communities can come into being and continue to hold together. These are the unacknowledged ago-ras of modern life. When the automobilecentric, suburban fast-food, shopping-mall way of life eliminated many of these "third places" from traditional towns and cities around the world, the social fabric of existing communities started shredding.

Oldenburg puts a name and a conceptual framework on a phenomenon that every virtual community member knows instinctively, the power of infor-mal public life:

> "Third places exist on neutral ground and serve to level their guests to a condi-
> tion of social equality. Within these places, conversation is the primary activity
> and the major vehicle for the display and appreciation of human personality

and individuality. Third places are taken for granted and most have a low profile. Since the formal institutions of society make stronger claims on the individual, third places are normally open in the off hours, as well as at other times. The character of a third place is determined most of all by its regular clientele and is marked by a playful mood, which contrasts with people's more serious involvement in other spheres. Though a radically different kind of setting for a home, the third place is remarkably similar to a good home in the psychological comfort and support that it extends.

"Such are the characteristics of third places that appear to be universal and essential to a vital informal public life. . . .

"The problem of place in America manifests itself in a sorely deficient informal public life. The structure of shared experience beyond that offered by family, job, and passive consumerism is small and dwindling. The essential group experience is being replaced by the exaggerated self-consciousness of individuals. American lifestyles, for all the material acquisition and the seeking after comforts and pleasures, are plagued by boredom, loneliness, alienation, and a high price tag. . . .

"Unlike many frontiers, that of the informal public life does not remain benign as it awaits development. It does not become easier to tame as technology evolves, as governmental bureaus and agencies multiply, or as population grows. It does not yield to the mere passage of time and a policy of letting the chips fall where they may as development proceeds in other areas of urban life. To the contrary, neglect of the informal public life can make a jungle of what had been a garden while, at the same time, diminishing the ability of people to cultivate it."

It might not be the same kind of place that Oldenburg had in mind, but many of his descriptions of third places could also describe the WELL. Perhaps cyberspace is one of the informal public places where people can rebuild the aspects of community that were lost when the malt shop became a mall. Or perhaps cyberspace is precisely the *wrong* place to look for the rebirth of community, offering not a tool for conviviality but a life-denying simulacrum of real passion and true commitment to one another. In either case, we need to find out soon.

Because we cannot see one another in cyberspace, gender, age, national origin, and physical appearance are not apparent unless a person wants to make such characteristics public. People whose physical handicaps make it difficult to form new friendships find that virtual communities treat them as they always wanted to be treated—as thinkers and transmitters of ideas and feeling beings, not carnal vessels with a certain appearance and way of walking and talking (or not walking and not talking).

One of the few things that enthusiastic members of virtual communities in places like Japan, England, France, and the United States all agree on is that expanding their circle of friends is one of the most important advantages of computer conferencing. It is a way to *meet* people, whether or not you feel the need to affiliate with them on a community level. It's a way of both making contact with and maintaining a distance from others. The way you meet people in cyberspace puts a different spin on affiliation: In traditional kinds of communities, we are accustomed to meeting people, then getting to know them; in virtual communities, you can get to know people and *then* choose to meet them. Affiliation also can be far more ephemeral in cyberspace because you can get to know people you might never meet on the physical plane.

How does anybody find friends? In the traditional community, we search through our pool of neighbors and professional colleagues, of acquaintances and acquaintances of acquaintances, in order to find people who share our values and interests. We then exchange information about one another, disclose and discuss our mutual interests, and sometimes we become friends. In a virtual community we can go directly to the place where our favorite subjects are being discussed, then get acquainted with people who share our passions or who use words in a way we find attractive. In this sense, the topic is the address: You can't simply pick up a phone and ask to be connected with someone who wants to talk about Islamic art or California wine, or someone with a 3-year-old daughter or a 40-year-old Hudson; you can, however, join a computer conference on any of those topics, then open a public or private correspondence with the previously unknown people you find there. Your chances of making friends are increased by several orders of magnitude over the old methods of finding a peer group.

You can be fooled about people in cyberspace, behind the cloak of words. But that can be said about telephones or face-to-face communication as well; computer-mediated communications provide new ways to fool people, and the most obvious identity swindles will die out only when enough people learn to use the medium critically. In some ways, the medium will, by its nature, be forever biased toward certain kinds of obfuscation. It will also be a place where people often end up revealing themselves far more intimately than they would be inclined to do without the intermediation of screens and pseudonyms.

Point of view, along with identity, is one of the great variables in cyberspace. Different people in cyberspace look at their virtual communities through differently shaped keyholes. In traditional communities, people have a strongly shared mental model of the sense of place—the room or village or city where their interactions occur. In virtual communities, the sense of place requires an individual act of imagination. The different mental models people have of the electronic agora complicate the question of why people seem to want to build societies mediated by computer screens. A question like that leads inexorably to the old fundamental questions of what forces hold any society together. The roots of these questions extend farther than the social upheavals triggered by modern communications technologies.

When we say "society," we usually mean citizens of cities in entities known as nations. We take those categories for granted. But the mass-psychological transition we made to thinking of ourselves as part of modern society and nation-states is historically recent. Could people make the transition from the close collective social groups, the villages and small towns of premodern and precapitalist Europe, to a new form of social solidarity known as society that transcended and encompassed all previous kinds of human association? Ferdinand Tönnies, one of the founders of sociology, called the premodern kind of social group *gemeinschaft,* which is closer to the English word *community,* and the new kind of social group he called *gesellschaft,* which can be translated roughly as *society.* All the questions about community in cyberspace point to a similar kind of transition, for which we have no technical names, that might be taking place now.

Sociology student Marc Smith, who has been using the WELL and the Net as the laboratory for his fieldwork, pointed me to Benedict Anderson's *Imagined Communities,* a study of nation-building that focuses on the ideological labor involved. Anderson points out that nations and, by extension, communities are imagined in the sense that a given nation exists by virtue of a common acceptance in the minds of the population that it exists. Nations must exist in the minds of their citizens in order to exist at all. "Virtual communities require an act of imagination," Smith points out, extending Anderson's line of thinking to cyberspace, "and what must be imagined is the idea of the community itself."

DISCUSSION QUESTIONS

1. What do you think of Rheingold's main thesis, that the "virtual community" can be a real community? Can you speak from experience?
2. What do you think of Oldenburg's concept of the "third place"? Have you found a "third place" on or off campus?
3. Do you have a preference for "informal written text" or "audible speech" when it comes to authentic communication?
4. How do you think college campuses have changed over the last five years as a result of the Internet? For better or worse?

SUGGESTIONS FOR JOURNAL ENTRIES

1. Write about a "third place" that you frequented before coming to college and why it was important.
2. Would you say that you are a member of a "virtual community"? If not, interview someone who is. Write about what it has contributed to your (their) life.
3. Some colleges like U. of Colorado at Boulder have a special cyberspace network for first-year students. Do you think this is a good idea? Why or why not?

CONFLICT

It is important to realize that conflict is not the opposite of community. Indeed conflict is inevitable and can be a positive agent for change. As the Chinese symbol emphasizes, conflict contains both crisis and opportunity. It is conflict that is hidden or denied that can erode community and healthy living.

The personal "conflicts" of pressures and stress have been a part of college life probably since the Middle Ages when the great universities of Europe were founded. But the group conflicts of the 80s and 90s are a more recent development on college campuses. I believe that there is a not-so-quiet revolution going on in how we relate to each other sexually, racially, and otherwise. As Ellen Goodman phrased it in Reading 18, we are indeed "training for real life," but that life is changing very rapidly as we stampede into the 21st century.

In the first essay, William Zinsser, formerly master of Branford College (one of 12 residences) of Yale University, discusses the four kinds of pressures that he sees being visited on Yalies and presumably other students as well: economic, parental, peer, and self-induced. Not only does Zinsser give some good advice but he shows that for students everywhere, the going gets tough.

The second essay is a cautionary tale of what can go wrong in a college dormitory when, as Ian Schreuder writes, "We drink ourselves into oblivion." Dr. Henry Wechsler of the Harvard School of Public Health conducted his College Alcohol Study in 1996 and discovered that 44 percent of college students regularly engage in heavy, episodic, or "binge" drinking—drinking that has harmful effects not only on those doing the drinking but on others in their immediate environment. Paul Keegan in "Inhuman Architecture, Bad Food, Boredom, Death by Fun and Games," recounts the nightmare of what happened at UMass in the spring of 1990.

In the third essay, Nancy Gibbs in *Time* gives some frightening statistics on the topic of "date" or "acquaintance rape" (terms that did not exist 15 years ago) on college campuses. While this topic has received much media attention recently, it is an ancient problem.

In the final piece, an untitled student dramatic production, Sylva Miller wrote and performed her final project in a seminar titled "Women and Theatre: the Politics of Representation." In it she recounts "stories" of confusion, sadness, pain, anger, strength, and power, rites of passage stories of the 90s that nearly everyone can relate to.

READING 25

College Pressures

William Zinsser

William Zinsser, Princeton '44, is a professional writer and former professor of writing in residence at Yale University and perhaps best known for his texts On Writing Well *(1976), and* Writing with a Word Processor *(1983). This essay is about the four kinds of pressures that Zinsser discovered to be plaguing undergraduates while serving as master at Branford College, one of the twelve residential colleges at Yale, and some good counsel about how to cope. It originally appeared in* Blair and Ketchum's Country Journal *(1979).*

DEAR CARLOS: I desperately need a dean's excuse for my chem midterm which will begin in about one hour. All I can say is that I totally blew it this week. I've fallen incredibly, inconceivably behind.

CARLOS: Help! I'm anxious to hear from you. I'll be in my room and won't leave it until I hear from you. Tomorrow is the last day for . . .

CARLOS: I left town because I started bugging out again. I stayed up all night to finish a take-home make-up exam and am typing it to hand in on the tenth. It was due on the fifth. P.S. I'm going to the dentist. Pain is pretty bad.

CARLOS: Probably by Friday I'll be able to get back to my studies. Right now I'm going to take a long walk. This whole thing has taken a lot out of me.

CARLOS: I'm really up the proverbial creek. The problem is I really bombed the history final. Since I need that course for my major I . . .

CARLOS: Here follows a tale of woe. I went home this weekend, had to help my Mom, and caught a fever so didn't have much time to study. My professor . . .

CARLOS: Aargh! Trouble. Nothing original but everything's piling up at once. To be brief, my job interview . . .

Hey Carlos, good news! I've got mononucleosis.

Who are these wretched supplicants, scribbling notes so laden with anxiety, seeking such miracles of postponement and balm? They are men and women who belong to Branford College, one of the twelve residential colleges at Yale University, and the messages are just a few of the hundreds that they left for their dean, Carlos Hortas—often slipped under his door at 4 a.m.—last year.

But students like the ones who wrote those notes can also be found on campuses from coast to coast—especially in New England and at many other private colleges across the country that have high academic standards and highly motivated students. Nobody could doubt that the notes are real. In their urgency and their gallows humor they are authentic voices of a generation that is panicky to succeed.

My own connection with the message writers is that I am master of Branford College. I live in its Gothic quadrangle and know the students well. (We have 485 of them.) I am privy to their hopes and fears—and also to their stereo music and their piercing cries in the dead of night ("Does anybody *ca-a-are?*"). If they went to Carlos to ask how to get through tomorrow, they come to me to ask how to get through the rest of their lives.

Mainly I try to remind them that the road ahead is a long one and that it will have more unexpected turns than they think. There will be plenty of time to change jobs, change careers, change whole attitudes and approaches. They don't want to hear such liberating news. They want a map—right now—that they can follow unswervingly to career security, financial security, Social Security and, presumably, a prepaid grave.

What I wish for all students is some release from the clammy grip of the future. I wish them a chance to savor each segment of their education as an experience in itself and not as a grim preparation for the next step. I wish them the right to experiment, to trip and fall, to learn that defeat is as instructive as victory and is not the end of the world.

My wish, of course, is naive. One of the few rights that America does not proclaim is the right to fail. Achievement is the national god, venerated in our media—the million-dollar athlete, the wealthy executive—and glorified in our praise of possessions. In the presence of such a potent state religion, the young are growing up old.

I see four kinds of pressure working on college students today: economic pressure, parental pressure, peer pressure, and self-induced pressure. It is easy to look around for villains—to blame the colleges for charging too much money, the professors for assigning too much work, the parents for pushing their children too far, the students for driving themselves too hard. But there are no villains; only victims.

"In the late 1960s," one dean told me, "the typical question that I got from students was 'Why is there so much suffering in the world?' or 'How can I make a contribution?' Today it's 'Do you think it would look better for getting into law school if I did a double major in history and political science, or just majored in one of them?'" Many other deans confirmed this pattern. One said: "They're trying to find an edge—the intangible something that will look better on paper if two students are about equal."

Note the emphasis on looking better. The transcript has become a sacred document, the passport to security. How one appears on paper is more important than how one appears in person. *A* is for Admirable and *B* is for Borderline, even though, in Yale's official system of grading, *A* means "excellent" and *B* means "very good." Today, looking very good is no longer good enough, especially for students who hope to go on to law school or medical school. They know that entrance into the better schools will be an entrance into the better law firms and better medical practices where they will make a lot of money. They also know that the odds are harsh. Yale Law School, for instance, matriculates 170 students from an applicant pool of 3,700; Harvard enrolls 550 from a pool of 7,000.

It's very well for those of us who write letters of recommendation for our students to stress the qualities of humanity that will make them good lawyers or doctors. And it's nice to think that admission officers are really reading our letters and looking for the extra dimension of commitment or concern. Still, it would be hard for a student not to visualize these officers shuffling so many transcripts studded with *A*s that they regard a *B* as positively shameful.

The pressure is almost as heavy on students who just want to graduate and get a job. Long gone are the days of the "gentleman's *C*," when students journeyed through college with a certain relaxation, sampling a wide variety of courses—music, art, philosophy, classics, anthropology, poetry, religion— that would send them out as liberally educated men and women. If I were an employer I would rather employ graduates who have this range and curiosity than those who narrowly pursued safe subjects and high grades. I know countless students whose inquiring minds exhilarate me. I like to hear the play of their ideas. I don't know if they are getting *A*s or *C*s, and I don't care. I also like them as people. The country needs them, and they will find satisfying jobs. I tell them to relax. They can't.

Nor can I blame them. They live in a brutal economy. Tuition, room, and board at most private colleges now comes to at least $7,000, not counting books and fees. This might seem to suggest that the colleges are getting rich. But they are equally battered by inflation. Tuition covers only 60 percent of what it costs to educate a student, and ordinarily the remainder comes from what colleges receive in endowments, grants, and gifts. Now the remainder keeps being swallowed by the cruel costs—higher every year—of just opening the doors. Heating oil is up. Insurance is up. Postage is up. Health-premium costs are up. Everything is up. Deficits are up. We are witnessing in America the creation of a brotherhood of paupers—colleges, parents, and students, joined by the common bond of debt.

Today it is not unusual for a student, even if he works part time at college and full time during the summer, to accrue $5,000 in loans after four years— loans that he must start to repay within one year after graduation. Exhorted at commencement to go forth into the world, he is already behind as he goes forth. How could he not feel under pressure throughout college to prepare for this day of reckoning? I have used "he," incidentally, only for brevity. Women at Yale are under no less pressure to justify their expensive education to themselves, their parents, and society. In fact, they are probably under more pressure. For although they leave college superbly equipped to bring fresh leadership to traditionally male jobs, society hasn't yet caught up with this fact.

Along with economic pressure goes parental pressure. Inevitably, the two are deeply intertwined.

I see many students taking pre-medical courses with joyless tenacity. They go off to their labs as if they were going to the dentist. It saddens me because I know them in other corners of their life as cheerful people.

"Do you want to go to medical school?" I ask them.

"I guess so," they say, without conviction, or "Not really."

"Then why are you going?"

"Well, my parents want me to be a doctor. They're paying all this money and . . ."

Poor students, poor parents. They are caught in one of the oldest webs of love and duty and guilt. The parents mean well; they are trying to steer their sons and daughters toward a secure future. But the sons and daughters want to major in history or classics or philosophy—subjects with no "practical" value. Where's the payoff on the humanities? It's not easy to persuade such loving parents that the humanities do indeed pay off. The intellectual faculties developed by studying subjects like history and classics—an ability to synthesize and relate, to weigh cause and effect, to see events in perspective—are just the faculties that make creative leaders in business or almost any general field. Still, many fathers would rather put their money on courses that point toward a specific profession—courses that are pre-law, pre-medical, pre-business, or, as I sometimes heard it put, "pre-rich."

But the pressure on students is severe. They are truly torn. One part of them feels obligated to fulfill their parents' expectations; after all, their parents are older and presumably wiser. Another part tells them that the expectations that are right for their parents are not right for them.

I know a student who wants to be an artist. She is very obviously an artist and will be a good one—she has already had several modest local exhibits. Meanwhile she is growing as a well-rounded person and taking humanistic subjects that will enrich the inner resources out of which her art will grow. But her father is strongly opposed. He thinks that an artist is a "dumb" thing to be. The student vacillates and tries to please everybody. She keeps up with her art somewhat furtively and takes some of the "dumb" courses her father wants her to take—at least they are dumb courses for her. She is a free spirit on a campus of tense students—no small achievement in itself—and she deserves to follow her muse.

Peer pressure and self-induced pressure are also intertwined, and they begin almost at the beginning of freshman year.

"I had a freshman student I'll call Linda," one dean told me, "who came in and said she was under terrible pressure because her roommate, Barbara, was much brighter and studied all the time. I couldn't tell her that Barbara had come in two hours earlier to say the same thing about Linda."

The story is almost funny—except that it's not. It's symptomatic of all the pressures put together. When every student thinks every other student is working harder and doing better, the only solution is to study harder still. I see students going off to the library every night after dinner and coming back when it closes at midnight. I wish they would sometimes forget about their peers and go to a movie. I hear the clacking of typewriters in the hours before dawn. I see the tension in their eyes when exams are approaching and papers are due: *"Will I get everything done?"*

Probably they won't. They will get sick. They will get "blocked." They will sleep. They will oversleep. They will bug out. *Hey Carlos, help!*

Part of the problem is that they do more than they are expected to do. A professor will assign five-page papers. Several students will start writing ten-page papers to impress him. Then more students will start writing ten-page papers, and a few will raise the ante to fifteen. Pity the poor student who is still just doing the assignment.

"Once you have twenty or thirty percent of the student population deliberately overexerting," one dean points out, "it's bad for everybody. When a teacher gets more and more effort from his class, the student who is doing normal work can be perceived as not doing well. The tactic works, psychologically."

Why can't the professor just cut back and not accept longer papers? He can, and he probably will. But by then the term will be half over and the damage done. Grade fever is highly contagious and not easily reversed. Besides, the professor's main concern is with his course. He knows his students only in relation to the course and doesn't know that they are also overexerting in their other courses. Nor is it really his business. He didn't sign up for dealing with the student as a whole person and with all the emotional baggage the student brought along from home. That's what deans, masters, chaplains, and psychiatrists are for.

To some extent this is nothing new: a certain number of professors have always been self-contained islands of scholarship and shyness, more comfortable with books than with people. But the new pauperism has widened the gap still further, for professors who actually like to spend time with students don't have as much time to spend. They also are overexerting. If they are young, they are busy trying to publish in order not to perish, hanging by their fingernails onto a shrinking profession. If they are old and tenured, they are buried under the duties of administering departments—as departmental chairmen or members of committees—that have been thinned out by the budgetary axe.

Ultimately it will be the students' own business to break the circles in which they are trapped. They are too young to be prisoners of their parents' dreams and their classmates' fears. They must be jolted into believing in themselves as unique men and women who have the power to shape their own future.

"Violence is being done to the undergraduate experience," says Carlos Hortas. "College should be open-ended: at the end it should open many, many roads. Instead, students are choosing their goal in advance, and their choices narrow as they go along. It's almost as if they think that the country has been codified in the type of jobs that exist—that they've got to fit into certain slots. Therefore, fit into the best-paying slot.

"They ought to take chances. Not taking chances will lead to a life of colorless mediocrity. They'll be comfortable. But something in the spirit will be missing."

I have painted too drab a portrait of today's students, making them seem a solemn lot. That is only half of their story; if they were so dreary I wouldn't so thoroughly enjoy their company. The other half is that they are easy to like. They are quick to laugh and to offer friendship. They are not introverts. They are unusually kind and are more considerate of one another than any student generation I have known.

Nor are they so obsessed with their studies that they avoid sports and extracurricular activities. On the contrary, they juggle their crowded hours to play on a variety of teams, perform with musical and dramatic groups, and write for campus publications. But this in turn is one more cause of anxiety. There are too many choices. Academically, they have 1,300 courses to select from; outside class they have to decide how much spare time they can spare and how to spend it.

This means that they engage in fewer extracurricular pursuits than their predecessors did. If they want to row on the crew and play in the symphony they will eliminate one; in the sixties they would have done both. They also tend to choose activities that are self-limiting. Drama, for instance, is flourishing in all twelve of Yale's residential colleges as it never had before. Students hurl themselves into these productions—as actors, directors, carpenters, and technicians—with a dedication to create the best possible play, knowing that the day will come when the run will end and they can get back to their studies.

They also can't afford to be the willing slave of organizations like the *Yale Daily News*. Last spring at the one-hundredth anniversary banquet of that paper—whose past chairmen include such once and future kings as Potter Stewart, Kingman Brewster, and William F. Buckley, Jr.—much was made of the fact that the editorial staff used to be small and totally committed and that "newsies" routinely worked fifty hours a week. In effect they belonged to a club; Newsies is how they defined themselves at Yale. Today's student will write one or two articles a week, when he can, and he defines himself as a student. I've never heard the word Newsie except at the banquet.

If I have described the modern undergraduate primarily as a driven creature who is largely ignoring the blithe spirit who keeps trying to come out and play, it's because that's where the crunch is, not only at Yale but throughout American education. It's why I think we should all be worried about the values that are nurturing a generation so fearful of risk and so goal-obsessed at such an early age.

I tell students that there is no one "right" way to get ahead—that each of them is a different person, starting from a different point and bound for a different destination. I tell them that change is a tonic and that all the slots are not codified nor the frontiers closed. One of my ways of telling them is to invite men and women who have achieved success outside the academic world to come and talk informally with my students during the year. They are heads of companies or ad agencies, editors of magazines, politicians, public officials, television magnates, labor leaders, business executives, Broadway producers, artists, writers, economists, photographers, scientists, historians—a mixed bag of achievers.

I ask them to say a few words about how they got started. The students assume that they started in the present profession and knew all along that it was what they wanted to do. Luckily for me, most of them got into their field by a circuitous route, to their surprise, after many detours. The students are startled. They can hardly conceive of a career that was not pre-planned. They can hardly imagine allowing the hand of God or chance to nudge them down some unforeseen trail.

DISCUSSION QUESTIONS

1. Do you think that Zinsser does a good job of analyzing the basic pressures of college today? Has he left anything of importance out? Are things any different on your campus (assuming it's not Yale)?
2. Were you surprised at Zinsser's characterization of the classes of 1979–83 as "more considerate of one another than any student generation I have known"? Would that characterization still fit your generation? Why or why not?
3. How do you feel about Yale's practice of having professors live in the dorms? Do you see any advantages or disadvantages?
4. Having read Zinsser's analysis of the problem and his suggestions for coping, are you going to change as a result? Were you persuaded to start doing anything differently? What are your resolutions, if any?

SUGGESTIONS FOR JOURNAL ENTRIES

1. Putting Zinsser's categories aside for the moment, analyze your own situation and make a list of all the things that contribute to feeling pressured at the moment. Do they fall neatly into Zinsser's four categories or are there others?
2. Discuss your list with either someone in authority on your campus (faculty, adviser, staff, etc.) or an upperclass student and write what you learned about how they dealt with some of the pressures you described.

READING 26

Inhuman Architecture, Bad Food, Boredom, Death by Fun and Games

Paul Keegan

This report on a student residence at UMass called "the Zoo" was written by a free-lance journalist who specializes in college culture stories, Paul Keegan, U. of New Hampshire '80, and originally appeared in Esquire *(1992).*

In the mid-sixties, small cities were created across America where young people could immerse themselves in higher learning in order to come of age, fully prepared for the adult world.

In one such city, in a tower named for President John F. Kennedy, the weekend rituals begin on Friday afternoon. The television teeters atop a small refrigerator stocked with cans of beer, and the clatter of *Wheel of Fortune* is drowned out by the angry guitars of Jane's Addiction. Citizens are discussing last weekend, when one of their number was so drunk and disturbed over a girl that he started karate-chopping a door and attempted to throw a table through a window. The constables showed up and handed out alcohol violations, which still pisses everybody off, just thinking about it.

Half of this tiny room is crowded with a bunk bed and two desks; the living room is carpeted with beer cans, pens, potato chip bags, a newspaper, cigarette butts, a roll of duct tape, two trash cans overflowing with beer cans, and *The Portable Voltaire.*

Sang Oh, who lives here, walks in and heads for a mattress in the corner. He's in jeans, high-tops, a gold chain around his neck, his hair shaved on the sides and rising into a stylish flattop. Sang has become fully acclimated to American life since his family moved from Korea to the Boston suburb of Newton eleven years ago.

A swimsuit model taped to his wall is falling to her knees, arms out for balance, hair flying, breasts heaving. There's a memorial collage of John Lennon, 1940–1980, and posters of the Beatles and Public Enemy's *Fear of a Black Planet.* The pinup belongs to Sang; the music posters, the *New York Times,* and the books on the floor belong to Sang's roommate, Val, an economics major who says he wants to be either an actor or a talk-show host. But when they are in their bunk beds late at night, Sang will say, "So what do you want to do?"

"I don't know," Val answers. "What do you want to do?"

Sang usually tells people he wants to be a lawyer, but in the honesty of the dark, he'll say, "I don't know."

Val's as loquacious as Sang is taciturn. He talks so fast that his friends have difficulty following his rants about the historic brutalities of the Catholic church or about racist students. Val couldn't believe it when he heard a kid on campus refer to Bill Cosby as a nigger.

Enter two girls, one sexy in tight jeans and halter, the other wholesome in an argyle sweater . . . .

Relationships between boys and girls who live on the same floor tend to be more sibling than sexual. The girls know they can call Sang late at night from the library and he'll walk them home. After a few beers, the boys will get huggy with the girls, but that's about as far as it goes.

After all, nothing could be worse for a boy who got drunk at a keg party and went hogging than to run into the girl the following day. It'll be bad enough having to face her in the dining commons. Living on the same floor? Nightmare! Except if it's serious. But how often does that happen?

The truly wild stories the boys like to tell are from last year, when most of them lived on the all-male sixteenth floor. Keg parties were popular that semester, in clear violation of university rules. A student resident assistant can lose his free room and board if a violation of such magnitude occurs while he's around. But neither does he want his peers to think he's a weenie. So if an RA sees his boys hefting a keg down the hall, he'll simply ask, "Does this mean I have to go to the library?"

When Sang moved into the Kennedy Tower, his roommate was a high school buddy named Joel. Sang and Joel were part of a clique at Newton North High School known for their pranks. Kid stuff compared to what they got away with in college, which had lots of beer and girls and no parents or curfew.

Sang would look forward to the morning discussions of the previous night's misadventures. He'd know instantly whether Joel made it home by looking up from the lower berth of their bunk bed for that familiar lump in the mattress.

Sung remembers the first keg party he went to. "Joel got to the keg first. He always did." Then they lost him in the crowd. "We were always losing Joel." So they left without him. Sang remembers catching a last glimpse of his buddy, fighting the crowds at the keg, laughing and pouring himself a beer.

When Sang and Joel entered the University of Massachusetts at Amherst as freshmen, they were just two of 5,400 students packed into a giant dormitory complex. The John F. Kennedy Tower is one of five twenty-two-story high-rises; surrounded by eleven low-rises, the towers look like a housing project dropped into the middle of the western Massachusetts countryside.

Like most state universities, UMass realized in the late Fifties that a tsunami of baby-boomer college students was headed its way. If the school wanted to keep the local talent at home, it had to grow huge in a hurry. President John W. Lederle transformed UMass from a tiny cow college of 6,495 students in 1960, when he took over, into a metropolis of more than 21,000 by 1970.

But somehow, amid the excitement of trying to build UMass into "one of the top ten public universities in America," as Lederle put it, they forgot about the students. There was no money left for the complex of smallish residential colleges originally envisioned. So UMass bought a thirty-five-acre parcel of land on which to house and feed 5,400 kids. An emerging Boston architect named Hugh Stubbins, who would later become one of the nation's most prominent architects, building the Ronald Reagan Presidential Library, was hired to design it.

It's hard to imagine what his firm's historians were thinking when they titled the chapter on his work from that period "Academic Restraint and Prescience." There was nothing restrained about the 205-foot towers into which nearly three thousand students were jammed, and nothing prescient about believing that students would behave themselves in there. Adults at UMass always seemed surprised when anything unpleasant happened in the Southwest Residential Area. Students knew better. They've always called it the Zoo.

Soon after moving into Southwest in 1966, students began to trash the place. Stubbins had ordered furniture "of many cheerful colors" for the lounges and designed two balconies in the towers where he imagined students sunning themselves and sipping soft drinks. Instead, the kids did drugs, guzzled beer, threw the pretty furniture out the windows, and vandalized the elevators. Some suicidal kids used the balconies as jumping-off spots. Emmett Glynn, one of the architects on the project, says American youth just hasn't been the same since John Kennedy was shot.

The Zoo's most famous incident came in 1986, just after the Red Sox lost the World Series to the Mets. A crowd of more than a thousand students started chanting "Red Sox! Mets Suck!" The campus cops were overpowered as fights broke out and a black student was beaten unconscious by whites.

Today, most big universities have a place like the Zoo, soaring stone monuments to America's dream of universal public higher education. The incidents that have taken place in these student ghettos for a quarter-century—rape, racial violence, alcoholism, drug abuse, dangerous pranks, vandalism, suicides—have only recently begun to be talked about. Colleges have tried for decades to suppress the truth about crime in dorm life. But that will change by 1993, when a new law will require colleges to publish annual security reports, including the numbers of violent crimes.

Studies show campus crime is nearly always student against student. Incredibly, the crime rate at the UMass Zoo is nearly identical to that of the high-rise housing projects they resemble. The Polo Grounds Towers in New York City, which has 5,500 residents jammed into four towers, did have more murders than the Zoo (2 to 0), robberies (38 to 0), assaults (98 to 24), and disorderly conducts (47 to 12) during 1990, the last year for which comparative statistics are available. But the Southwest Residential Area, with 5,400 people spread over five high-rises and eleven low-rises, had more larcenies (135 to 54), burglaries (103 to 20), car thefts (25 to 7), and DWI arrests (10 to 1). The two finished in nearly a dead heat in sexual offenses, including rape/sexual assault (Zoo 6, Polo Grounds 8), arson (3 to 2), drug offenses (16 to 18), and weapons charges (6 to 5). UMass spends nearly twice as much on security per resident, $200 to $120.

The Polo Grounds and Southwest towers also share a passion for a bizarre sport played in high-rise buildings. Ghetto kids call it elevator action. Suburban teenagers in the Zoo call it elevator surfing. UMass housing director Joe Zannini remembers kids boasting about getting their "elevator wings" when he was a residence director at the University of Nebraska–Lincoln in the early Seventies.

Lederle remembers hearing about it in the late Sixties. Paul Lawler, UMass's director of elevator maintenance, says he's received evidence of kids riding on top of elevators at least once a week since he started back in 1966, when the towers opened. "It's been like a war," he says wearily. "They attack, we counterattack." Once, Lawler found a chair tied like a gondola to the underside of a tower car.

In New York City housing projects, thirty people were injured and two killed from riding on top of elevators last year. The problem has become so widespread that the New York City Housing Authority has produced a chilling, nineteen-minute educational video called *Children Are Too Young to Die.*

Umass has considered borrowing the grisly film and piping it into TV sets in campus dorm rooms. Students in the Southwest towers should have no problem identifying with the nine-year-olds depicted in the program—restless kids stuck in high-rise towers, largely ignored, with no backyard to play in, left to create their own increasingly dangerous coming-of-age rituals.

Tower windows flash with beer signs and strobe lights, and the air is pulsing with rap music. Cars whip through the parking lot and boys jump out carrying duffel bags lumpy with beer cans. Kids roam the quadrangle in packs.

A campus police car speeds across the courtyard at 2:30, trying to catch a nude boy hiding behind a tower, laughing, stepping into his underwear. A chubby, middle-aged campus cop runs after him and the streaker tucks his clothes under his arm like a football and scampers away, his lean, muscular body easily outpacing the constable. The boy slips in a puddle, still laughing, dashing away just before the cop grabs his arm. Another boy wearing only shorts and a baseball cap was not so lucky. He's getting handcuffed.

Here also is a date rape in the making, a typical horny, drunk, violent boy and girl too ashamed to ask for help. The barrel-chested guy skips down a sidewalk alongside the girl, whispering to her. She is clearly mad about something, refusing to slow down or speak. The girl takes a shortcut between two dorms, and once they're in a secluded area, the boy grabs her from behind, still whispering. She listens for a moment, then shouts, "Let me go!" and breaks free. When two campus cops become suspicious and start following them, the boy puts his arm around her affectionately, until the cops give up. Then she tries to escape, and he grabs her again from behind. They repeat this dance several times. Students of both sexes stroll by without saying a word. Finally, she breaks free and almost reaches her low-rise dorm, just as two girls emerge. Helpfully, they hold the door open as the boy and the girl silently disappear inside.

At 6:00 P.M. Sang, Val, and the guys walk next door to the dining commons. They bolt their machine-cut slices of turkey, glutinous beige gravy, stuffing, and pumpkin pie and are out in twenty minutes.

The guy with the fake ID makes a run to the liquor store. They drink until about 9:30, when Sang, Val, and two other boys, and three girls squeeze into somebody's car. They pull into a parking lot where about fifteen kids are waiting for a friend, who is next to some bushes, throwing up. Val is disgusted with his technique. "He's doing it all wrong. You don't throw up right where everybody can see you," he says. "I should write a book on how to throw up."

The group eventually arrives at a big white house in Amherst rented by somebody named Murph. They buy plastic cups for three dollars apiece from a guy in the hallway, then head for the kitchen, where the keg is. It's a relaxed, quiet party, but less than an hour later, Sang is outside, pacing, furious. At the keg, an immense, drunk boy-giant called him a "f---ing gook."

This isn't the first racial slur Sang's heard since he went to college. Sang says his friends usually get madder about these things than he does. But this time he's pissed. "I should go deck him," he keeps saying. Val dances around, swinging at the air, and says, "Hey Sang, why don't you give him some of that kung-fu-s--t?"

Now the mood's ruined and nobody feels like sticking around. Even though it's only about 11:30, they head back to Kennedy, where they can sit around smoking, watching TV, and listening to the Smiths: *I want to live and I want to love/I want to catch something I might be ashamed of.* At about 1:00 they all head for a tiny house, where a guy at the door is asking three dollars for admission. Sang and Val push through the packed living room and into the kitchen, but getting near the keg is out of the question. Sang pulls out some cold ones he brought for just such emergencies and hands them to friends. Most of the crowd is chanting along to a Beastie Boys song: *"Ali Baba and the forty thieves!"* The floor is wet and the stench of beer is choking. Soon the crowd is so dense it's impossible to move.

By 2:00, the Stones are singing *Baby, you're a fool to cry . . .* Standing in a narrow hallway, Val starts talking to a short, slim girl with teased hair who's having trouble standing. They brush up against one another, hands touching, then holding. It looks a sure thing, but then she walks away.

Val is bewildered. He says he offered to take her home and she said yes, but first she had to tell her roommate. "Then she turns around and starts talking to some other guy!" he says. It's getting kind of late, so the gang gets back in the car and returns to the dorm.

At 3:00, Val gets undressed for bed. "Life's a big bowl of s--t, sexually," he says. "The rest of it's fine." He drifts off to sleep.

But where's Sang?

Joel pulled one of these roommate-disappearing stunts the previous March on the sixteenth floor. It was exactly this time of the morning, somewhere between 3:00 and 4:00. Sang had already gone to bed. *Your roommate could be anywhere at this hour . . . maybe he's partying in somebody's room . . . or maybe he's off getting lucky. . . .*

Sang remembers Joel being especially pumped up that night. The hometown boys had driven out from Newton for a weekend of partying. It was great to see those guys again. Just when you're sure those high school days are gone forever, they'll show up at your door and it all comes back.

They arrived about 7:00 P.M., picked up Sang on the sixteenth floor of Kennedy, and met Joel at an off-campus keg party.

Joel was an honors student, but he could drink anybody under the table. At off-campus parties, he learned to do "kegstands," standing on his head atop the keg while someone pours beer from the hose into your mouth.

At 9:45, the boys went to a sub shop, then returned to the party until the keg ran dry at about 12:30. As they were walking toward their car, they noticed a party at another apartment in the same complex. They went inside and drank more. At about 3:00, the boys staggered off to Sang and Joel's room on the sixteenth floor of the Kennedy Tower. When his friends from Newton began fighting over pillows and floor space, Sang decided to go to bed. That's when Joel said something like, "You wimps, it's too early to go to bed. Let's do something wild, for old times' sake."

They'd heard Joel rave about riding on top of the elevators before. He supposedly learned the technique from some guys on the twenty-second floor: You wait until the elevator is between floors, then pry open the inside doors with your hands, which makes the car stop. Then you take a broom and reach up until it touches a latch, drawing open the outside doors as easily as you might pull back a window curtain. You crawl out—the lobby floor is now chest high—climb on top of the elevator, and close the doors behind you.

It's pitch black in there, silent except for the low hiss of the moving cars. You hold onto the cluster of metal hoist cables affixed to the top of the car. There's also a bare light bulb you can turn on. The car moves at a crawl compared to those big-city 'vators that really fly at one thousand feet per minute. Some kids like to smoke a bone as they climb slowly into the blackness.

Looking through a slit at your feet, you can see kids walking into the elevator after a night of partying. There's also a tiny red switch that shuts the car on and off. It's fun to stop the car with people inside and listen to them yelling. You can get off the elevator and stand on the horizontal crossbeams that run between shafts and watch the car dropping down the tunnel. If you're feeling wild, you can jump from the crossbeam onto the elevator car while it's moving. If you're totally insane, you can try to leap from one moving car to another and hope you don't get tangled up in the curtain of cables. You realize you're carrying on an American rite of passage when you notice the ancient cave markings flashing by: JERRY G. '69 . . . STEVE '69 . . . BALLS . . . JFK 22 RULES THE TOWERS . . . I WANT HER SO BAD . . . DO ME . . .

No elevator surfing tonight, said two of the boys from Newton. Joel walked over to his buddy Sang, who was in bed. No way, man. "Oh, come on, you baby," Joel said. Sang was not even tempted. Dave was Joel's last hope. They'd raced across a dangerous bridge together in high school, hadn't they?

Joel had consumed the equivalent of a case of beer, but his friends didn't consider him any drunker than usual.

Joel and Dave walked into the sixteenth-floor elevator.

Few places on earth feel as dangerous as standing on the greasy top of an elevator car. Walls slide by on two sides, inches away. An empty shaft beckons. And down the fourth wall slides the black guillotine of the counterweight.

That's the first way you imagine yourself dying, looking up and seeing the counterweight dropping from the murky darkness toward you. An optical illusion caused by the narrowness of the shaft makes it appear to be coming straight for your head. Only at the last moment does it glide past you, not more than four feet away.

You could also be killed by falling into the empty shaft. But that would be pleasant compared to the truly nasty way to go: snagging your sleeve or shoelace or sneaker in the matrix of wheels, pulleys, cables, and hooks that surround you. Or becoming caught in small cracks and gaps that open and close like a vise as the car moves. You could be pulled off-balance, or spun around and tumble, getting snagged further, held in place just long enough for this machine to slowly tear your body apart at a leisurely 250 feet per minute.

Oddly, fear dissipates quickly, replaced by a childlike awe at the elevator's sheer immensity and power. As you're being hoisted two hundred feet into the darkness, the silence broken only by a gentle *shhhhhhhhhh,* you suddenly feel pathetically small and helpless, utterly alone. And so you surrender, safe and snug, floating through black space. Perhaps that's what Joel loved most about the elevator shaft. Not only was he a prankster and risk-taker, but a poet:

> There is a place, where no wind blows
> The calm of earth abound
> There grows a thinking, floating rose
> Which I have often found. . . .

Sang woke up to pounding on his door.

He ignored it for a long time. Finally, Steve dragged himself off the floor and opened the door. Some guy named Dave was downstairs, a kid said. Dave was yelling something about Joel.

Steve and Sang ran downstairs to the fourteenth-floor lobby and found Dave pounding the walls with his fists. "I can't find Joel," he said. He had already looked on top of both elevators. So Steve climbed onto the elevators, too, and rode them until they were side by side. No sign. There was blood on top of one of the cars.

Somebody called the cops, and they started looking, too. Then Sang heard a police walkie-talkie say they found something in the pit. Sang rushed down the stairs, but he was stopped by a cop who said, "There's nothing you can do."

Nobody except Dave knows exactly what happened inside the shaft during the early morning hours of March 11, 1990. He broke numerous appointments with the authorities to tell his story. They finally gave up—no charges were being pressed and nobody blamed him. Their only clue is a barely legible statement the boy wrote in the police station that night, which reads, in part:

". . . Joel got on the beem in the middle of the elevator and watched me go up and down and I told Joel to get off and he did . . . but he slipped and fell between the elevator and the elevator door . . . and I grabbed his hand, but it was to late he was getting forced Down and he fell . . ."

Today, inside the John F. Kennedy elevator shaft, there is a dark green divider beam smeared, from the seventh floor to the third, with the blood of Joel

Mangion. His body struck a horizontal metal beam in the pit, pushing it down by two feet. When they found Joel, his eyes and mouth were open in horror, his body severed in half.

Sang cried the next day at the sound of Mr. Mangion's voice on the phone, "Don't blame yourself; there's nothing you could have done," Joel's father told him.

For years, Paul Lawler couldn't get anybody to show up for meetings to talk about elevator surfing. But forty people showed up in the sixteenth-floor lounge that night to discuss Joel's death with the dorm's resident director, a priest, and psychologist. That night, a friend drove Sang home to Newton.

For a long time, Sang couldn't really believe that Joel was dead. At the open-casket funeral, it hit him. He took one look at Joel's face and tried to run outside, but Mr. Mangion stopped him. "So I went to the casket and prayed," Sang says. "It didn't look like Joel. But I talked to him like he was there and told him I'd miss him."

Sang stayed home for two weeks. Finally, he drove back to Amherst and rode the elevator up to the sixteenth floor. He felt sick, so he went to bed early. He woke up the next morning and instinctively looked up. There was no lump in the mattress.

Unable to bring himself to drink, Sang missed most of the parties. When he did go, he'd stand in a corner by himself. Sang's grades plummeted as he wandered through the semester, wondering who he was, why it happened, what the goddamn point of life was, anyway. He'd open a book but be unable to concentrate, torturing himself: *Why didn't I stop him?*

There were eulogies in the student newspaper, and a memorial event was held in Kennedy. But the university seemed like a big, cold, impersonal place when Sang read Dennis Madson, vice-chancellor of student affairs, telling the student newspaper, "This just shows that bad judgments are made when people have too much to drink. People are smart enough to know that climbing on an elevator is a dumb, stupid thing to do."

Why was everybody being so insensitive, looking for blame and scapegoats? "Nobody came out and said it was a tragedy," Sang says, still bitter. "They just wanted to make an example out of what happened, which was rude. It seemed like they didn't care."

In all, it was a rough semester for UMass. Tuition went up and some kids couldn't afford to come back. Police were unable to come up with any clues in the case of a twenty-year-old Chi Omega sorority girl, who was brutally murdered that December in her car parked at a nearby mall. After Joel's death, a sophomore apparently hanged himself.

Then one night, something happened to Sang. It was Sunday, and he'd been left alone in his room. He was in utter despair, wanting to quit school and succumb to the meaninglessness of life. "I wanted to call my father and go home," he says. "I decided I couldn't take it anymore."

Sang revealed his plans to his resident assistant, who gave him a pad of paper and said, "Write down how you feel. It's worked for me plenty of times."

Sang sat down and wrote a one-page letter to himself. "Why did it have to be Joel?" he wrote "It's not fair. So many other people deserve to die. If there's a god, why would he do that to such a bright kid? Why?" In the end, that was his biggest question: WHY?

Sang folded the note, shoved it into his desk drawer, and went to bed. That night, he was visited by a force as mysterious and powerful as that wicked evilness that invaded his dreams on March 11, 1990, the last day of his childhood.

When Sang woke up, the world was different. "The next day was the best one I ever had," he says. Sang sat in class taking notes without falling asleep, read his economics chapters, saw his friends, and didn't even think about what happened.

Sang's greatest source of strength, remarkably, was the dead boy's father. "I remembered what Mr. Mangion said, that life goes on," he says. "That really helped."

"I said, 'Would Joel want me to sit around feeling sorry about what happened?' No way. If I was dead, I wouldn't want Joel to just sit around. I'd want him to go on."

Sang doesn't describe himself as religious, but he'd lie in bed and say out loud, into the darkness, "If you're up there, God, take care of him. I'll see you up there, Joel."

He made up the midterms he'd missed and pulled his grades up to passing. He even went to a couple of keg parties and had fun. Sang still gets depressed about what happened to Joel sometimes, especially when he's drunk. But that's not often. Joel's part of another life that seems long ago.

Today when Sang walks through the lobby of the John F. Kennedy Tower and out the front door, he never looks up at the photograph of his friend standing on a rock, clouds full and rippling behind him on a sunny day, squinting off into the distance, forever a boy.

As for the other five thousand kids who live in the Zoo, and those in student ghettos across the country, their future was presaged in a tiny news item in the UMass student newspaper. Four days after Joel Mangion's body was found, a student told police that something odd happened as she boarded the elevator on the nineteenth floor of the John F. Kennedy Tower:

"She heard someone knocking on the roof . . . ."

DISCUSSION QUESTIONS

1. What do you think is Keegan's message about why high-rise college dorms have so many problems? Do you agree with him?
2. Why do you think so many college students abuse alcohol? What can be done about it?
3. What is a "rite of passage"? Can you think of some other examples besides elevator surfing?
4. What is the meaning of the story at the end of the essay?

SUGGESTIONS FOR JOURNAL ENTRIES

1. Write about a "rite of passage" experience you have had.
2. Interview at least five students who drink and write their answers as to why. Be sure to include both sexes in your sample. What did you learn?
3. Every campus has a "culture." How would you describe yours? How is it similar and different from the one depicted at UMass?

When Is It Rape?

Nancy Gibbs

A report in Time *magazine in 1991 on the apparently growing phenomenon of "acquaintance or date rape" on college campuses and elsewhere and how the culture is struggling to adjust to this new sensitivity about an ancient crime.*

Be careful of strangers and hurry home, says a mother to her daughter, knowing that the world is a frightful place but not wishing to swaddle a child in fear. Girls grow up scarred by caution and enter adulthood eager to shake free of their parents' worst nightmares. They still know to be wary of strangers. What they don't know is whether they have more to fear from their friends.

Most women who get raped are raped by people they already know—like the boy in biology class, or the guy in the office down the hall, or their friend's brother. The familiarity is enough to make them let down their guard, sometimes even enough to make them wonder afterward whether they were "really raped." What people think of as "real rape"—the assault by a monstrous stranger lurking in the shadows—accounts for only one out of five attacks.

So the phrase "acquaintance rape" was coined to describe the rest, all the cases of forced sex between people who already knew each other, however casually. But that was too clinical for headline writers, and so the popular term is the narrower "date rape," which suggests an ugly ending to a raucous night on the town.

These are not idle distinctions. Behind the search for labels is the central mythology about rape; that rapists are always strangers, and victims are women who ask for it. The mythology is hard to dispel because the crime is so rarely exposed. The experts guess—that's all they can do under the circumstances—that while one in four women will be raped in her lifetime, less than 10 percent will report the assault, and less than 5 percent of the rapists will go to jail.

Women charge that date rape is the hidden crime; men complain it is hard to prevent a crime they can't define. Women say it isn't taken seriously; men say it is a concept invented by women who like to tease but not take the consequences. Women say the date-rape debate is the first time the nation has talked frankly about sex; men say it is women's unconscious reaction to the excesses of the sexual revolution. Meanwhile, men and women argue among themselves about the "gray area" that surrounds the whole murky arena of sexual relations, and there is no consensus in sight.

In court, on campus, in conversation, the issue turns on the elasticity of the word *rape*, one of the few words in the language with the power to summon a shared image of a horrible crime.

At one extreme are those who argue that for the word to retain its impact, it must be strictly defined as forced sexual intercourse: a gang of thugs jumping a jogger in Central Park, a psychopath preying on old women in a housing complex, a man with an ice pick in a side street. To stretch the definition of the word risks stripping away its power. In this view, if it happened on a date, it wasn't rape. A romantic encounter is a context in which sex *could* occur, and so what omniscient judge will decide whether there was genuine mutual consent?

Others are willing to concede that date rape sometimes occurs, that sometimes a man goes too far on a date without a woman's consent. But this infraction, they say, is not as ghastly a crime as street rape, and it should not be taken as seriously. The New York *Post,* alarmed by the Willy Smith case, wrote in a recent editorial, "If the sexual encounter, *forced or not,* has been preceded by a series of consensual activities—drinking, a trip to the man's home, a walk on a deserted beach at three in the morning—the charge that's leveled against the alleged offender should, it seems to us, be different than the one filed against, say, the youths who raped and beat the jogger."

This attitude sparks rage among women who carry scars received at the hands of men they knew. It makes no difference if the victim shared a drink or a moonlit walk or even a passionate kiss, they protest, if the encounter ended with her being thrown to the ground and forcibly violated. Date rape is not about a misunderstanding, they say. It is not a communications problem. It is not about a woman's having regrets in the morning for a decision she made the night before. It is not about a "decision" at all. Rape is rape, and any form of forced sex—even between neighbors, co-workers, classmates and casual friends—is a crime.

A more extreme form of that view comes from activists who see rape as a metaphor, its definition swelling to cover any kind of oppression of women. Rape, seen in this light, can occur not only on a date but also in a marriage, not only by violent assault but also by psychological pressure. A Swarthmore College training pamphlet once explained that acquaintance rape "spans a spectrum of incidents and behaviors, ranging from crimes legally defined as rape to verbal harassment and inappropriate innuendo." No wonder, then, that the battles become so heated. When innuendo qualifies as rape, the definitions have become so slippery that the entire subject sinks into a political swamp. The only way to capture the hard reality is to tell the story.

A 32-year-old woman was on business in Tampa last year for the Florida Supreme Court. Stranded at the courthouse, she accepted a lift from a lawyer involved in her project. As they chatted on the ride home, she recalls, "he was saying all the right things, so I started to trust him." She agreed to have dinner, and afterward, at her hotel door, he convinced her to let him come in to talk. "I went through the whole thing about being old-fashioned," she says. "I was a virgin until I was twenty-one. So I told him talk was all we were going to do."

But as they sat on the couch, she found herself falling asleep. "By now, I'm comfortable with him, and I put my head on his shoulder. He's not tried anything all evening, after all." Which is when the rape came. "I woke up to find him on top of me, forcing himself on me. I didn't scream or run. All I could think about was my business contacts and what if they saw me run out of my room screaming rape.

"I thought it was my fault. I felt so filthy, I washed myself over and over in hot water. Did he rape me? I kept asking myself. I didn't consent. But who's gonna believe me? I had a man in my hotel room after midnight." More than a year later, she still can't tell the story without a visible struggle to maintain her composure. Police referred the case to the state attorney's office in Tampa, but without more evidence it decided not to prosecute. Although her attacker has admitted that he heard her say no, maintains the woman, "he says he didn't know that I meant no. He didn't feel he'd raped me, and he even wanted to see me again."

Her story is typical in many ways. The victim herself may not be sure right away that she has been raped, that she had said no and been physically forced into having sex anyway. And the rapist commonly hears but does not heed the protest. "A date rapist will follow through no matter what the woman wants because his agenda is to get laid," says Claire Walsh, a Florida-based consultant on sexual assaults. "First comes the dinner, then a dance, then a drink, then the coercion begins." Gentle persuasion gives way to physical intimidation with alcohol as the ubiquitous lubricant. "When that fails, force is used," she says. "Real men don't take no for an answer."

The Palm Beach case serves to remind women that if they go ahead and press charges, they can expect to go on trial along with their attacker, if not in a courtroom then in the court of public opinion. The *New York Times* caused an uproar on its own staff not only for publishing the victim's name but also for laying out in detail her background, her high-school grades, her driving record, along with an unattributed quote from a school official about her "little wild streak." A freshman at Carleton College in Minnesota, who says she was repeatedly raped for four hours by a fellow student, claims that she was asked at an administrative hearing if she performed oral sex on dates. In 1989 a man charged with raping at knife point a woman he knew was acquitted in Florida because his victim had been wearing lace shorts and no underwear.

From a purely legal point of view, if she wants to put her attacker in jail, the survivor had better be beaten as well as raped, since bruises become a badge of credibility. She had better have reported the crime right away, before taking the hours-long shower that she craves, before burning her clothes, before curling up with the blinds down. And she would do well to be a woman of shining character. Otherwise the strict constructionist definitions of rape will prevail in court. "Juries don't have a great deal of sympathy for the victim if she's a willing participant up to the nonconsensual sexual intercourse," says Norman Kinne, a prosecutor in Dallas. "They feel that many times the victim has placed herself in the situation." Absent eyewitnesses or broken bones, a case comes down to her word against his, and the mythology of rape rarely lends her the benefit of the doubt.

She should also hope for an all-male jury, preferably composed of fathers with daughters. Prosecutors have found that women tend to be harsh judges of one another—perhaps because to find a defendant guilty is to entertain two grim realities: that anyone might be a rapist, and that every woman could find herself a victim. It may be easier to believe, the experts muse, that at some level the victim asked for it. "But just because a woman makes a bad judgment, does that give the guy a moral right to rape her?" asks Dean Kilpatrick, director of the Crime Victim Research and Treatment Center at the Medical University of South Carolina. "The bottom line is, Why does a woman's having a drink give a man the right to rape her?"

Last week the Supreme Court waded into the debate with a 7-to-2 ruling that protects victims from being harassed on the witness stand with questions about their sexual history. The Justices, in their first decision on "rape shield laws," said an accused rapist could not present evidence about a previous sexual relationship with the victim unless he notified the court ahead of time. In her decision, Justice Sandra Day O'Connor wrote that "rape victims deserve heightened protection against surprise, harassment, and unnecessary invasions of privacy."

That was welcome news to prosecutors who understand the reluctance of victims to come forward. But there are other impediments to justice as well. An internal investigation of the Oakland police department found that officers ignored a quarter of all reports of sexual assaults or attempts, though 90 percent actually warranted investigation. Departments are getting better at educating officers in handling rape cases, but the courts remain behind. A New York City task force on women in the courts charged that judges and lawyers were routinely less inclined to believe a woman's testimony than a man's.

The present debate over degrees of rape is nothing new; all through history, rapes have been divided between those that mattered and those that did not. For the first few thousand years, the only rape that was punished was the defiling of a virgin, and that was viewed as a property crime. A girl's virtue was a marketable asset, and so a rapist was often ordered to pay the victim's father the equivalent of her price on the marriage market. In early Babylonian and Hebrew societies, a married woman who was raped suffered the same fate as an adulteress—death by stoning or drowning. Under William the Conqueror, the penalty for raping a virgin was castration and loss of both eyes—unless the violated woman agreed to marry her attacker, as she was often pressured to do. "Stealing an heiress" became a perfectly conventional means of taking—literally—a wife.

It may be easier to prove a rape case now, but not much. Until the 1960s it was virtually impossible without an eyewitness; judges were often required to instruct jurors that "rape is a charge easily made and hard to defend against; so examine the testimony of this witness with caution." But sometimes a rape was taken very seriously, particularly if it involved a black man attacking a white woman—a crime for which black men were often executed or lynched.

Susan Estrich, author of *Real Rape,* considers herself a lucky victim. This is not just because she survived an attack 17 years ago by a stranger with an ice pick, one day before her graduation from Wellesley. It's because police, and her friends, believed her. "The first thing the Boston police asked was whether it was a black guy," recalls Estrich, now a University of Southern California law professor. When she said yes and gave the details of the attack, their reaction was, "So, you were really raped." It was an instructive lesson, she says, in understanding how racism and sexism are factored into perceptions of the crime.

A new twist in society's perception came in 1975, when Susan Brownmiller published her book *Against Our Will: Men, Women and Rape.* In it she attacked the concept that rape was a sex crime, arguing instead that it was a crime of violence and power over women. Throughout history, she wrote, rape has played a critical function. "It is nothing more or less than a conscious process of intimidation, by which *all men* keep *all women* in a state of fear."

Out of the contention was born a set of arguments that have become politically correct wisdom on campus and in academic circles. This view holds that rape is a symbol of women's vulnerability to male institutions and attitudes. "It's sociopolitical," insists Gina Rayfield, a New Jersey psychologist. "In our culture men hold the power, politically, economically. They're socialized not to see women as equals."

This line of reasoning has led some women, especially radicalized victims, to justify flinging around the term rape as a political weapon, referring to everything from violent sexual assaults to inappropriate innuendos, Ginny, a college senior who was really raped when she was sixteen, suggests that false accusations of rape can serve a useful purpose, "Penetration is not the only form of violation," she explains. In her view, *rape* is a subjective term, one that women must use to draw attention to other, nonviolent, even nonsexual forms of oppression. "If a woman did falsely accuse a man of rape, she may have had reasons to," Ginny says. "Maybe she wasn't raped, but he clearly violated her in some way."

Catherine Comins, assistant dean of student life at Vassar, also sees some value in this loose use of "rape." She says angry victims of various forms of sexual intimidation cry rape to regain their sense of power. "To use the word carefully would be to be careful for the sake of the violator, and the survivors don't care a hoot about him." Comins argues that men who are unjustly accused can sometimes gain from the experience. "They have a lot of pain, but it is not a pain that I would necessarily have spared them. I think it ideally initiates a process of self-exploration. 'How do I see women?' 'If I didn't violate her, could I have?' 'Do I have the potential to do to her what they say I did?' Those are good questions."

Taken to extremes, there is an ugly element of vengeance at work here. Rape is an abuse of power. But so are false accusations of rape, and to suggest that men whose reputations are destroyed might benefit because it will make them more sensitive is an attitude that is sure to backfire on women who are seeking justice for all victims. On campuses where the issue is most inflamed, male students are outraged that their names can be scrawled on a bathroom-wall list of rapists and they have no chance to tell their side of the story.

"Rape is what you read about in the New York *Post* about seventeen little boys raping a jogger in Central Park" says a male freshman at a liberal-arts college, who learned that he had been branded a rapist after a one-night stand with a friend. He acknowledges that they were both very drunk when she started kissing him at a party and ended up back in his room. Even through his haze, he had some qualms about sleeping with her: "I'm fighting against my hormonal instincts, and my moral instincts are saying, 'This is my friend and if I were sober, I wouldn't be doing this.'" But he went ahead anyway. "When you're drunk and there are all sorts of ambiguity, and the woman says 'Please, please' and then she says no sometime later, even in the middle of the act, there still may very well be some kind of violation, but it's not the same thing. It's not rape. If you don't hear her say no, if she doesn't say it, if she's playing around with you—oh, I could get squashed for saying it—there is an element of say no, mean yes."

The morning after their encounter, he recalls, both students woke up hung over and eager to put the memory behind them. Only months later did he learn that she had told a friend that he had torn her clothing and raped her. At this point in the story, the accused man starts using the language of rape. "I felt violated," he says, "I felt like she was taking advantage of me when she was very drunk. I never heard her say 'No!', 'Stop!,' anything." He is angry and hurt at the charges, worried that they will get around, shatter his reputation and force him to leave the small campus.

So here, of course, is the heart of the debate. If rape is sex without consent, how exactly should consent be defined and communicated, when and by whom? Those who view rape through a political lens tend to place all responsibility on men to make sure that their partners are consenting at every point of a sexual encounter. At the extreme, sexual relations come to resemble major surgery, requiring a signed consent form. Clinical psychologist Mary P. Koss of the University of Arizona in Tucson, who is a leading scholar on the issue, puts it rather bluntly: "It's the man's penis that is doing the raping, and ultimately he's responsible for where he puts it."

Historically, of course, this has never been the case, and there are some who argue that it shouldn't be—that women too must take responsibility for their behavior, and that the whole realm of intimate encounters defies regulation from on high. Anthropologist Lionel Tiger has little patience for trendy sexual politics that make no reference to biology. Since the dawn of time, he argues, men and women have always gone to bed with different goals. In the effort to keep one's genes in the gene pool, "it is to the male advantage to fertilize as many females as possible, as quickly as possible and as efficiently as possible." For the female, however, who looks at the large investment she will have to make in the offspring, the opposite is true. Her concern is to "select" who "will provide the best set up for their offspring." So, in general, "the pressure is on the male to be aggressive and on the female to be coy."

No one defends the use of physical force, but when the coercion involved is purely psychological, it becomes hard to assign blame after the fact. Journalist Stephanie Gutmann is an ardent foe of what she calls the date-rape dogmatists. "How can you make sex completely politically correct and completely safe?" she asks. "What a horribly bland, unerotic thing that would be! Sex is, by nature, a risky endeavor, emotionally. And desire is a violent emotion. These people in the date-rape movement have erected so many rules and regulations that I don't know how people can have erotic or desire-driven sex."

Nonsense, retorts Cornell professor Andrea Parrot, co-author of *Acquaintance Rape: The Hidden Crime*. Seduction should not be about lies, manipulation, game playing or coercion of any kind, she says. "Too bad that people think that the only way you can have passion and excitement and sex is if there are mis-communications, and one person is forced to do something he or she doesn't want to do." The very pleasures of sexual encounters should lie in the fact of mutual comfort and consent: "You can hang from the ceiling, you can use fruit, you can go crazy and have really wonderful sensual erotic sex, if both parties are consenting."

It would be easy to accuse feminists of being too quick to classify sex as rape, but feminists are to be found on all sides of the debate, and many protest the idea that all the onus is on the man. It demeans women to suggest that they are so vulnerable to coercion or emotional manipulation that they must always be escorted by the strong arm of the law. "You can't solve society's ills by making everything a crime," says Albuquerque attorney Nancy Hollander. "That comes out of the sense of overprotection of women, and in the long run that is going to be harmful to us."

What is lost in the ideological debate over date rape is the fact that men and women, especially when they are young, and drunk, and aroused, are not very good at communicating. "In many cases," says Estrich, "the man thought it was sex, and the woman thought it was rape, and they are both telling the truth." The man may envision a celluloid seduction, in which he is being com-manding; she is being coy. A woman may experience the same event as a de-grading violation of her will. That some men do not believe a woman's protests is scarcely surprising in a society so drenched with messages that women have rape fantasies and a desire to be overpowered.

By the time they reach college, men and women are loaded with cultural baggage, drawn from movies, television, music videos and "bodice ripper" ro-mance novels. Over the years they have watched Rhett sweep Scarlett up the stairs in *Gone With the Wind;* or Errol Flynn, who was charged twice with statutory rape, overpower a protesting heroine who then melts in his arms; or Stanley rape his sister-in-law Blanche du Bois while his wife is in the hospital giving birth to a child in *A Streetcar Named Desire.* Higher up the cultural food chain, young people can read of date rape in Homer or Jane Austen, watch it in *Don Giovanni* or *Rigoletto.*

The messages come early and often, and nothing in the feminist revolu-tion has been able to counter them. A recent survey of sixth- to ninth-graders in Rhode Island found that a fourth of the boys and a sixth of the girls said it was acceptable for a man to force a woman to kiss him or have sex if he has spent money on her. A third of the children said it would not be wrong for a man to rape a woman who had had previous sexual experiences.

Certainly cases like Palm Beach, movies like *The Accused* and novels like Avery Corman's *Prized Possessions* may force young people to reexamine as-sumptions they have inherited. The use of new terms, like acquaintance rape and date rape, while controversial, has given men and women the vocabulary they need to express their experiences with both force and precision. This dia-logue could be useful if it helps strip away some of the dogmas, old and new, surrounding the issue. Those who hope to raise society's sensitivity to the problem of date rape would do well to concede that it is not precisely the same sort of crime as street rape, that there may be very murky issues of intent and degree involved.

On the other hand, those who downplay the problem should come to realize that date rape is a crime of uniquely intimate cruelty. While the body is violated, the spirit is maimed. How long will it take once the wounds have healed, before it is possible to share a walk on a beach, a drive home from work or an evening's conversation without always listening for a quiet alarm to start ringing deep in the back of the memory of a terrible crime?

WHAT IF A WIFE SAYS NO?

"But if you can't rape your wife, who can you rape?" A crude joke, but a fair reflection of a common attitude for most of history. Until 1979, most states had rape laws that explicitly protected husbands from prosecution for even the most violent rapes of their wives. For a woman to refuse to sleep with her husband was grounds for divorce. But over the past decade, the attitudes and the laws have slowly shifted. A generation that saw an epidemic of wife beating and wife murder could hardly pretend that sexual violence within marriage was not also a crime. In a 1990 study a House committee estimated that one in seven married women will be raped by their spouses. Very few crimes will be reported, however, since women assume that no one will believe them. "People think marital rape is she has a headache and doesn't want to have sex and she gives in," says Ann Marie Tucker, executive director of the Citizens Committee on Rape, Sexual Assault and Sexual Abuse in Buffalo. "That isn't it at all. The sexual abuse is often part of an ongoing pattern of physical intimidation and violence."

Women who do press charges face a heavy burden of proof. The National Clearinghouse on Marital and Date Rape in Berkeley reports that though twenty states have completely eliminated preferential treatment for husbands, twenty-six other states hover in a gray zone; without gross brutality, the husband has the benefit of the doubt. If prosecutors decide they have enough for a case, however, they usually win; between 1978 and 1985, only 118 cases of spousal rape went to trial, but 104 wound up with a conviction.

CAN A MAN BE RAPED?

One answer, of course, is yes—by another man. In fact by some estimates, 10 percent of rape victims are men, though they rarely report the crime. But the interesting question, in light of the current debate, is how a man could be raped by a woman.

Most men would say, with physiological confidence, that if a man doesn't want to have sex, he can't be tied down and forced. Human anatomy provides him a special protection. But there are sex therapists who dispute this notion; some point to "masochistic titillation," while others speculate that panic, along with fear of bodily harm, does not necessarily rule out sexual arousal and may even increase it in some cases.

In any event, the most expansive definitions of rape include psychological coercion, which raises the question, Couldn't a woman emotionally pressure a man to have sex, by, for instance, impugning his manhood if he refused, and thus be guilty of rape?

If the word is given to mean unwanted sex, then men are vulnerable too. A 1988 study of sexually active college students found that 46.3 percent of the women and 62.7 percent of the men reported having had unwanted inter-course. Peer pressure, coercion, intimidation—all led students into situations they later regretted.

Some researchers fear that even raising the question trivializes the whole issue of rape. But there are paradoxes here that might shed light on the issue. How is it that when an adolescent boy is coerced into sleeping with an older woman, it is viewed with a wink as an accepted rite of passage, while the reverse—the coercion of a girl by an older man—is clearly not?

DISCUSSION QUESTIONS

1. *Time* suggests that date rape is a major social problem on college campuses today. Why do you think it has become such a problem?
2. Do you agree with the implication that we are all burdened with "cultural
   baggage" with regard to rape and as a result we have what feminists call a
   "rape culture"?
3. What effect has consciousness-raising on the issue of date rape had on
   your campus?
4. If you were the Dean of Students on your campus what would you do
   about this issue, if anything?

SUGGESTIONS FOR JOURNAL ENTRIES

1. Write about an experience you have had or know about in which someone
   was coerced into sexual behavior against their will.
2. Attend some kind of anti-rape program on your campus and write about
   what you have learned.

READING 28
Untitled Student Dramatic Production

Sylva Miller

Sylva Miller is a student who graduated from Western College Program, a residential college within Miami University (Ohio) in 1995, and who wrote this as a final project in a seminar, "Women and Theatre: the Politics of Representation," in her sophomore year. The assignment was to develop a six-minute theater performance that addressed the question, "What does feminism mean to me?" Peter M. Magolda, professor of education at Miami University, included it in a summary of his ethnographic study of college students, "Life As I Don't Know It," which appeared in About Campus *in 1997.*

How do I feel about this class? What do I think?

CONFUSION.

It was the summer after my first year of college and my mother and I were sitting in a cafe. She asked me to see her psychiatrist with her. I didn't even know she was seeing one.

"Why?"

"Because we fight so much."

"We don't fight enough to need a psychiatrist, mom."

"Well, maybe you can tell her things you don't like about me and we can work through things."

"I tell you what I don't like about you and that's the part you don't like."

"Oh."

"Why are you seeing a psychiatrist anyway?"

"I guess you are old enough to know."

"Know what?"

"That I was sexually abused as a child."

"By who?"

"A neighbor boy and an uncle."

"How old were you?"

"Seven."

"What did he do?"

"He would take my clothes off and touch me, and make me touch him."

"Did you actually have sex with him?"

"No, well, I don't know. We are working through that right now."

"And the uncle?"

"He used to touch me also.

"How old were you then?"

"Three."

"How can you remember? I can't remember anything from when I was three."

"I just know, and when I asked my mom about it she said it happened and never brought it up again."

SADNESS.

I didn't even care. My mom was telling me this and I felt nothing. I wasn't angry or mad. I didn't blame anyone. All I felt was sadness. I thought, Oh, this is why she's so weird. This is why she has no self-worth and does self-destructive things like overeat. Then she throws herself into things like Weight Watchers and Overeaters Anonymous and reads books like the *Courage to Heal* and *Adults Dealing with Childhood Sexual Abuse*. The sad thing is that I am just like her. I do self-destructive things and I don't like myself very much. I am my mother.

ME.

Something did happen to me once. It was my sophomore year in high school. He asked me to the prom; I said Yes. It'd be cool to go. None of my friends were going. I knew I wasn't his first choice; in fact, I knew I was his third. We left the dance an hour early. I knew something was going to happen; I could have said something. But we walked along Lake Michigan in the sand and it was beautiful, and I was beautiful, and I felt wonderful, and I felt wanted. Most importantly, I felt wanted. He ripped my dress in the car, my dress that cost $160. I stopped him before any "real" damage was done, before he actually raped me. What was worse than what happened in the car was the hour-and-a-half ride home. He drove 100 miles an hour down the highway while staring at me with stone-cold eyes, blaming me. I didn't care if I died. I didn't care if he killed me. All I felt was pain.

PAIN.

That night I sewed my dress so my mom wouldn't know what happened. Once again I wasn't angry, or mad, or upset. I just sat there and felt sad. All I know is that I never felt beautiful again and I sure as hell wasn't going to be alone again with a man who thought I was. I let him make choices for me. He chose that I would only go out with men who were weaker than me, men I could control. Not physically weaker, but mentally and emotionally weak. He made decisions that weren't his to make.

Now I can see that I have a right to be angry and a right to be mad. I know that other women are angry and are willing to help me and to wait for me to understand this.

ANGER.

I'm angry because I wasn't there for my mom when she came to me as a friend, a woman, and most importantly as a daughter. I'm angry because I wasn't there for myself when I needed me. I just wasn't there. Now I can see that I have strength, strength all women have, if only they knew it.

STRENGTH.

I have the power to stand up for myself and care about myself and my mother. I have the power to know that the asshole who hurt me is an individual, and I don't blame all men for what he did to me. The funny thing is that I had the power all along, I just didn't know it. I just couldn't see it.

POWER.

DISCUSSION QUESTIONS

1. What emotions did you experience as you read Sylva's production? What do you think your experience would have been had you been present for Sylva's performance?
2. As Professor Magolda exited the class after Sylva's performance, a student commented, "That's why theater class is so difficult. It's an exercise in self-exploration. It's like a big therapy group. It forces people to investigate who they are." Why do you think theater classes are like this?
3. How do you feel about sharing such personal material in a classroom? Have you ever done so? If so, what happened?
4. What do you think the connection was for Sylva between feminism and her production?

SUGGESTIONS FOR JOURNAL ENTRIES

1. Pick one emotion and write about it from a personal experience perspective à la Sylva.
2. Write about a time when you had power all along but "just didn't know it . . . just couldn't see it."

RESOURCES

Students need to learn how to take care of themselves, and colleges have responded by developing a huge array of programs and services to help them to
do so. Nevertheless, I see too many students jeopardizing their health through
a combination of alcohol and/or drug abuse, insufficient sleep and exercise,
poor diet, and dependence on caffeine. This is especially true for traditional-
aged first-year students.

One of the biggest challenges for many first-year students is living away
from home for the first time. I never realized just how much of a challenge
until my own daughter went away to college and developed a life-threatening
stress-related illness. The first essay by Philip Zimbardo, "A Practical Guide to
Sources of Help," talks about the importance of knowing when and where to
go for help when the usual support network of family or friends is no longer
available or sufficient. The essay also attempts to remove any stigma from getting professional help.

The second essay, "A Hug for All Reasons," is an excerpt from Kathleen
Keating's classic, *The Hug Therapy Book,* which describes the power of touch in
maintaining psychological health in both the hugger and the hugged, critical
whether living at or away from home and family. A minimum daily hug requirement of four has been attributed to the late Virginia Satir, a pioneer of
family therapy.

READING 29

A Practical Guide to Sources of Help

Philip Zimbardo

Philip Zimbardo, Brooklyn College '54, now a very popular professor of psychology at Stanford University, has written many books including Psychology and Life *(1975), an introductory psychology textbook. The following is an excerpt addressed to college students on getting psychological help and removing any stigma that students might have about doing so.*

Many of us have developed (or been taught) the feeling that we ought to be able to work out our own problems and not burden others with our troubles. It somehow seems inappropriate, or a sign of weakness, to admit that we might need help. There is little doubt, however, that almost everyone sometimes experiences feelings of depression or loneliness, or the inability to cope. Numerous life experiences have the potential of inducing such personal crises. It is important to realize that everyone faces such crises at one time or another and that there is nothing wrong or unusual about reacting to them emotionally. Seeking help at such times may not be easy, but it seems preferable to muddling through alone.

When our usual emotional supports, such as parents or close friends, are absent or unavailable, we should not hesitate to seek help from other sources. The duration of crisis is usually short for most people (from four to six weeks) and contains both the danger of increased psychological vulnerability and the opportunity for personal growth. The outcome seems to depend to a large degree on the availability of appropriate help and one's own attitude and definition of the "problem."

In terms of prevention, however, it would make better sense to seek out sources of help *before* they are needed. An interesting and worthwhile project would be to identify various sources of psychological support available to you now. First of all, you should list the available sources of help outside the mental health profession, such as family, friends, teachers, clergy, "rap centers," etc. Perhaps a visit to a local church or drop-in center would be instructive in terms of whether or not you think these places could be of help to you. You need not feel that you should make up a story to hide the exploratory nature of your visit; you can simply explain that you are trying to identify sources of emotional support in the community.

Most problems are in fact minor ones that will go away in time, that diminish in intensity as we look back on them. But the process of working them through helps us get in touch with ourselves and perhaps reduces the stressfulness of such problems in the future. However, there are also cases of real distress where perhaps you or a friend might become severely depressed, seriously contemplate suicide, or else begin to develop paranoid feelings of persecution, hallucinations, or other signs of major psychological stress. For such problems you should go at once to an accredited professional therapist for help. Ideally, it should be someone you have identified earlier as a person whom you can respect and trust, and with whom you can deal openly. Go early, before the symptoms themselves become problems (causing poor grades, etc.).

It is not unreasonable to talk ahead of time about the "therapeutic contract"—what you get for what you give. If you think it appropriate, you might want to explore the therapist's personal philosophy; his or her view of human nature and the causes of emotional and behavioral disturbance. Of course, feeling comfortable with the therapist and being able to develop feelings of trust are more important than knowing the therapist's philosophy. This can best be accomplished through sharing your problems and concerns and gauging the helpfulness of the response you get. Remember though, most therapists refrain from giving advice, but seek to help the client achieve his or her own resolution to the problem. You may judge for yourself whether or not this is what you need.

Therapy is an intimate social exchange in which you pay for a service. If you feel the service is not benefiting you, discuss this openly with the therapist, expose the possibility that failure of therapy represents the *therapist's failure* as well as your own. Discuss criteria for successful termination of therapy—when will the two of you know you are "really" better? Also discuss the issue of terminating therapy if you are unsatisfied with it. This may itself be a positive step toward self-assertion. There is an almost universal understanding among professionals that no therapist relates well with everyone, and a good one will sometimes suggest that a client might do better with another therapist.

DISCUSSION QUESTIONS

1. Why do you think there is such a strong bias in our culture against seeking help? Are there gender, racial, or ethnic differences?
2. How do you feel about Zimbardo's suggestion that a crisis contains not only increased vulnerability but also the opportunity for personal growth? Can you think of an example of how this was true for you?
3. Are you familiar with all of the potential sources of help on your campus? If not, do you know where you could get more information?
4. What would you do if your best friend began to talk about suicide?

SUGGESTIONS FOR JOURNAL ENTRIES

1. Interview one of the counselors on campus about their "personal philosophy" and therapeutic orientation, and write about what you learned.
2. Think of a crisis that you experienced in high school and write about all of the things you did in order to resolve it.

READING 30

A Hug for All Reasons

Kathleen Keating

Kathleen Keating, R.N., is a psychiatric and mental health counselor, educator, and consultant living in Canada. The following is an excerpt from The Hug Therapy Book *(drawings by Mimi Noland) published in 1983, describing the theory and rationale of hugging as well as illustrating four main types of hugs.*

THEORY

Touch is not only nice. It's needed. Scientific research supports the theory that stimulation by touch is absolutely necessary for our physical as well as our emotional well-being.

Therapeutic touch, recognized as an essential tool for healing, is now part of nurses training in several large medical centers. Touch is used to help relieve pain and depression and anxiety, to bolster patients' will to live, to help premature babies—who have been deprived of touch in the incubators—grow and thrive.

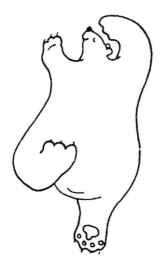

A hug makes you feel good all day!

Various experiments have shown that touch can:

Make us feel better about ourselves and our surroundings;

Have a positive effect on children's language development and IQ;

Cause measurable physiological changes in the toucher and the touched.

We are just beginning to understand the power of touch.

While there are many forms of touching, we propose that hugging is a very special one that contributes in a major way to healing and health.

RATIONALE

HUGGING

Feels good

Dispels loneliness

Overcomes fears

Opens doors to feelings

Builds self-esteem ("Wow! *She* actually wants to hug *me!*")

Fosters altruism ("I can't believe it, but I actually *want* to hug that old son-of-a-gun!")

Slows down aging; huggers stay younger longer.

Helps curb appetite; we eat less when we are nourished by hugs—and when our arms are busy wrapped around others.

Eases tension

Fights insomnia

Keeps arm and shoulder muscles in condition

Provides stretching exercise if you are short

Provides stooping exercise if you are tall

Offers a wholesome alternative to promiscuity

HUGGING ALSO

Offers a healthy, safe alternative to alcohol and other drug abuse *(better hugs than drugs!)*

Affirms physical being

Is democratic; anyone is eligible for a hug

Is ecologically sound, does not upset the environment

Is energy-efficient, saves heat

Is portable

Requires no special equipment

Demands no special setting; anyplace from a doorstep to an executive conference room, from a church parlor to a football field, is a fine place for a hug!

Makes happy days happier

Makes impossible days possible

Imparts feelings of belonging

Fills up empty places in our lives

Keeps on working to dispense benefits even after the hug's release

Besides, hugging prevents war.

BEAR HUG

In the traditional bear hug (named for members of the family Ursidae, who do it best), one hugger usually is taller and broader than the other, but this is not necessary to sustain the emotional quality of bear-hugging. The taller hugger may stand straight or slightly curved or over the shorter one, arms wrapped firmly around the other's shoulders. The shorter of the pair stands straight with head against the taller hugger's shoulder or chest, arms wrapped—also firmly!—around whatever area between waist and chest that they will reach. Bodies are touching in a powerful, strong squeeze that can last five to ten seconds or more.

We suggest you use skill and forbearance in making the hug firm rather than breathless. Always be considerate of your partner, no matter what style of hug you are sharing.

The feeling during a bear hug is warm, supportive, and secure.

Bear hugs are for:

Those who share a common feeling or a common cause.

Parents and offspring. Both need lots of reassuring bear hugs.

Grandparents and grandoffspring. Don't leave grandparents out of family bear hugs.

Friends (this includes marrieds and lovers, who hopefully are friends too).

Anyone who wants to say, wordlessly, "You're terrific!" Or, "I'm your friend; you can count on me." Or, "I share whatever pain or joy you're feeling."

What can a bear hug say for you?

BACK-TO-FRONT-HUG

In the back-to-front hug (also known as the waist-grabber), the hugger approaches the other from the back, folds arms around his or her waist and gives
a gentle hug.

The back-to-front waist-grabber is the perfect hug to give someone who is
peeling potatoes, scrubbing pans over a kitchen sink, or otherwise engaged in
some routine stand-up chore. A somewhat old-fashioned hug, this was practiced more extensively before the invention of the automatic dishwasher. But
most of the time a waist-grabber is still welcome as a brief, playful gesture.
The feeling behind it is happy and supportive.*

Back-to-front hugs are for:

Househusbands, housewives, and other live-ins.

Co-workers on an assembly line.

Friends whose occupations require that they face mostly in one
direction—like raspberry-pickers or mail sorters.

Do you know someone who would appreciate a waist-grabber?

---

*Even more supportive would be the back-to-front hug *followed* by the picking up of a dishtowel
and applying it to the pans.

THE A-FRAME HUG

Stand facing each other, wrapping arms around shoulders, sides of heads pressed together and bodies leaning forward and not touching at all below shoulder level. There. You have an A-frame hug. The length of time spent in the A formation is usually brief, since this is often a "hello" or "goodbye" hug.

The underlying feeling may be one of polite caring or detached warmth.

The A-frame hug is most appropriate for new acquaintances or professional colleagues, or in situations that require a degree of formality. Because it is relatively nonthreatening, it is comfortable for shy or unpracticed huggers.

This is a classic hug and should not be discounted because of its formal quality. It has broad application and is therefore beneficial to a wide range of huggers.

An A-frame hug is particularly apt for:

A great-aunt whom you haven't seen since you were a toddler.

Your spouse's employer's husband.

Your former academic adviser.

A new daughter-in-law.

Who else?

Like this.

HEART-CENTERED HUG

Many consider the heart-centered hug to be the highest form of hugging, and official Hug Therapists feel, too, that it is indeed very powerful.

The heart-centered hug begins with direct eye contact as the two huggers stand facing each other. Then the arms are wrapped around shoulders or back. Heads are together, and there is full body contact. The hug is firm, yet gentle. As the two breathe slowly and easily together, they focus on the compassion that is flowing from one heart into the other.

There is no limit on this hug; it may last several moments, shutting out all nearby distractions. The heart-centered hug is full and lingering, caring and tender, open and genuine, supportive and strong.

The heart-centered hug feels right:

When the huggers are very old friends with a long history of crisscrossing paths.

When the huggers are very new friends brought together by a shared experience and a strong, shared emotion.

When might you share a heart-centered hug?

It may last several moments, shutting out all distractions.

DISCUSSION QUESTIONS

1. A number of years ago, Virginia Satir, the late founder of family therapy, is rumored to have said that we all have a minimum requirement of something like four hugs a day. Why do you think she said that and do you agree?
2. It has been observed that our culture gives more permission to women to hug each other than to men. Why do you think that is so and do you think that is beginning to change?
3. How can you tell if someone is going to be receptive to a hug?
4. What are some other types of hugs that do not appear in this excerpt?
5. Do you think it is coincidental that a nurse wrote this excerpt?

SUGGESTIONS FOR JOURNAL ENTRIES

1. Try the four different types of hugs described by Keating and write about the difference in experience for each one.
2. Write about the most important hug that you've ever experienced in your life.

Personal Development

As should be obvious, the demarcation between Section I, "Campus Culture," and Section II, "Personal Development," is somewhat arbitrary. However, this section is a little removed from the campus, as the readings explore issues of family, identity, and spirituality. Nonetheless, personal development is a large part of adolescence, and college life provides great opportunities as well as great hazards for its accomplishment. The following readings offer a sampling of professional recommendations as well as some personal statements about the inherent difficulties of achieving self-identity in a society that is rapidly becoming more diverse.

FAMILY TIES

Most students are naive about the impact of parents upon their lives. I have found these readings to have a powerfully corrective influence on my students. There is an essay on each of the four primary binary relationships—mother-daughter, mother-son, father-daughter, and father-son—in addition to a short story that explores a mother's regret in not meeting the needs of her daughter.

Much of the adolescent journey is coming to terms with the discovery that our parents are not perfect but neither are they monsters. As you read these selections, reflect upon your own family and the degree to which you have been shaped and influenced by your parents, siblings, and extended family.

The first essay describes a daughter's experience of being dropped off at college by her parents and discovering the ambiguity of her new-found freedom. The second essay describes a mother's poignant goodbye to her son who is about to drive across country from California to Harvard. There is much in these two essays about the difference between a mother's perspective and that of the child.

The third essay is written by a father who must face the fact that he is no longer the only man in his daughter's life. The fourth essay completes the binary possibilities with a college professor's groundbreaking investigation of the phenomenon of "father hunger" in men, a malady that only recently has been acknowledged and addressed.

The essays are followed by a short story. The story, by the well-known Tillie Olsen, is an intensely personal reflection by a woman on her guilt and frustration in being an inadequate mother to a gifted daughter.

READING 31

Untitled

Amy Corey

Amy Corey, UVM '96, was a student in a course (AGRI 99—Beginnings: First-Year Seminar) required of all first-year students in the College of Agriculture and Life Sciences at the University of Vermont, where the first edition of College 101 *was a required text. Her professor, Thomas Patterson, Jr., sent me a copy of Amy's essay in January 1993 as a sample of students' responses to my book. This is a story of a daughter coming to terms with her mother as a result of leaving home for college.*

Adjusting to the life at UVM was relatively easy for me. I was not at all homesick in the beginning, but after a couple of weeks I began to think about my family and friends back home. I realized how much I missed them. I also realized that before I came to UVM I had taken them for granted. My feelings for them, my mom in particular, have changed drastically. From talking to my friends I know that this situation is not unique to me. Most of them feel differently about their families as well. I think many people have this change of heart once they are away from someone they think they don't like. That's why this piece would make a good addition to the "Family Ties" section in Lawry's book, *College 101: A Freshman Reader.* Many people would be able to relate to it, especially teenagers. The readings currently in this section are written by adults, for adults. A piece by someone a bit younger, giving a perspective on adults, might be more useful to teenagers.

As I said before, many students feel differently about their home life once they go away to college. Usually, it is their attitude toward their parents that changes the most. This is what happened to me. I feel completely different toward my parents now, mainly toward my mom. We've always had a one-sided relationship. She was always the one to start a conversation, give a hug, or say I love you. I always shied away from her, pushed her away, or avoided her. Now that I've been away from her for a while, I miss her and I regret the way I've acted toward her. I never thought I'd be hearing myself say this, but it's true. I don't think she knows how I feel now, and, unfortunately, I'm not the type of person to tell her all this straight out. She must notice something because I am more talkative and more receptive to her on the phone. I don't get irritated just by listening to her anymore. And for the first time in my life I actually enjoy talking with her and value her opinion.

From what you've read so far, you must think I'm a rotten child. Unfortunately, there is reason for my past behavior. My mom is not the most stable person in the world. Her childhood was pretty messed up by a bitter mother and an alcoholic father. On top of that, she was an only child who was supposed to be a boy. Expectedly, the effects ran deep, so deep that she is still trying to deal with them. Over the years she had periodic breakdowns in which she would go into deep depression or into tantrums; then she would tell my sisters, my brother, and I how much she hated us and what terrible, ungrateful children we were. Other than these digressions she was really an understanding, fair mother with a good sense of humor. Needless to say, these "episodes," as we called them, pitted my siblings and me against her. We learned to stick together, unable to go to Dad because he always sided with Mom, no matter what.

Being the youngest by quite a few years, I always took what Mom said the hardest. I guess that's because the other three were more mature and had a better understanding of why she acted the way she did. As we grew up they just seemed to ignore her episodes and acted like nothing had happened. Because I didn't feel right being the only one to speak out, I kept what I felt inside and alienated her instead. My sisters and my brother even started to get along with her after a while. This frustrated me and, now that I think back, it made me feel really guilty. While they were calling a truce, I was still resentful and unforgiving.

My bitterness mellowed out a little at the end of my senior year in high school, probably because my mom mellowed out, too. I think she realized this was the end of my childhood and after I left for college she wouldn't have anyone completely dependent upon her anymore. When she and my dad dropped me off at my dorm, she was in kind of a daze. I could tell she was thinking back on the years and how fast time had gone by, just as I was. As they drove away, I stood quietly and watched. A year ago, a month ago, I pictured myself jumping for joy, ecstatic to be rid of them and on my own. But now that the time had come I couldn't tell if I was happy or sad to see them go.

I've been at UVM for almost three months now. I called my mom the other day to say hi and ask her how she was doing. I told her that I want to change my major, to what I don't know, and I listened to some of the possibilities she gave me. I took her advice on one and, ironically, I'll be going into her field— psychology. I'm looking forward to starting over with her when I come home for Thanksgiving. It'll be strange at first but I really want to make an effort to understand what she has to cope with. Maybe I can help her in some way. Coming to college was obviously a good thing for me to do. It's strange, though, that coming to UVM made me adjust to my life at home. It's strange that I needed adjustment to a place I've lived for 18 years, rather than to a place I'd hardly been.

DISCUSSION QUESTIONS

1. Amy describes how her feelings toward her family, especially her mother, began to change within a couple of weeks after leaving home for college. Whether commuter or resident student, has this been true for you as well? In what ways?

2. How similar to or different from Amy's was your experience of saying goodbye to your parents?

3. Amy recommends that I should consider incorporating some student-authored work into the new edition of this book. Assuming you have read some of the other student essays (Readings 5, 22, 23, 28, 36, 46) by now, how do you feel about this suggestion?

SUGGESTIONS FOR JOURNAL ENTRIES

1. Reflect upon your relationship with your mother. Write about your own struggles in terms of adjustment and separation.
2. Amy reports that her mother's childhood was "pretty messed up by a bitter mother and an alcoholic father." Interview your mother about her relationship with her mother. Write a report about what you learned that you never knew before.

READING 32

Sons and Mothers

Susan Moon

Susan Moon is a writer who lives in Berkeley, California, where she teaches writing in an adult education program. The following is a poignant essay by a mother who experiences the difficulty of letting go—even when he's off to Harvard. This essay appeared in Ms. Magazine *in 1988.*

When Noah recently left home for his sophomore year at Harvard, we had a really good good-bye. These days I'm studying what it is to have my children grow up and go away. Noah is the first one, so this story is about him, but in a couple of years his brother, Sandy, will graduate from high school, and then I'll have another good-bye story to tell. That will be the real empty nest story.

One thing I've found out: we middle-aged moms are shy to tell how we feel when our kids leave home. Our culture doesn't give us a lot of help with this transition. Being a middle-aged mom is bad enough in itself, but being upset when your children leave home seems downright pathetic. But if I miss Noah, and I do, it isn't because I haven't "cultivated interests outside the home." I could probably get into the *Guinness Book of World Records* for having the most outside interests of any mother in my category of age and weight. Another thing our sadness doesn't mean—it doesn't mean our kids are "tied to our apron strings," it doesn't mean we aren't proud and happy to see them becoming adults, and it doesn't mean we have nothing more fulfilling to do than go fishing with a bent coat hanger in the dust behind the dryer for missing socks. I'm happy to have more time for other activities. Only you get used to having somebody around.

So I welcome my grief. And with this good-bye, I learned that a good good-bye makes a big difference.

It was a Berkeley end-of-summer sunny day, one of those really hot September days. I was puttering around in my study, trying to concentrate on my work, but I was distracted by anticipating Noah's departure, listening to his preparations, hearing his footsteps up and down the stairs, the front door opening and closing. He's loading up the car he's about to drive across the country, the fancy car of a grown-up friend. In the kitchen he's packing up a cooler, putting in juice and ice. Does he remember the chocolate bar I got him for a treat? And the "coffee nips" to help him stay awake? He calls me: "Well, I'm taking off now."

I go out to the kitchen, and he hugs me. We just stand there clinging to each other, a good hard hug. "I sure hate to say good-bye to you," I say, and suddenly begin to cry. My tears fall on his neck. I hear him crying, too, and he holds me tighter. And so we stand, weeping, saying nothing, for the longest time I've ever held him still in all his nineteen years. When he was an infant, he squirmed in my arms, arched his back, waved his feet at the ceiling.

The corner of the kitchen looks different over Noah's shoulder. Everything shifts slightly as he holds me, as if it were two-dimensional before, and now it's become three-dimensional. Everything looks so cozy, even the smudge of fingerprints on the wall beside the light switch. It's so hot, I stroke his hair, and pull my head back far enough to kiss his cheek, then put my chin back on his shoulder. We don't quite want to look at each other, wanting to give privacy to each other's tears. "You're a good boy . . . I mean man." He's six feet tall, which means he has a couple of inches on me.

I think of the Russian movie I saw a few days before: *Ballad of a Soldier,* about a soldier (also nineteen years old) who gets leave from the front to visit his mother, because he never had a chance to say good-bye to her. He has so many misadventures along the way that by the time he gets home and finds his mother in the field where she is working, he only has a few moments to spend with her. They stand together in the road, embracing, while the jeep and driver that will take him away wait beside them, and the mother weeps with grief and joy: "My son, my son. How can I let you go, my son?" I like how the Russians think it's okay to show all that love between mother and son. When I saw the movie I saw myself and Noah standing in that field. And now they are standing with us, in us, here by the refrigerator.

I have a moment of humility, comparing my experience to the Russian mother's. Noah is going to Harvard (what more could a mother want?), not to war, and every cell in my body appreciates that.

But Noah is about to pull away from a Berkeley curb, and drive off through smoky California, burning up with forest fires, all the way across the United States to shady maple trees, dark green before they turn; to steer a heavy, humming white machine over three thousand miles of roadway. A big, fast fish in a dangerous river. The exit signs will flash by, and the drone of tires will be punctuated now and then by the ticking of a turn signal. Yesterday he told me that you are thirty times more likely to die in a car than a plane, traveling over the same distance. And this means, he said, that if it's a half mile to the co-op, you are two hundred times more likely to die in a plane flying across country than if you take the car to get groceries. This is supposed to make me feel safe when I go shopping.

Noah's a good driver, but he thinks hard, and sometimes this causes him to miss a turn. He brings true meaning to the phrase "lost in thought." Still, a person can't exactly get lost driving across the country. Imagine him calling up Harvard, "I'm sorry I'm late—I must have missed my exit, and now I'm lost, somewhere, in thought, or maybe Nebraska. Can you tell me how to get there from here?"

I've never had such a good good-bye. A year ago he literally flew out of the nest. That was the real threshold, his first time leaving for college—scarier for me, and probably for him too—but at Oakland Airport we couldn't say good-bye like this, in our own sweet time. His plane left early in the morning. We had a few minutes to stand around together at the gate, shifting our weight from one foot to the other, making good-bye noises: "Have you got something to read?" I might have said, to the boy with the ever-present pack of books on his back. He nodded and grinned and pointed to the backpack. "What are you reading now?" I think it was a book about Japanese design, or else it was Wittgenstein. Something very intellectual that made me proud of him, but that I didn't want to read myself.

They were starting to board the plane. A quick hug. "I love you, Noah." "I love you, too," and he held me by the shoulders and looked at me hard, for just a split second, his head slightly cocked to the side, with a look that seemed to say, "I'm going to miss you a lot, but I'm happy and excited about going to college. Miss me back, be sad but not too sad. You won't forget to keep on loving me?" Then we broke apart, like what? Not like a cell dividing—we have different chromosomes. Did he leave like a cowbird leaving a cow? That's silly. More like a wave curling back from a rock, while I stood rooted to the spot—but now I'm talking of a tree, mixing metaphors. Well, like a son leaving his mother, then, he entered the big accordion tube, while I stood still, my sad hands in my pockets, and just before he disappeared around the bend, he turned, waved, smiled. He turned away again—I got a last glimpse of his tall, thin form, with his old, mended day pack heavy with books on his back, and his shoulders slightly hunched—at once the familiar body of my son, and the unknown body of a man—and he was gone. I walked back to the car, through the airport that smelled of new carpeting, crying wretchedly, but silently, so nobody would notice. I cried on and off for a week. And now he goes again.

Massachusetts is so far away. Why do we put these miles between us, all three thousand of them? What kind of crazy society do we live in? Where *is* my family? I have a mother in Illinois; a sister in New Mexico; a father, brother, and now a son in Massachusetts. Thank goodness I have a sister in Berkeley, too. And in two years I'll be saying good-bye to the other one. How will I be able to bear it? What a strange kind of intimacy—to be so very close to another person, and the whole time, starting with conception, you are teaching them to leave you. Even birth, that great arrival, is the first of many separations. First they leave your body; then they leave your home. Think of an intimate relationship between adults. What if at the beginning you set a marriage or a close friendship on a compass course toward separation, as we do with our children?

"Why is it like this?" I wailed to a friend soon after Noah left. "Why do we raise our children up so that they can leave us?"

She had just returned from a visit with her aging parents. "That's not all," she said. "Then we grow old and die, and we leave *them*. It's like Dear Abby says. We should tell people we love them now, before they go." She laughed. "I love you, Sue."

"I'm not going anywhere," I said.

"Oh, well, I love you anyway."

DISCUSSION QUESTIONS

1. Do you agree with Moon that "Our culture doesn't give us a lot of help with this transition"?
2. How might Noah's goodbye with his father been different?
3. What does Moon's reminiscence of *Ballad of a Soldier* add to the feeling tone of the essay? What is she trying to say?
4. Why is it so difficult for most of us to tell our parents that we love them? Is it more difficult for sons than for daughters?

SUGGESTIONS FOR JOURNAL ENTRIES

1. Reflect back on your own good-byes with your parents and write about how they were in contrast with Noah's.
2. Whether commuter or resident student, write about the advantages and disadvantages of each. Which would be your preference and why?

READING 33

Daughters, Fathers, & Dancing

John D. Lawry

This essay was occasioned by an annual Women's Day at the women's college where I teach. The topic was "Daughters and Fathers" and I was a member of a three-person panel of two professor/fathers and a professor/daughter. It was published in the New York Times *in 1989. The following interview by Celine Allen, Marymount '66, was published in the alumnae magazine,* Marymount Tarrytown, *in 1990.*

As I was thinking about what I would say on the topic of "Daughters and Fathers" at our yearly Women's Day at the women's college where I teach, I met a young woman who told me that she used to dread high school dances. When I asked her why, she said that her father died when she was young and as a result she had never learned to dance.

This poignant revelation reminded me of two things. One, the fact that my mother taught me to dance and I had completely forgotten that until I heard this woman's story. The second thing I was reminded of was how much I have enjoyed dancing with my daughter from that first, awkward father-daughter dance in junior high school to the mirthful parents' weekends at the college she graduated from this year.

When the day arrived for Women's Day '89, I was not prepared for the large turnout of students for what I, along with two colleagues (another father and a daughter), would have to say about that which Joyce Carol Oates has called one of the central mysteries of her life. Of all the possible binary family configurations, father-daughter is the least written about and what little is written is primarily from the daughter's viewpoint.

Little wonder that these students were eager to hear what two fathers had to say. (The original title was "Fathers and Daughters," but I was discreetly asked by a feminist colleague if I would mind reversing the order. "It's a subtle but important part of what we are trying to accomplish with the day," she argued. Being a feminist myself, I thought the point well taken.)

I gave a creditable summary of the research findings on the importance of fathering, voicing my opposition to Margaret Mead, who once expressed the folk wisdom of an earlier time when she said that fathers are a "biological necessity but a social accident." Beginning with the early research (1970s and earlier) on fathers being absent, I spoke about how the absence of fathers seemed to correlate with difficulties in the areas of sex-role development, moral development, cognitive competence, and social adjustment—no small matters in this society of achievers.

I went on to talk about the newer research on the presence of fathers: for example, how fathers can learn to be just as competent a parent as mothers and to bond as well with their babies, provided that they have time alone together. On the other hand, I reported how fathers seem to be sexist, in that they prefer male offspring and talk more to their sons than to daughters.

I could see some nodding heads in agreement with this painful reality. I pointed out, however, that androgynous men do not seem to fit the stereotype and that perhaps that was the hope for the future. "Of course, we must teach our sons to be men in this new age, but we also have the capacity and obligation to teach our daughters how to dance." Thus, I concluded to spirited applause.

But I was not yet off the hook. It was time for questions and I could tell the students were trying to be sensitive. Finally, one brave student asked the question all the students had come to hear answered. "Dr. Lawry, how do you feel about your daughter's boyfriend?"

Luckily, I came prepared. I showed them two photographs taken at the same time over a Christmas vacation. It was the first time I had met my daughter's boyfriend. The two photos included my daughter, one with me and one with her boyfriend. Looking at them one day, I suddenly realized that my daughter was standing much closer to her boyfriend than she was to me. It came as quite a shock, and yet the evidence was there.

I told the students that, initially, it was hard for me to acknowledge being replaced as the "man" in my daughter's life, but I think I have worked it through.

In retrospect, I realize that my daughter has been very sensitive to not forcing the issue of my replacement by avoiding any public displays of affection with her boyfriend in my presence. I had not realized this until recently, when I visited her in Boston and her boyfriend came over in the afternoon to visit.

We were in the backyard and I went into the house to get some refreshments. From the kitchen window I could see my daughter in a playful embrace with her boyfriend. It was the first time I had ever witnessed my daughter in any man's arms other than my own. It caught me by surprise and I started to cry. For some reason, I was reminded of Patricia Bosworth writing about her father: "It's an impossible passion . . . a perilous love, an unrequited love." That's so and yet I truly rejoice in my daughter's blossoming womanhood. May she never stop dancing.

What do you mean by "dancing"? . . .

It's a metaphor for living life to the fullest, as I say in the introduction to my book. I wanted to title the book "May You Never Stop Dancing," but the marketing people at the publishing house changed it to "How to Succeed at School." In fact, the dedication in the book is to my daughter, who danced the role of a soldier in the Nutcracker at Lincoln Center, and to my mother, who taught me how to dance. That dedication really doesn't mean very much with this new title.

How come it was your mother who taught you how to dance?

I've assumed it was commonplace in my generation, and that most of my male friends learned to dance from their mothers. I haven't seen any surveys to validate that, and I may or may not be typical, but I just assumed that's how it was, and vice versa, that daughters learned to dance from their fathers. Many daughters I know learned to dance from their fathers. I would suspect, though, that there are very few men who learned to dance from their fathers in our culture.

Why?

I don't know. It's just a gut feeling. Perhaps it's because of the kind of dancing we do in our culture, namely ballroom dancing. It would be harder for a man to teach another man the reverse steps, whereas in, let's say, some of the Mediterranean cultures, where group dances are typical, I think it would be more natural. I could see Zorba the Greek teaching his son to dance.

Remember Rain Man? He teaches his brother how to dance.

Yes. But he's not his father.

Let's get back to the father-daughter relationship. Although we hear and read a lot these days about mother-daughter relationships, the father-daughter relationship is obviously a real concern for daughters. Look at the large turnout for your seminar on Women's Day.

From what I've observed among my students, the relationship that is more wounded—that's the word I would use—is the one with their fathers rather than the one with their mothers, even though their relationship with their mothers is often more problematic. A Jungian analyst, Linda Leonard, has even written a book entitled *The Wounded Woman: Healing the Father-Daughter Relationship.**

I'm interested in the terms "problematic" and "wounded." How do they differ?

I think daughters expect more from their mothers. In fact I even chided my students in developmental psychology a couple of weeks ago and I said, "Come on, you're easier on your fathers than you are on your mothers." And they all agreed. It's like a double standard. They expect their mothers to be more perfect than their fathers.

That helps explain why the mother-daughter relationship is problematic, but why is the father-daughter relationship wounded?

It's as if the father hasn't been able to give whatever the daughter needs, and I suspect that probably begins somewhere around adolescence. From what I hear, most of them have had good fathering through their childhood, but as soon as they begin to enter adolescence there is a change. I'm just speculating now, but I suspect it's because fathers feel threatened by their daughters' sexuality, and the way they deal with it is to withdraw. I've heard even grown women say they can remember the day when their fathers pushed them away and said, "You're too old for that now, sitting on my lap"—or whatever—"You're too old for that now." And they experience it as rejection, because they don't understand.

In your article you talk very honestly about your own feelings.

I was referring to the feelings I had when I looked out the window and for the first time saw my daughter in the arms of another man. I suspect that many fathers have had similar feelings about their daughters when they're

*Leonard, Linda. *The Wounded Woman: Healing the Father-Daughter Relationship*. London, Boulder, Boston: Shambhala, 1983.
(Distributed by Random House.)

growing up. But fathers tend to be somewhat reticent. That's the point of the article. I haven't seen many fathers write about this. A lot of the literature on father-daughter relationships seems to have been written by daughters rather than by fathers.

Do you think it's a cultural thing? Fathers are more reticent in our society?

I think so. Well, men are more reticent; therefore I think fathers are more reticent, especially when it comes to feelings.

What do you mean by "teaching our sons to be men in this new age"?

I think it's an obligation of fathers to teach their sons how to be men, period. A recent article in *Time* magazine quoted a retired Army officer who said that the Panama invasion provided an opportunity for American soldiers to show their manhood in ways that have been challenged since our "failure" in Vietnam—as if this is the way to prove their manhood, as if that is what "manhood" is all about. I think it's passe. That's what I'm getting at by the "new age."

So, teaching our sons how to be men would involve presenting a different model. You've implied what that model isn't. Could you say a little more about what it would be?

Well, the word "androgyny" comes to mind. A lot of the things that we've identified as womanly or feminine I think we're beginning to recognize are valuable for men as well. These things don't have to be the prerogative of women. And some of the characteristics that have traditionally been considered masculine—like assertiveness, ambition, being a success in the world—are beginning to be seen as individual traits, rather than gender-related.

In your article, you mention that men tend to favor their male offspring and talk to them more, but you note that the androgynous male doesn't seem to fit that stereotype.

I think younger fathers are changing, and the new research will probably show less favoritism of male children. My sense is that there's a kind of revolution going on for men as well as for women. I think it's more subtle and more silent and slower, and it's not getting much publicity, but I think there's no question that it's going on.

Do you think you and I will see the new age?

I think we've already begun to see it.

DISCUSSION QUESTIONS

1. Who taught you to dance?
2. Why do you think the father-daughter relationship is possibly the least written about of all the possible binary configurations in the family?
3. Joyce Carol Oates, the author, is quoted as saying that her relationship with her father is one of the "central mysteries" of her life. What do you think she means?
4. Many students resist the implication that parents, especially fathers, play an important role in their lives. How much importance has your relationship with your father had on your life?

SUGGESTIONS FOR JOURNAL ENTRIES

1. Whether son or daughter, write about the difference between the role your father has played in your life and the role your mother has played.
2. Write about whether you agree with the author that the definition of "manhood" is changing for your generation.

READING 34

Father Hunger

Andrew Merton

*Professor Andrew Merton, University of New Hampshire '67, runs the
composition program at the University of New Hampshire. This essay
appeared in* New Age Journal *in 1986 and explores father-son relationships
and their importance in how young men relate to women and how a new
generation of men are struggling to become the father they never had.*

I am going to tell you a secret about men. But first let me remind you of something you already know, although, if you are a woman, part of you keeps
denying it—the part that takes over late at night as you are drifting off to
sleep, alone, and whispers things like, *How come I never have any luck with men?
How come the only guys I ever meet are insensitive louts or oversensitive wimps or
both rolled into one?* The implication being that everybody else is meeting men
who are wonderful.

Here is the good news: There's nothing wrong with *you.*

The bad news (and this is what you already knew) is that the kind of man
you want—one who is strong yet sensitive, virile, yet faithful, decisive yet
considerate—really is in short supply. When it comes to intimacy—sustained,
egalitarian intimacy—men are incompetent.

Maybe not *all* men. But a lot of them. Probably most of them. And (this
may or may not comfort you) this condition is not confined to available men.
A lot of married men are afflicted as well. Unfortunately, the same problems
that prevent them from becoming truly intimate with their wives also frustrate
their attempts to establish close relationships with their children—and this is
true even if the men intend to take active roles in child rearing.

Now, here is the secret. It has two parts. Part one is dark, so dark that a lot
of tough guys, men with well-developed pectorals and lots of notches on their
bedposts, will go to great lengths to deny it, but it is true nonetheless: In terms
of psychological development, there is not much difference between a macho
and a wimp.

Oh, I know. On the surface they are opposites. Sylvester Stallone and
Woody Allen. One uses force to achieve his goals, while the other manipulates
through weakness. The wimp may be harder to spot, because he does seem
genuinely concerned about *you:* only later do you realize that when he asks
about your feelings, it's a cue to answer quickly and then ask him about *his.*

They have this in common: Both are incapable of dealing with a woman as
an equal. Therefore, neither is able to enter into an intimate, stable partnership
with a woman.

Experts have been telling us about men's inability to connect with women
for a while now. In *The Seasons of a Man's Life,* psychologist Daniel J. Levinson
warns, "Most men in their twenties are not ready to make an enduring inner
commitment to wife and family, and they are not capable of a highly loving,

sexually free, and emotionally intimate relationship." His studies show that, in this regard, a lot of men never *leave* their twenties. In her book *In a Different Voice,* psychologist Carol Gilligan pinpoints the different qualities men and women value in establishing relationships: "male and female voices typically speak of the importance of different truths, the former of the role of separation as it defines and empowers the self, the latter of the ongoing process of attachment that creates and sustains the human community." Levinson, Gilligan, and others point out that from the day he is born a boy is conditioned to be strong, stoic, and independent. Little in the culture at large tells him he should value intimacy or nurturing. The male cartoon heroes on television are lone warriors. (Voltron? He-Man? Tom Selleck? You might as well share your feelings with a B-52.) Girls' and women's magazines are full of articles about relationships. But you will not find articles on "How to Make This Relationship Last" in *Playboy.*

But here is something that, from experience, you may have trouble believing: A lot of men, deep down, want intimacy as much as you do. The trouble is, they don't know how to go about achieving it. And while the culture around them has a lot to do with this, some researchers are concluding that for an enormous number of men the inability to form intimate relationships may be traced to flawed relationships with their own fathers.

Which brings us to the second part of the secret: It is likely that both wimp and macho behavior are different manifestations of the same underlying psychological problem—the yearning for a father who never was.

Four years ago Harvard University psychoanalyst James Herzog invented the term *father hunger* to describe the psychological state of young children who had been deprived of their fathers through separations, divorce, or death. In his study, "On Father Hunger," published in *Father and Child,* he found that children thus affected—particularly boys—tended to have trouble controlling their aggressive impulses. He speculated that on a long-term basis "father hunger appears to be a critical motivational variable in matters as diverse as caretaking, sexual orientation, moral development, and achievement."

In that study Herzog applied the term *father hunger* to men whose fathers had been physically absent. But based on recent work by psychoanalyst John Munder Ross and psychologist Samuel Osherson, as well as on my own interviews with fifty men, the term can be expanded to include the offspring of fathers who were physically present, but *psychologically* absent or inadequate. We can define father hunger as a subconscious yearning for an ideal father that results in behavior ranging from self-pity to hypermasculinity and frustrates attempts to achieve intimacy.

If a father is bad enough, he can short-circuit his daughter's capacity for intimacy as well. But that's another story. And while inadequate fathering may do damage to a daughter, it is more likely to wound a son—and the wound is likely to be deeper and longer lasting.

And this is for the simple reason that a daughter can identify with her mother, while a son, at least beyond the age of two, can't. For it is at that age a boy begins to understand that he cannot be a woman. That is to say, he learns he cannot satisfy his creative and nurturing instincts directly by bearing a child. He must separate his own identity from that of his mother. He needs someone else to identify with.

According to John Ross of Cornell Medical College, the boy lucky enough to have a good father will develop a broad and flexible concept of what being a man is all about—a concept that includes tenderness, vulnerability, and open displays of feelings, alongside strength and fortitude. He will be secure enough to "expand and deepen his concept of manhood to encompass a variety of affects and activities that might otherwise become associated with the mother's exclusive province, with being womanly."

But chances are that if you are an adult between twenty and fifty-five, your father was not a big part of your childhood, or big only in a negative way; remote, angry, repressed, vindictive.

Maybe you have met a guy like Paul O'Shea. The image that comes to Paul's mind when he thinks of the pace of his life just before his breakdown in 1967 is the collage on the cover of the Beatles' *Sgt. Pepper* album: All those faces! Early Beatles, middle Beatles (John, somber in his epaulets, carrying a French horn), Diana Dors in gold lamé, the Mona Lisa, fifty, sixty faces jammed in next to one another. And the vaguely funereal floral arrangement on the foreground, with BEATLES spelled out in red hyacinths. An album cover to linger over, yet one must keep one's eyes moving, the way O'Shea himself was moving, trying to ward off failure and death.

Always he was extraordinarily handsome in an ascetic way, with a lean face softened by dark, liquid eyes. He grew up in New England, the son of a contractor. What went on between father and son was unspoken and horrible. The irregular beatings were the least of it. There was a house rule in matters involving the father: "You had to lose. Whatever it was. If you won, it was a violation of the family rule, and you don't . . . the consequences are too terrible to contemplate." He fixed a toaster once and was beaten for his troubles. His father had been unable to fix the toaster, had declared the toaster unfixable, and had been shown up. When things got unbearable, Paul took refuge with his mother, a stolid woman willing to deflect some of her husband's rage from her son to herself.

Paul had a high IQ, but he barely made it through college. At twenty-five, he found work teaching math and science at a private high school in Washington, D.C. The year was 1967. Antiwar fever was rising quickly. O'Shea plunged in—to the politics and the counterculture that went along with them. A new drug, a new woman every night. He was learning firsthand what Camus knew about debauchery: "One plays at being immortal, and after a few weeks one doesn't even know whether one can hang on till the next day." One night at a party he took LSD laced with angel dust. He was babbling, out of his head. The women he was with fled. But another woman stayed and talked him down. Her name was June. She took him home, and for two months she nursed him through seizures, out-of-body experiences, paranoia. At night, when he woke up screaming, she held him. At the end of it they were married. "She took over as my mother," says O'Shea.

A boy with an inflexible, authoritarian father might go one of two ways: He might rebel against his father with such rage that, in his rebelling, he becomes just as macho as the father. Or like Paul, he might succumb to his father's bullying, take shelter with his mother, and perpetually seek women who will mother him.

A boy with a father who is not a strong presence in the home is likely to have a dominant, if not domineering, mother. He, too, can go one of two ways: If he is strong, he will strive to become the man his father is not and in doing so, become overly aggressive, macho. Or he can succumb to his mother's will and perpetually seek women who will give him direction.

Terry Leonard's father was not a bad man—just a weak one with a tendency to exaggerate his abilities. Terry found this out early, with the help of the Brooklyn Dodgers. It was on a summer day in 1952, Ebbets Field, with the Cubs leading 5-2 in the eighth inning. Terry's father said, "Let's get out of here and beat the traffic."

"But the meat of the order is coming up," Terry said. "Furillo, Snider, Campanella!"

"I know this game," said the father. "They won't score."

"Are you sure?"

"I'm sure."

Reluctantly, Terry accompanied his father out of the stadium.

One of the worst feelings in the world happens when you are walking away from the ballpark before the game is over and from inside you hear a roar. Campy hit one over the wall with two men on, and the Dodgers went on to win. Terry, thirteen, turned to his father and said, "You promised! You promised!" He hasn't forgiven the old man yet.

The father was a wholesale furrier who worked most of the time and spent the rest promoting himself. Once when the family was vacationing at the beach, Terry overheard his father chatting with a man. "My father was talking about his business, and he said, 'I have forty employees.' He had four. I couldn't believe it. Later I said, 'How come you told him you have forty employees?' He just smiled. 'Did I say that?' He disappointed me. I felt something profound. My father let me down."

Terry's father had a coronary when Terry was thirteen and subsequently began to drink and womanize. In 1964 his parents were divorced after thirty-seven years of marriage. Terry sought situations and relationships that would be unlike his parents' in any respect. The idea of marriage appealed to him in the abstract, but "when I was in high school I just thought about fucking as much as I could." In college and later as an administrator for a city welfare program, he made it a point to go to bed with women of every ethnic and religious background he could find. "It was a smorgasbord. Orientals, blacks . . . I also came into contact with gays and lesbians." And his career changed almost as often as his girlfriends. He left social work to manage a motel. Then he became a stockbroker. Nor was this to be the final change.

And then suddenly, a few weeks before his thirtieth birthday, he married. It was time. He married a nice, quiet woman who he thought would be a good wife. And she thought he would be a good husband. It was as though they had read each other's resumes and each had thought, "Yeah, this ought to work." And it worked for a while, the way a machine works. But there is no intimacy in resumes or machines. After one child, they were divorced. They arranged joint custody of their son. Terry's wife became a radical feminist who wore bib overalls. Terry became a psychologist. In the process he learned that in trying to be someone other than his father—in trying to be first a stud and then a model husband and father—he was actually trying to *re-create* his father through himself in ideal form, which never works. He also learned this about both his father and himself: You cannot develop intimacy while attempting to project an image. The two are mutually exclusive, since image is concerned only with what is on the surface, while intimacy depends on the ability to share what is beneath.

Terry yearned for a father strong enough not to have to lie about his accomplishments. But even when a father has enough self-esteem to be honest with his children, father hunger is possible.

Frank Snyder, thirty-six, a successful lawyer, remembers worshipping his father and is happy with many of the values his father preached. "The force that drove him forward was not to make money, but to do the right thing. And to make a mark. I translated that into seeking justice. My father was an athlete, a big-time college football coach, and an airforce pilot. He came from the slums and made good. He was gone a lot. I remember him coming home from trips . . . He had the right stuff, like Chuck Yeager. Trying to live up to him was a crushing feeling, although it might have been easier for me because I was not a good athlete, so there was no possibility of competing."

But intimacy was not something Frank thought about. "As a kid I didn't see getting married and having a family as a positive value. The things I did were masculine kinds of things . . . Women were always interesting to me. I liked them. But I had difficulty with relationships. I always thought women needed relationships, settling down, more than men did." Frank's father's world was different from his own, remote and abstract. There was casual affection between father and son, but no intimacy in the sense of sharing their lives with one another. And Frank perceived this same relationship between his father and mother. The main business of the father's life was not here with the family, but somewhere else, somewhere outside, where life was played out in a broader sphere, which in his son's imagination was much more fascinating, much more exciting. But intimacy is not something that can be learned from an abstraction.

And this is why father hunger tends to be passed from generation to generation—why the son of a father-hungry father will be father hungry himself. For a man who fails to develop an intimate relationship with his wife has an extremely poor chance of doing so with his children. James Herzog is certain that, with men (but not necessarily with women), "adult-adult interaction predicts adult-child interaction"—that is, if a man is in touch with his own feelings and those of his wife, he is likely to be attuned to his children as well, but if his relationship with his wife is poor to begin with, the odds of his becoming a good father are long. Which is why the idea of having a baby to solidify a relationship is almost always a bad one. Even for a well-adjusted man, the transition from husband to husband-and-father, starting with pregnancy, can be daunting. Suddenly he is no longer the center of his wife's attention. He has fulfilled his biological function in reproduction and is reduced to a supporting role. His wife may become moody. Lovemaking is likely to become less frequent. "There's just some existential pain in becoming a father," Samuel Osherson says. "You're a deeply feeling person who's on the periphery."

Herzog studied a group of men whose wives had recently given birth and found that those who had been most supportive of their wives during pregnancy tended to be able to come to terms with their feelings about their own fathers (living or dead), while men who had never resolved these feelings "seemed to become progressively less able to participate in their expectant fatherhood." During the third trimester, many of these men, he says, "seemed . . . to make a career of the pursuit of . . . maleness." And he stresses again "that the male's caretaking line of development is fatefully affected by the presence of a good-enough male mentor-father, who helps the boy grieve the loss of his earlier identification [with his mother] and helps him see what a man is and what a man does."

Once the child is born, the problems are likely to intensify. The father, already insecure, feels displaced by the child. Ed Wyzanski, a computer technician in his late thirties, said his relationship with his wife deteriorated dangerously following the birth of their first child: "I remember being very angry at times. Holding the baby, trying to get him to stop crying, bouncing him, being so mad I wanted to do something violent. That was scary. I had never seen that in myself. I'd swing him around out of desperation, slam him back into the crib."

"I saw him as a rival for my wife's affections. Here was someone else getting the affection I had gotten . . . I pushed myself on her sexually shortly after the birth. I regret that."

Wyzanski, who is in therapy, describes his own father as an insecure manipulator and misogynist. "If my mother was saying something he didn't like, he would glare and purse his lips. 'Shut up.' It was a very destructive relationship. I learned insecurity from him."

In his new book, *Finding Our Fathers,* Samuel Osherson sums up persuasive evidence of the psychological gap between men and their fathers:

> Shere Hite's survey of 7,239 men revealed that "almost no men said they had been or were close to their fathers." Judith Arcana writes that in interviews for her book on mothers and sons only "about 1 percent of the sons had good relations with their fathers."
>
> The psychologist Jack Sternbach examined the father-son relationship in seventy-one of his male clients. He found fathers were physically absent for 23 percent of the men; 29 percent had psychologically absent fathers who were too busy with work, uninterested in their sons, or passive at home; 18 percent had psychologically absent fathers who were austere, moralistic, and emotionally

uninvolved; and 15 percent had fathers who were dangerous, frightening to their sons, and seemingly out of control. Only 15 percent of Sternbach's cases showed evidence of fathers appropriately involved with their sons, with a history of nurturance and trustworthy warmth and connection.

Osherson adds that his own interviews with men in their thirties and forties convinced him "that the psychological or physical absence of fathers from their families is one of the great underestimated tragedies of our times."

The American man who grew up with a father who was affectionate, strong, and significantly involved in the upbringing of his children is so rare he is a curiosity. It has not always been this way. At the turn of the century the average father who, whether affectionate or not, at least provided a concrete role model for his sons. Typically he worked on a farm or ran a store or business near home; typically, as a matter of course, he included his sons in his affairs. They went to work with him and were expected to follow in his footsteps or urged to do better.

But a series of historical events beginning with World War I altered this state of affairs dramatically. Beginning in 1917 and again in 1941, millions of U.S. men went off to war, leaving their families for as long as four years. They came home to sons who had grown up in their absence. And they came home to a changed society.

For a sizable portion of American men, the nature of work itself changed drastically after 1946. The ideal living situation was no longer an apartment next to the store but a house in the suburbs. In addition to spending eight or more hours away from his family at work, a man now spent an additional two, three, or even four hours commuting to and from his job. He came home to sleep. And on weekends he went bowling or golfing with his buddies. To his family he was a phantom.

And the nature of his job had changed from something that his son could identify with to something rendering the father even more remote, mysterious, and abstract than he already was. No longer could a boy say with confidence that his father was a cobbler or a merchant; now he might scratch his head and say, "Well, he deals in futures." or "He's a consultant," with no understanding of what that meant. In his 1968 book, *Fatherhood: A Sociological Perspective,* Leonard Benson declared the separation of the father from the rest of the family complete and self-perpetuating:

> Mother is the primary parent. She is first by popular acclaim, in actual household practice, and in the minds of students of family life . . . The fact that the father is assigned the role of breadwinner rather than that of caring for the children guarantees that boys will not develop and cultivate skills appropriate to child care. The primary skills of fathers are often beyond the understanding or even appreciation of contemporary children, and their style in social relations is usually conditioned by the demanding, singularly adult world of "work."

Today's adult males grew to maturity under those conditions. But Benson was wrong to predict that the situation would remain unchanged forever, because even when a man is pigeonholed as the worker, the achiever, the distant voice of authority, he has creative and nurturing instincts: to the extent that they are suppressed in the service of a macho image, he is not whole. All it takes are the right conditions to bring these instincts to the surface. And those conditions now exist.

The women's movement was in its infancy when Benson wrote his book. Women were only beginning to discover that they were not whole, that they too possessed traits encouraged only in men: assertiveness, independence, aptitudes for an enormous variety of occupations outside the home. During the intervening eighteen years they have done something about it—in schools, in consciousness-raising groups, in therapy. In unprecedented numbers women have tapped these previously latent reserves, have made themselves whole. And men in large numbers are beginning to understand: Whole women want whole men. Macho men and wimps need not apply.

Despite Rambo, values are changing. In 1970 only 30 percent of Americans believed that it was important for fathers to spend as much time with their children as mothers do. In 1986 the figure is 91 percent, according to the Ethan Allen Report on the Status of the American Family. Another recent study by *USA Today* found that 65 percent of men think they are closer to their kids than their fathers were. Within the past fifteen years scholars and the media have pronounced men's private and family lives fit subjects for investigation. The pressure is on for men to change. And men who grew up in the sixties and seventies have a hunger to *be* the father they never had.

Were it not for this pressure, father hunger as a concept probably would not exist. The raw material was supplied by men going into therapy, talking about their difficulties in forming and maintaining relationships and with fathering.

Fortunately, once a man discovers that his unresolved frustrations about his relationship with his father are causing some of his distress, he is in a position to change. Terry Leonard, Paul O'Shea, Frank Snyder, and Ed Wyzanski are among thousands of men who are working to come to terms with these feelings. They have had varying degrees of success, but in each case the recognition of a problem and the desire to resolve it has forced the man to move and to change.

By coming to terms with their feelings about their fathers, men are becoming better fathers themselves. And in doing so, they are breaking the cycle of father hunger.

Paul O'Shea no longer treats June like his mother. The change has been recent, and June is not sure she trusts it yet. But she says she's enjoying it while she can. They have a son and a daughter now, and Paul is working hard to be the kind of father his own father was not. The transition has not been simple. He's been in and out of therapy for years. And he's come to an understanding with his father.

Shortly before Christmas, Paul sat in his small apartment with his two children in his arms. "I have been a little-boy husband for a lot of years. Never again. I have made it. With a little boy of my own and a baby girl sleeping on my shoulder." He sat silently for a while. Then he said, "My father is over seventy now. He's mellowed a bit. He told me that when *his* father was dying, he wanted to tell him he loved him, but he couldn't. He cried about that. I took a chance, sitting with him at the kitchen table." He paused, took a deep breath. "I told him I loved him."

DISCUSSION QUESTIONS

1. Do you agree with Merton's contention that, "In terms of psychological development, there is not much difference between a macho and a wimp"?
2. Merton refers to a psychoanalyst who speculates that fathers are critical in their sons' lives with regard to such diverse characteristics as ability to nurture, sexual orientation, moral development and ability to achieve. Have you ever thought of the importance of your father in this regard?
3. Levinson in *The Seasons of a Man's Life* warns, "Most men in their twenties are not ready to make an enduring inner commitment to wife and family . . ." Do you agree?
4. Merton concludes on a note of optimism: "By coming to terms with their feelings about their fathers, men are becoming better fathers themselves." Do you believe that the men of your generation will be better fathers? Why?

SUGGESTIONS FOR JOURNAL ENTRIES

1. Shere Hite's survey of over seven thousand men revealed that "almost no men said they had been or were close to their father." Whether son or daughter, write about how close you are to your father. Would you like to be closer?
2. As a result of reading Merton's article, reflect upon the importance of your father in your own development.

READING 35

I Stand Here Ironing

Tillie Olsen

Tillie Olsen (b. 1912) has received many honorary doctorates and has taught at many colleges and universities, but she never attended college. This short story about a mother's anguish over not meeting her adolescent daughter's needs was originally published in 1956 and later collected in a volume of Olsen's short stories, Tell Me a Riddle, *which received the O. Henry Award in 1961.*

I stand here ironing, and what you asked me moves tormented back and forth with the iron.

"I wish you would manage the time to come in and talk with me about your daughter. I'm sure you can help me understand her. She's a youngster who needs help and whom I'm deeply interested in helping."

"Who needs help." . . . Even if I came, what good would it do? You think because I am her mother I have a key, or that in some way you could use me as a key? She has lived for nineteen years. There is all that life that has happened outside of me, beyond me.

And when is there time to remember, to sift, to weigh, to estimate, to total? I will start and there will be an interruption and I will have to gather it all together again. Or I will become engulfed with all I did or did not do, with what should have been and what cannot be helped.

She was a beautiful baby. The first and only one of our five that was beautiful at birth. You do not guess how new and uneasy her tenancy in her now-loveliness. You did not know her all those years she was thought homely, or see her poring over her baby pictures, making me tell her over and over how beautiful she had been—and would be, I would tell her—and was now, to the seeing eye. But the seeing eyes were few or non-existent. Including mine.

I nursed her. They feel that's important nowadays. I nursed all the children, but with her, with all the fierce rigidity of first motherhood, I did like the books then said. Though her cries battered me to trembling and my breasts ached with swollenness, I waited till the clock decreed.

Why do I put that first? I do not even know if it matters, or if it explains anything.

She was a beautiful baby. She blew shining bubbles of sound. She loved motion, loved light, loved color and music and textures. She would lie on the floor in her blue overalls patting the surface so hard in ecstasy her hands and feet would blur. She was a miracle to me, but when she was eight months old I had to leave her daytimes with the woman downstairs to whom she was no miracle at all, for I worked or looked for work and for Emily's father, who "could no longer endure" (he wrote in his good-bye note) "sharing want with us."

I was nineteen. It was the pre-relief, pre-WPA world of the depression. I would start running as soon as I got off the streetcar, running up the stairs, the place smelling sour, and awake or asleep to startle awake, when she saw me she would break into a clogged weeping that could not be comforted, a weeping I can hear yet.

After a while I found a job hashing at night so I could be with her days, and it was better. But it came to where I had to bring her to his family and leave her.

It took a long time to raise the money for her fare back. Then she got chicken pox and I had to wait longer. When she finally came, I hardly knew her, walking quick and nervous like her father, looking like her father, thin, and dressed in a shoddy red that yellowed her skin and glared at the pockmarks. All the baby loveliness gone.

She was two. Old enough for nursery school they said, and I did not know then what I know now—the fatigue of the long day, and the lacerations of group life in the kinds of nurseries that are only parking places for children.

Except that it would have made no difference if I had known. It was the only place there was. It was the only way we could be together, the only way I could hold a job.

And even without knowing, I knew. I knew the teacher that was evil because all these years it has curdled into my memory, the little boy hunched in the corner, her rasp, "why aren't you outside, because Alvin hits you? that's no reason, go out, scaredy." I knew Emily hated it even if she did not clutch and implore "don't go Mommy" like the other children, mornings.

She always had a reason why we should stay home. Momma, you look sick, Momma. I feel sick. Momma, the teachers aren't there today, they're sick. Momma, we can't go, there was a fire there last night. Momma, it's a holiday today, no school, they told me.

But never a direct protest, never rebellion. I think of our others in their three-, four-year-oldness—the explosions, the tempers, the denunciations, the demands—and I feel suddenly ill. I put the iron down. What in me demanded that goodness in her? And what was the cost, the cost to her of such goodness?

The old man living in the back once said in his gentle way: "You should smile at Emily more when you look at her." What was in my face when I looked at her? I loved her. There were all the acts of love.

It was only with the others I remembered what he said, and it was the face of joy, and not of care or tightness or worry I turned to them—too late for Emily. She does not smile easily, let alone almost always as her brothers and sisters do. Her face is closed and sombre, but when she wants, how fluid. You must have seen it in her pantomimes, you spoke of her rare gift for comedy on the stage that rouses a laughter out of the audience so dear they applaud and applaud and do not want to let her go.

Where does it come from, that comedy? There was none of it in her when she came back to me that second time, after I had had to send her away again. She had a new daddy now to learn to love, and I think perhaps it was a better time.

Except when we left her alone nights, telling ourselves she was old enough.

"Can't you go some other time, Mommy, like tomorrow?" she would ask. "Will it be just a little while you'll be gone? Do you promise?"

The time we came back, the front door open, the clock on the floor in the hall. She rigid awake. "It wasn't just a little while, I didn't cry. Three times I called you, just three times, and then I ran downstairs to open the door so you could come faster. The clock talked loud. I threw it away; it scared me what it talked."

She said the clock talked loud again that night I went to the hospital to have Susan. She was delirious with the fever that comes before red measles, but she was fully conscious all the week I was gone and the week after we were home when she could not come near the new baby or me.

She did not get well. She stayed skeleton thin, not wanting to eat, and night after night she had nightmares. She would call for me, and I would rouse from exhaustion to sleepily call back: "You're all right, darling, go to sleep, it's just a dream," and if she still called, in a sterner voice, "now go to sleep, Emily, there's nothing to hurt you." Twice, only twice, when I had to get up for Susan anyhow, I went in to sit with her.

Now when it is too late (as if she would let me hold and comfort her like I do the others) I get up and go to her at once at her moan or restless stirring. "Are you awake, Emily? Can I get you something?" And the answer is always the same: "No, I'm all right, go back to sleep, Mother."

They persuaded me at the clinic to send her away to a convalescent home in the country where "she can have the kind of food and care you can't manage for her, and you'll be free to concentrate on the new baby." They still send children to that place. I see pictures on the society page of sleek young women planning affairs to raise money for it, or dancing at the affairs, or decorating Easter eggs or filling Christmas stockings for the children.

They never have a picture of the children so I do not know if the girls still wear those gigantic red bows and the ravaged looks on the every other Sunday when parents can come to visit "unless otherwise notified"—as we were notified the first six weeks.

Oh, it is a handsome place, green lawns and tall trees and fluted flower beds. High up on the balconies of each cottage the children stand, the girls in their red bows and white dresses, the boys in white suits and giant red ties. The parents stand below shrieking up to be heard and the children shriek down to be heard, and between them the invisible wall "Not to Be Contaminated by Parental Germs or Physical Affection."

There was a tiny girl who always stood hand in hand with Emily. Her parents never came. One visit she was gone. "They moved her to Rose Cottage." Emily shouted in explanation. "They don't like you to love anybody here."

She wrote once a week, the labored writing of a seven-year-old. "I am fine. How is the baby. If I write my leter nicly I will have a star. Love." There never was a star. We wrote every other day, letters she could never hold or keep but only hear read—once. "We simply do not have room for children to keep any personal possessions," they patiently explained when we pieced one Sunday's shrieking together to plead how much it would mean to Emily, who loved so to keep things, to be allowed to keep her letters and cards.

Each visit she looked frailer. "She isn't eating," They told us.

(They had runny eggs for breakfast or mush with lumps, Emily said later, I'd hold it in my mouth and not swallow. Nothing ever tasted good, just when they had chicken.)

It took us eight months to get her released home, and only the fact that she gained back so little of her seven lost pounds convinced the social worker.

I used to try to hold and love her after she came back, but her body would stay stiff, and after a while she'd push away. She ate little. Food sickened her, and I think much of life too. Oh she had physical lightness and brightness, twinkling by on skates, bouncing like a ball up and down, up and down over the jump rope, skimming over the hill; but these were momentary.

She fretted about her appearance, thin and dark and foreign-looking at a time when every little girl was supposed to look or thought she should look a chubby blonde replica of Shirley Temple. The doorbell sometimes rang for her, but no one seemed to come and play in the house or be a best friend. Maybe because we moved so much.

There was a boy she loved painfully through two school semesters. Months later she told me how she had taken pennies from my purse to buy him candy. "Licorice was his favorite and I bought him some every day, but he still liked Jennifer better'n me. Why, Mommy?" The kind of question for which there is no answer.

School was a worry to her. She was not glib or quick in a world where glibness and quickness were easily confused with ability to learn. To her over-worked and exasperated teachers she was an overconscientious "slow learner" who kept trying to catch up and was absent entirely too often.

I let her be absent, though sometimes the illness was imaginary. How different from my now-strictness about attendance with the others. I wasn't working. We had a new baby, I was home anyhow. Sometimes after Susan grew old enough, I would keep her home from school, too, to have them all together.

Mostly Emily had asthma, and her breathing, harsh and labored, would fill the house with a curiously tranquil sound. I would bring the two old dresser mirrors and her boxes of collections to her bed. She would select beads and single earrings, bottle tops and shells, dried flowers and pebbles, old post-cards and scraps, all sorts of oddments; then she and Susan would play King-dom, setting up landscapes and furniture, peopling them with action.

Those were the only times of peaceful companionship between her and Susan, no, Emily toward Susan that poisonous feeling between them, that ter-rible balancing of hurts and needs I had to do between the two, and did so badly, those earlier years.

Oh there are conflicts between the others too, each one human, needing, demanding, hurting, taking—but only between Emily and Susan. I have edged away from it, that no, Emily toward Susan that corroding resentment. It seems so obvious on the surface, yet it is not obvious. Susan, the second child, Susan, golden- and curly-haired and chubby, quick and articulate and assured, everything in appearance and manner Emily was not; Susan, not able to resist Emily's precious things, losing or sometimes clumsily breaking them; Susan telling jokes and riddles to company for applause while Emily sat silent (to say to me later: that was *my* riddle, Mother, I told it to Susan); Susan, who for all the five years' difference in age was just a year behind Emily in developing physically.

I am glad for that slow physical development that widened the difference between her and her contemporaries, though she suffered over it. She was too vulnerable for that terrible world of youthful competition, of preening and parading, of constant measuring of yourself against every other, of envy, "If I had that copper hair," "If I had that skin. . . ." She tormented herself enough about not looking like the others; there was enough of the unsureness, the having to be conscious of words before you speak, the constant caring—what are they thinking of me? without having it all magnified by the merciless physical drives.

Ronnie is calling. He is wet and I change him. It is rare there is such a cry now. That time of motherhood is almost behind me when the ear is not one's own but must always be racked and listening for the child cry, the child call. We sit for a while and I hold him, looking out over the city spread in charcoal with its soft aisles of light. "*Shoogily,*" he breathes and curls closer. I carry him back to bed, asleep. *Shoogily.* A funny word, a family word, inherited from Emily, invented by her to say: *comfort.*

In this and other ways she leaves her seal, I say aloud. And startle at my saying it. What do I mean? What did I start to gather together, to try and make coherent? I was at the terrible, growing years. War years. I do not remember them well. I was working, there were four smaller ones now, there was not time for her. She had to help be a mother, and housekeeper, and shopper. She had to set her seal. Mornings of crisis and near hysteria trying to get lunches packed, hair combed, coats and shoes found, everyone to school or Child Care on time, the baby ready for transportation. And always the paper scribbled on by a smaller one, the book looked at by Susan then mislaid, the homework not done. Running out to that huge school where she was one, she was lost, she was a drop; suffering over the unpreparedness, stammering and unsure in her classes.

There was so little time left at night after the kids were bedded down. She would struggle over books, always eating (it was in those years she developed her enormous appetite that is legendary in our family) and I would be ironing, or preparing food for the next day, or writing V-mail to Bill, or tending the baby. Sometimes, to make me laugh, or out of her despair, she would imitate happenings or types at school.

I think I said once: "Why don't you do something like this in the school amateur show?" One morning she phoned me at work, hardly understandable through the weeping: "Mother, I did it. I won; they gave me first prize; they clapped and clapped and wouldn't let me go."

Now suddenly she was Somebody, and as imprisoned in her difference as she had been in anonymity.

She began to be asked to perform at other high schools, even in colleges, then at city and statewide affairs. The first one we went to, I only recognized her that first moment when thin, shy, she almost drowned herself into the curtains. Then: Was this Emily? The control, the command, the convulsing and deadly clowning, the spell, then the roaring, stamping audience, unwilling to let this rare and precious laughter out of their lives.

Afterwards: You ought to do something about her with a gift like that—but without money or knowing how, what does one do? We have left it all to her, and the gift has as often eddied inside, clogged and clotted, as been used and growing.

She is coming. She runs up the stairs two at a time with her light, graceful step, and I know she is happy tonight. Whatever it was that occasioned your call did not happen today.

"Aren't you ever going to finish the ironing, Mother? Whistler painted his mother in a rocker. I'd have to paint mine standing over an ironing board." This is one of her communicative nights and she tells me everything and nothing as she fixes herself a plate of food out of the icebox.

She is so lovely. Why did you want me to come in at all? Why were you concerned? She will find her way.

She starts up the stairs to bed. "Don't get me up with the rest in the morning." "But I thought you were having midterms." "Oh, those," she comes back in, kisses me, and says quite lightly, "in a couple of years when we'll all be atom-dead they won't matter a bit."

She has said it before. She *believes it.* But because I have been dredging the past, and all that compounds a human being is so heavy and meaningful in me, I cannot endure it tonight.

I will never total it all. I will never come in to say: She was a child seldom smiled at. Her father left me before she was a year old. I had to work her first six years when there was work, or I sent her home and to his relatives. There were years she had care she hated. She was dark and thin and foreign-looking in a world where the prestige went to blondeness and curly hair and dimples; she was slow where glibness was prized. She was a child of anxious, not proud, love. We were poor and could not afford her the soil of easy growth. I was a young mother, I was a distracted mother. There were the other children pushing up, demanding. Her younger sister seemed all that she was not. There were years she did not want me to touch her. She kept too much in herself; her life was such she had to keep too much in herself. My wisdom came too late. She has much to her and probably little will come of it. She is a child of her age, of depression, of war, of fear.

Let her be. So all that is in her will not bloom—but in how many does it? There is still enough left to live by. Only help her to know—help make it so there is cause for her to know—that she is more than this dress on the ironing board, helpless before the iron.

DISCUSSION QUESTIONS

1. To whom is the mother speaking in the story and why?
2. What feelings toward the mother does the story elicit for you? The daughter?
3. Why do you think Olsen chose the metaphor of ironing? What does it mean? Does it still work in this virtual non-ironing age?
4. How do you feel about the last paragraph? "Let her be. So all that is in her will not bloom—but in how many does it? There is still enough to live by."

SUGGESTIONS FOR JOURNAL ENTRIES

1. Write about what insight this story has given you about your own mother.
2. Share this story with your mother and interview her afterwards about her response.

IDENTITY

Developmental psychologists tell us that personality is not completely formed in childhood as Freud thought, but is rather a process that continues throughout life. According to the late Erik Erikson, the life cycle goes through eight stages and the particular task of adolescence is identity formation. In fact, Erikson coined the term *identity crisis* to describe the typical adolescent search for and confusion about who one is. The next six readings all speak to issues of identity: sexual orientation, class, ethnicity, body image and appearance, and risk-taking.

In the first essay, a gay college student writes about how and why he "came out" to his parents and what happened as a result. The second essay describes the coming-of-age of Mexican-American Richard Rodriguez, when in a summer job at the end of his senior year at Stanford University he engages in hard labor and discovers the differences between himself and the Mexican laborers with whom he comes in contact.

The third essay is by Elizabeth Wong, a Chinese-American who writes about her struggle to be assimilated into American culture and the resultant loss of her Chinese identity.

The next reading is a short story, "The Fat Girl," by Andre Dubus. It is the story of a college student who struggles with body image and the cultural image of perfection.

The first poem, "If I Had My Life to Live Over," is a celebration of life written by an anonymous eighty-five-year-old woman who encourages us to take the risks described in the second poem, "Risks," lest we grow old before we have had time to live.

READING 36

How I Came Out to My Parents

Kenneth Kohler

Kenneth Kohler was a student at Middlesex County College when he wrote this essay about coming out in 1994.

Being a minority within your own family can be a source of conflict. I had always known that I was different from my brother and my sister. My parents, too, may have sensed the difference, but they never acknowledged it to me. For many years, I had struggled with the idea of letting them know how different I was from my older brother. I was gay and didn't know how they would react if they ever found out.

My struggle to "come out of the closet" grew out of several needs. First, I wanted to be closer with my parents and to be honest about who I was. Second, I needed to let them know that there was someone special in my life. Finally, I had agreed to speak at my church about being gay, and I felt it important to tell my parents about my lifestyle before informing my congregation.

Rejection was my greatest fear. At the time, I had friends who had not spoken to their families for years after revealing they were gay. Their parents could not understand how their children could be "fags" or "dykes." These were terms their families had previously applied only to strangers. Some friends even told me about the violent reactions their families had had to the news. One of them said his father chased him around the house with a butcher knife. I had also known people who had used their homosexuality as a weapon against their families. Never did I want to hurt my parents; I merely wanted to break down the barriers between us.

I had no idea how they might react when I came out to them. I knew that if they responded violently or negatively it could take years to heal the damage. I also knew that I might never see them again. It was for this reason that I had avoided coming out to them before. However, because of my pending public announcement, the time had come to let them know.

I planned what I had to say carefully. Something so important could not simply be announced and forgotten. I had actually begun to prepare for this moment years before by reading as much as I could about homosexuality and by talking to gay friends. It was necessary for me to accept myself as a gay man before expecting others to do so. I had to develop a positive self-image, and this took several years. Then, in the week prior to my announcement, I began to rehearse my lines. I made notes for various approaches I could take. I wanted to feel secure in my delivery and didn't want to appear ashamed of my lifestyle. "Why should I be?" I thought. I had never felt differently. I imagined my parents' every reaction and tried to predict my responses. I even prepared myself for the worst, afraid they would tell me to "Get out and never come back!"

6   I also knew it was possible that none of the negative things that had happened to my friends would happen to me. In fact, I thought my parents might have already suspected I was gay. After all, I had been living with a man for three years. My partner at the time said, "They probably already know about you, the way you swish around!" I knew he could be right, but I was still afraid. Would my disclosure actually draw me closer to them as I had hoped, or would it push me away? Would they accept my partner as they had in the past? How would I cope with the loss of their love? These were just a few of the many questions that swept through my mind as I called my mother to ask if I could visit and talk about something important.

7   My heart was racing and my palms were sweating as I stopped the car in front of their house. I turned off the ignition, took a deep breath, and stepped out. "This is it." I thought. "This is what I've been thinking about doing for years." The walk to the front door had never seemed so long. I was acutely aware of my heartbeat pounding in my ears. My breath seemed suspended in the frigid February night air. Time seemed to stop as I nervously straightened my jacket, threw my shoulders back, swallowed hard, and opened the front door.

8   My father was sitting in the recliner watching the television. My mother was folding laundry. "Hi, how are you doing?" I said, trying to hide my nervousness. They both looked up and smiled. As I walked over to give each of them a hug, I wondered if they would ever smile at me again.

9   I took off my coat, sat down next to my mother, and began to help her fold the laundry. We talked about how fast my niece was growing up. While we spoke, I tried to form the words that I feared would hurt them irreparably, but I realized there was only one way to say it. "Mom. Dad. I've been thinking about telling you this for some time now." I swallowed hard and took a good look at them. "I'm not telling you this because I want to hurt you. I love you. Please try to understand." I paused and took a deep breath. "I'm gay."

10   There was silence. Finally, with much hesitation, my mother asked, "Are you sure?"

11   There was still no response from my father. I wondered what was racing through his head. His silence was deeper than I could remember. Again my mother spoke. "Are you happy?"

12   "Yes," I replied with hesitation. I was not sure what would happen next. I could almost hear the silent screams that I imagined howling in each of them.

13   "Well," she paused, "you've always been good to us, and you've never given us any problems."

14   "Here it comes," I thought, "the guilt trip."

15   "I guess if you're happy," she continued slowly as if weighing every word, "then I'll try to understand."

16   A smile spread over my face as I leaned over and gave her a long, warm hug. Never had I felt so close to her. It was only then that my father piped up, "I hope you aren't sleeping with someone new every night." I assured him that I wasn't as I gave him a hug.

"You know, it's funny," my mother said. "We always thought your friend 17 was gay, but we didn't know you were." I tried hard to keep from laughing as I thought of my partner's remarks. Deep down, I suspected that they had always known but had denied it.

When I explained that I was going to speak at my church about what it 18 was like to be gay, my mother's brow became dark and furrowed. "Do you think you should? What if you lose your job? What if someone tries to hurt you?" she responded.

I tried to assure her that everything would be all right, but I really had no 19 idea what might happen. Of course, I knew my parents would struggle with my gayness just as I had, but I was overjoyed that they were asking such questions. A great burden had been lifted from my shoulders; I felt like laughing and dancing around the room. I realized I no longer had to hide my private life, to change pronouns, or to avoid questions about whom I was dating. More important, I had discovered how deeply my parents loved me.

DISCUSSION QUESTIONS

1. Were you surprised at Kohler's parents' reaction to his announcement? How would your parents have responded?
2. Why do you think there is still so much prejudice against gay people in our society?
3. What do we know about the incidence of homosexuality and its cause?
4. Darling (Reading 19) wrote that the Bi-Gay-Lesbian Student Association at Harvard provoked the most hostility and the most admiration on campus. Is there a similar organization on your campus? How is it viewed?

SUGGESTIONS FOR JOURNAL ENTRIES

1. Write about a time when you had to tell your parents something to which you weren't sure how they would react.
2. Write about a friend or acquaintance you know who is gay and how that has influenced your attitudes toward homosexuality.

READING 37

The Workers

Richard Rodriguez

Richard Rodriguez, Stanford '67, is a first generation Mexican-American, who wrote an autobiography titled, Hunger of Memory: The Education of Richard Rodriguez *in 1981. The following excerpt captures the author's struggle for personal and ethnic identity upon coming face to face with Mexican laborers,* los pobres, *on a summer construction job.*

It was at Stanford, one day near the end of my senior year, that a friend told me about a summer construction job he knew was available. I was quickly alert. Desire uncoiled within me. My friend said that he knew I had been looking for summer employment. He knew I needed some money. Almost apologetically he explained: It was something I probably wouldn't be interested in, but a friend of his, a contractor, needed someone for the summer to do menial jobs. There would be lots of shoveling and raking and sweeping. Nothing too hard. But nothing more interesting either. Still, the pay would be good. Did I want it? Or did I know someone who did? I did. Yes, I said, surprised to hear myself say it.

In the weeks following, friends cautioned that I had no idea how hard physical labor really is. ("You only *think* you know what it is like to shovel for eight hours straight.") Their objections seemed to me challenges. They resolved the issue. I became happy with my plan. I decided, however, not to tell my parents. I wouldn't tell my mother because I could guess her worried reaction. I would tell my father only after the summer was over, when I could announce that, after all, I did know what "real work" is like.

The day I met the contractor (a Princeton graduate, it turned out), he asked me whether I had done any physical labor before. "In high school, during the summer," I lied. And although he seemed to regard me with skepticism, he decided to give me a try. Several days later, expectant, I arrived at my first construction site. I would take off my shirt to the sun. And at last grasp desired sensation. No longer afraid. At last become like a *bracero*. "We need those tree stumps out of here by tomorrow," the contractor said. I started to work.

I labored with excitement that first morning—and all the days after. The work was harder than I could have expected. But it was never as tedious as my friends had warned me it would be. There was too much physical pleasure in the labor. Especially early in the day, I would be most alert to the sensations of movement and straining. Beginning around seven each morning (when the air was still damp but the scent of weeds and dry earth anticipated the heat of the sun), I would feel my body resist the first thrusts of the shovel. My arms, tightened by sleep, would gradually loosen; after only several minutes sweat would gather in beads on my forehead and then—a short while later—I would feel my chest silky with sweat in the breeze. I would return to my work. A nervous spark of pain would fly up to my arm and settle to burn like an ember in the thick of my shoulder. An hour, two passed. Three. My whole body would assume regular movements; my shoveling would be described by identical, even movements. Even later in the day, my enthusiasm for primitive sensation would survive the heat and the dust and the insects pricking my back. I would strain wildly for sensation as the day came to a close. At three-thirty, quitting time, I would stand upright and slowly let my head fall back, luxuriating in the feeling of tightness relieved.

Some of the men working nearby would watch me and laugh. Two or three of the older men took the trouble to teach me the right way to use a pick, the correct way to shovel. "You're doing it wrong, too fucking hard," one man scolded. Then proceeded to show me—what persons who work with their bodies all their lives quickly learn—the most economical way to use one's body in labor.

"Don't make your back do so much work," he instructed. I stood impatiently listening, half listening, vaguely watching, then noticed his work-thickened fingers clutching the shovel. I was annoyed. I wanted to tell him that I enjoyed shoveling the wrong way. And I didn't want to learn the right way. I wasn't afraid of back pain. I liked the way my body felt sore at the end of the day.

I was about to, but, as it turned out, I didn't say a thing. Rather it was at that moment I realized that I was fooling myself if I expected a few weeks of labor to gain me admission to the world of the laborer. I would not learn in three months what my father had meant by "real work." I was not bound to this job; I could imagine its rapid conclusion. For me the sensations of exertion and fatigue could be savored. For my father or uncle, working at comparable jobs when they were my age, such sensations were to be feared. Fatigue took a different toll on their bodies—and minds.

It was, I know, a simple insight. But it was with this realization that I took my first step that summer toward realizing something even more important about the "worker," In the company of carpenters, electricians, plumbers, and painters at lunch, I would often sit quietly, observant. I was not shy in such company. I felt easy, pleased by the knowledge that I was casually accepted, my presence taken for granted by men (exotics) who worked with their hands. Some days the younger men would talk and talk about sex, and they would howl at women who drove by in cars. Other days the talk at lunchtime was subdued; men gathered in separate groups. It depended on who was around. There were rough, good-natured workers. Others were quiet. The more I remember that summer, the more I realize that there was no single *type* of worker. I am embarrassed to say, I had not expected such diversity. I certainly had not expected to meet, for example, a plumber who was an abstract painter in his off hours and admired the work of Mark Rothko. Nor did I expect to meet so many workers with college diplomas. (They were the ones who were not surprised that I intended to enter graduate school in the fall.) I suppose what I really want to say here is painfully obvious, but I must say it nevertheless: The men of that summer were middle-class Americans. They certainly didn't constitute an oppressed society. Carefully completing their work sheets; talking about the fortunes of local football teams; planning Las Vegas vacations; comparing the gas mileage of various makes of campers—they were not *los pobres* my mother had spoken about.

On two occasions, the contractor hired a group of Mexican aliens. They were employed to cut down some trees and haul off debris. In all, there were six men of varying age. The youngest in his late twenties; the oldest (his father?) perhaps sixty years old. They came and they left in a single old truck. Anonymous men. They were never introduced to the other men at the site. Immediately upon their arrival, they would follow the contractor's directions, start working—rarely resting—seemingly driven by a fatalistic sense that work which had to be done was best done as quickly as possible.

I watched them sometimes. Perhaps they watched me. The only time I saw them pay me much notice was one day at lunchtime when I was laughing with the other men. The Mexicans sat apart when they ate, just as they worked by themselves. Quiet. I rarely heard them say much to each other. All I could hear were their voices calling out sharply to one another, giving directions. Otherwise, when they stood briefly resting, they talked among themselves in voices too hard to overhear.

The contractor knew enough Spanish, and the Mexicans—or at least the oldest of them, their spokesman—seemed to know enough English to communicate. But because I was around, the contractor decided one day to make me his translator. (He assumed I could speak Spanish.) I did what I was told. Shyly I went over to tell the Mexicans that the *patrón* wanted them to do something else before they left for the day. As I started to speak, I was afraid with my old fear that I would be unable to pronounce the Spanish words. But it was a simple instruction I had to convey. I could say it in phrases.

The dark sweating faces turned toward me as I spoke. They stopped their work to hear me. Each nodded in response. I stood there. I wanted to say something more. But what could I say in Spanish, even if I could have pronounced the words right? Perhaps I just wanted to engage them in small talk, to be assured of their confidence, our familiarity. I thought for a moment to ask them where in Mexico they were from. Something like that. And maybe I wanted to tell them (a lie, if need be) that my parents were from the same part of Mexico.

I stood there.

Their faces watched me. The eyes of the man directly in front of me moved slowly over my shoulder, and I turned to follow his glance toward *el patrón* some distance away. For a moment I felt swept up by that glance into the Mexican's company. But then I heard one of them returning to work. And then the others went back to work. I left them without saying anything more.

When they had finished, the contractor went over to pay them in cash. (He later told me that he paid them collectively—"for the job," though he wouldn't tell me their wages. He said something quickly about the good rate of exchange "in their own country." I can still hear the loudly confident voice he used with the Mexicans. It was the sound of the *gringo* I had heard as a very young boy. And I can still hear the quiet, indistinct sounds of the Mexican, the oldest who replied. At hearing that voice I was sad for the Mexicans. Depressed by their vulnerability. Angry at myself. The adventure of the summer seemed suddenly ludicrous. I would not shorten the distance I felt from *los pobres* with a few weeks of physical labor. I would not become like them. They were different from me.

After that summer, a great deal—and not very much really—changed in my life. The curse of physical shame was broken by the sun: I was no longer ashamed of my body. No longer would I deny myself the pleasing sensations of my maleness. During those years when middle-class black Americans began to assert with pride, "Black is beautiful," I was able to regard my complexion without shame. I am today darker than I ever was as a boy. I have taken up the middle-class sport of long-distance running. Nearly every day now I run ten or fifteen miles, barely clothed, my skin exposed to the California winter rain and wind or the summer sun of late afternoon. The torso, the soccer player's calves and thighs, the arms of the twenty-year-old I never was, I possess now in my thirties. I study the youthful parody shape in the mirror, the stomach lipped tight by muscle; the shoulders rounded by chin-ups; the arms veined strong. This man. A man. I meet him. He laughs to see me, what I have become.

The dandy. I wear double-breasted Italian suits and custom made English shoes. I resemble no one so much as my father—the man pictured in those honeymoon photos. At that point in life when he abandoned the dandy's posture, I assume it. At the point when my parents would not consider going on a vacation, I register at the Hotel Carlyle in New York and the Plaza Athenée in Paris. I am as taken by the symbols of leisure and wealth as they were. For my parents, however, those symbols became taunts, reminders of all they could not achieve in one lifetime. For me those same symbols are reassuring reminders of public success. I tempt vulgarity to be reassured. I am filled with the gaudy delight, the monstrous grace of the *nouveau riche*.

In recent years I have had occasion to lecture in ghetto high schools. There I see students of remarkable style and physical grace. (One can see more dandies in such schools than one ever will find in middle-class high schools.) There is not the look of casual assurance I saw students at Stanford display. Ghetto girls mimic high-fashion models. Their dresses are of bold, forceful color; their figures elegant, long; the stance theatrical. Boys wear shirts that grip at their overdeveloped muscular bodies. (Against a powerless future, they engage images of strength.) Bad nutrition does not yet tell. Great disappointment, fatal to youth, awaits them still. For the moment, movements in school hallways are dancelike, a procession of postures in a sexual masque. Watching them, I feel a kind of envy. I wonder how different my adolescence would have been had I been free. . . . But no, it is my parents I see—their optimism during those years when they were entertained by Italian grand opera.

The registration clerk in London wonders if I have just been to Switzerland. And the man who carries my luggage in New York guesses the Caribbean. My complexion becomes a mark of my leisure. Yet no one would regard my complexion the same way if I entered such hotels through the service entrance. That is only to say that my complexion assumes its significance from the context of my life. My skin, in itself, means nothing. I stress the point because I know there are people who would label me "disadvantaged" because of my color. They make the same mistake I made as a boy, when I thought a disadvantaged life was circumscribed by particular occupations. That summer I worked in the sun may have made me physically indistinguishable from the Mexicans working nearby. (My skin was actually darker because, unlike them, I worked without wearing a shirt. By late August my hands were probably as tough as theirs.) But I was not one of *los pobres*. What made me different from them was an attitude of *mind*, my imagination of myself.

I do not blame my mother for warning me away from the sun when I was young. In a world where her brother had become an old man in his twenties because he was dark, my complexion was something to worry about. "Don't run in the sun," she warns me today. I run. In the end, my father was right—though perhaps he did not know how right or why—to say that I would never know what real work is. I will never know what he felt at his last factory job. If tomorrow I worked at some kind of factory, it would go differently for me. My long education would favor me. I could act as a public person—able to defend my interests, to unionize, to petition, to speak up—to challenge and demand. (I will never know what real work is.) I will never know what the Mexicans knew, gathering their shovels and ladders and saws.

Their silence stays with me now. The wages those Mexicans received for their labor were only a measure of their disadvantaged condition. Their silence is more telling. They lack a public identity. They remain profoundly alien. Persons apart. People lacking a union obviously, people without grounds. They depend upon the relative good will or fairness of their employers each day. For such people, lacking a better alternative, it is not such an unreasonable risk.

Their silence stays with me. I have taken these many words to describe its impact. Only: the quiet. Something uncanny about it. Its compliance. Vulnerability. Pathos. As I heard their truck rumbling away, I shuddered, my face mirrored with sweat. I had finally come face to face with *los pobres*.

DISCUSSION QUESTIONS

1. Rodriguez describes the pure physical pleasure of hard labor. Have you ever had the opportunity to engage in hard labor and, if so, was your experience similar to Rodriguez's? Why or why not?
2. What does this essay say about the importance of education in affecting people's lives?

3. What do you think Rodriguez means when he writes, "I wonder how different my adolescence would have been had I been free"?

4. At the end of the essay, Rodriguez describes the pathos and vulnerability of people who have no voice. What is he trying to say and what is the lesson for you in this story, whether you are a member of a minority or not?

SUGGESTIONS FOR JOURNAL ENTRIES

1. Write about a job (summer or part-time after school) you have had in which you came to an important realization about yourself or life.

2. Write about an experience in which you lacked a voice and how you were taken advantage of as a result.

READING 38

The Struggle to Be an All-American Girl
Elizabeth Wong

Elizabeth Wong, USC '80, was a newspaper reporter and is presently a playwright having received her M.F.A. degree in 1991 from NYU, Tisch School of the Arts. This piece, originally appearing in 1981 in the Los Angeles Times, *is an autobiographical account of the typical first-generational struggle for assimilation and the resultant feeling of loss of ethnic and cultural heritage.*

It's still there, the Chinese school on Yale Street where my brother and I used to go. Despite the new coat of paint and the high wire fence, the school I knew ten years ago remains remarkably stoically the same.

Every day at five P.M., instead of playing with our fourth- and fifth-grade friends or sneaking out to the empty lot to hunt ghosts and animal bones, my brother and I had to go to Chinese school. No amount of kicking, screaming, or pleading could dissuade my mother, who was solidly determined to have us learn the language of our heritage.

Forcibly, she walked us the seven long, hilly blocks from our home to school, depositing our defiant tearful faces before the stern principal. My only memory of him is that he swayed on his heels like a palm tree, and he always clasped his impatient twitching hands behind his back. I recognized him as a repressed maniacal child killer, and knew that if we ever saw his hands we'd be in big trouble.

We all sat in little chairs in an empty auditorium. The room smelled like Chinese medicine, an imported faraway mustiness. Like ancient mothballs or dirty closets. I hated that smell. I favored crisp new scents. Like the soft French perfume that my American teacher wore in public school.

There was a stage far to the right, flanked by an American flag and the flag of the Nationalist republic of China, which was also red, white and blue but not as pretty.

Although the emphasis at the school was mainly language—speaking, reading, writing—the lessons always began with an exercise in politeness. With the entrance of the teacher, the best student would tap a bell and everyone would get up, kowtow, and chant, "Sing san ho," the phonetic for "How are you, teacher?"

Being ten years old, I had better things to learn than ideographs copied painstakingly in lines that ran right to left from the tip of a *moc but,* a real ink pen that had to be held in an awkward way if blotches were to be avoided. After all, I could do the multiplication tables, name the satellites of Mars, and write reports on *Little Women* and *Black Beauty.* Nancy Drew, my favorite book heroine, never spoke Chinese.

The language was a source of embarrassment. More times than not, I had tried to disassociate myself from the nagging loud voice that followed me wherever I wandered in the nearby American supermarket outside Chinatown.

The voice belonged to my grandmother, a fragile woman in her seventies who could outshout the best of the street vendors. Her humor was raunchy, her Chinese rhythmless, patternless. It was quick, it was loud, it was unbeautiful. It was not like the quiet, lilting romance of French or the gentle refinement of the American South. Chinese sounded pedestrian. Public.

In Chinatown, the comings and goings of hundreds of Chinese on their daily tasks sounded chaotic and frenzied. I did not want to be thought of as mad, as talking gibberish. When I spoke English, people nodded at me, smiled sweetly, said encouraging words. Even the people in my culture would cluck and say that I'd do well in life. "My, doesn't she move her lips fast," they would say, meaning that I'd be able to keep up with the world outside Chinatown.

My brother was even more fanatical than I about speaking English. He was especially hard on my mother, criticizing her, often cruelly, for her pidgin speech—smatterings of Chinese scattered like chop suey in her conversation. "It's not 'What it is,' Mom," he'd say in exasperation. "It's 'What *is* it, what *is* it, what *is* it!'" Sometimes Mom might leave out an occasional "the" or "a," or perhaps a verb of being. He would stop her in mid-sentence: "Say it again, Mom. Say it right," When he tripped over his own tongue, he'd blame it on her: "See, Mom, it's all your fault. You set a bad example."

What infuriated my mother most was when my brother cornered her on her consonants, especially "r." My father had played a cruel joke on Mom by assigning her an American name that her tongue wouldn't allow her to say. No matter how hard she tried, "Ruth" always ended up "Luth" or "Roof."

After two years of writing with a *moc but* and reciting words with multiples of meanings, I finally was granted a cultural divorce. I was permitted to stop Chinese school.

I thought of myself as multicultural. I preferred tacos to egg rolls; I enjoyed Cinco de Mayo more than Chinese New Year.

At last, I was one of you; I wasn't one of them.

Sadly, I still am.

DISCUSSION QUESTIONS

1. What does Wong mean by a "cultural divorce"?
2. What do you think are the advantages and disadvantages (if any) of being bilingual?
3. Do you notice any difference between Rodriguez (Reading 37) and Wong with respect to their attitude toward their cultural heritage? What are they?
4. What do you think Wong is telling the reader in the last sentence?

SUGGESTIONS FOR JOURNAL ENTRIES

1. Whether a member of a minority or not, write about how your cultural heritage has affected you.
2. Write about your own struggle to be an "all-American girl/boy."

The Fat Girl

Andre Dubus

This short story is about a girl who grows up the victim of what has been called the last prejudice in our society: obesity. Andre Dubus, McNeese State College '58, is a retired professor of modern fiction and creative writing at Branford College in Massachusetts. This short story was taken from an anthology, Selected Stories of Andre Dubus, *published in 1988.*

Her name was Louise. Once when she was sixteen a boy kissed her at a barbecue; he was drunk and he jammed his tongue into her mouth and ran his hands up and down her hips. Her father kissed her often. He was thin and kind and she could see in his eyes when he looked at her the lights of love and pity.

It started when Louise was nine. You must start watching what you eat, her mother would say. I can see you have my metabolism. Louise also had her mother's pale blonde hair. Her mother was slim and pretty, carried herself erectly, and ate very little. The two of them would eat bare lunches, while her older brother ate sandwiches and potato chips, and then her mother would sit smoking while Louise eyed the bread box, the pantry, the refrigerator. Wasn't that good, her mother would say. In five years you'll be in high school and if you're fat the boys won't like you; they won't ask you out. Boys were as far away as five years, and she would go to her room and wait for nearly an hour until she knew her mother was no longer thinking of her, then she would creep into the kitchen and, listening to her mother talking on the phone, or her footsteps upstairs, she would open the bread box, the pantry, the jar of peanut butter. She would put the sandwich under her shirt and go outside or to the bathroom to eat it.

Her father was a lawyer and made a lot of money and came home looking pale and happy. Martinis put color back in his face, and at dinner he talked to his wife and two children. Oh give her a potato, he would say to Louise's mother. She's a growing girl. Her mother's voice then became tense: If she has a potato she shouldn't have dessert. She should have both, her father would say, and he would reach over and touch Louise's cheek or hand or arm.

In high school she had two girl friends and at night and on weekends they rode in a car or went to movies. In movies she was fascinated by fat actresses. She wondered why they were fat. She knew why she was fat: she was fat because she was Louise. Because God had made her that way. Because she wasn't like her friends Joan and Marjorie, who drank milk shakes after school and were all bones and tight skin. But what about those actresses, with their talents, with their broad and profound faces? Did they eat as heedlessly as Bishop Humphries and his wife who sometimes came to dinner and, as Louise's mother said, gorged between amenities? Or did they try to lose weight, did they go about hungry and angry and thinking of food? She thought of them eating lean meats and salads with friends, and then going home and building strange large sandwiches with French bread. But mostly she believed they did not go through these failures; they were fat because they chose to be. And she was certain of something else too: she could see it in their faces: they did not eat secretly. Which she did: her creeping to the kitchen when she was nine became, in high school, a ritual of deceit and pleasure. She was a furtive eater of sweets. Even her two friends did not know her secret.

Joan was thin, gangling, and flat-chested; she was attractive enough and all she needed was someone to take a second look at her face, but the school was large and there were pretty girls in every classroom and walking all the corridors, so no one ever needed to take a second look at Joan. Marjorie was thin too, an intense, heavy-smoking girl with brittle laughter. She was very intelligent, and with boys she was shy because she knew she made them uncomfortable, and because she was smarter than they were and so could not understand or could not believe the levels they lived on. She was to have a nervous breakdown before earning her Ph.D. in philosophy at the University of California, where she met and married a physicist and discovered within herself an untrammelled passion: she made love with her husband on the couch, the carpet, in the bathtub, and on the washing machine. By that time much had happened to her and she never thought of Louise. Joan would finally stop growing and begin moving with grace and confidence. In college she would have two lovers and then several more during the six years she spent in Boston before marrying a middle-aged editor who had two sons in their early teens, who drank too much, who was tenderly, boyishly grateful for her love, and whose wife had been killed while rock-climbing in New Hampshire with her lover. She would not think of Louise either, except in an earlier time, when lovers were still new to her and she was ecstatically surprised each time one of them loved her and, sometimes at night, lying in a man's arms, she would tell how in high school no one dated her, she had been thin and plain (she would still believe that: that she had been plain; it had never been true) and so had been forced into the weekend and night-time company of a neurotic smart girl and a shy fat girl. She would say this with self-pity exaggerated by Scotch and her need to be more deeply loved by the man who held her.

She never eats, Joan and Marjorie said of Louise. They ate lunch with her at school, watched her refusing potatoes, ravioli, fried fish. Sometimes she got through the cafeteria line with only a salad. That is how they would remember her: a girl whose hapless body was destined to be fat. No one saw the sandwiches she made and took to her room when she came home from school. No one saw the store of Milky Ways, Butterfingers, Almond Joys, and Hersheys far back on her closet shelf, behind the stuffed animals of her childhood. She was not a hypocrite. When she was out of the house she truly believed she was dieting; she forgot about the candy, as a man speaking into his office dictaphone may forget the lewd photographs hidden in an old shoe in his closet. At other times, away from home, she thought of the waiting candy with near lust. One night driving home from a movie, Marjorie said: "You're lucky you don't smoke; it's incredible what I go through to hide it from my parents." Louise turned to her a smile which was elusive and mysterious; she yearned to be home in bed, eating chocolate in the dark. She did not need to smoke; she already had a vice that was insular and destructive.

She brought it with her to college. She thought she would leave it behind. A move from one place to another, a new room without the haunted closet shelf, would do for her what she could not do for herself. She packed her large dresses and went. For two weeks she was busy with registration, with shyness, with classes; then she began to feel at home. Her room was no longer like a motel. Its walls had stopped watching her, she felt they were her friends, and she gave them her secret. Away from her mother, she did not have to be as elaborate; she kept the candy in her drawer now.

The school was in Massachusetts, a girls' school. When she chose it, when she and her father and mother talked about it in the evenings, everyone so carefully avoided the word boys that sometimes the conversations seemed to be about nothing but boys. There are no boys there, the neuter words said; you will not have to contend with that. In her father's eyes were pity and encouragement; in her mother's was disappointment, and her voice was crisp. They spoke of courses, of small classes where Louise would get more attention. She imagined herself in those small classes; she saw herself as a teacher would see her, as the other girls would; she would get no attention.

The girls at the school were from wealthy families, but most of them wore the uniform of another class: blue jeans and work shirts, and many wore overalls. Louise bought some overalls, washed them until the dark blue faded, and wore them to classes. In the cafeteria she ate as she had in high school, not to lose weight nor even to sustain her lie, but because eating lightly in public had become as habitual as good manners. Everyone had to take gym, and in the locker room with the other girls, and wearing shorts on the volleyball and badminton courts, she hated her body. She liked her body most when she was unaware of it: in bed at night, as sleep gently took her out of her day, out of herself. And she liked parts of her body. She liked her brown eyes and sometimes looked at them in the mirror: they were not shallow eyes, she thought; they were indeed windows of a tender soul, a good heart. She liked her lips and nose, and her chin, finely shaped between her wide and sagging cheeks. Most of all she liked her long pale blonde hair, she liked washing and drying it and lying naked on her bed, smelling of shampoo, and feeling the soft hair at her neck and shoulders and back.

Her friend at college was Carrie, who was thin and wore thick glasses and often at night she cried in Louise's room. She did not know why she was crying. She was crying, she said, because she was unhappy. She could say no more. Louise said she was unhappy too, and Carrie moved in with her. One night Carrie talked for hours, sadly and bitterly, about her parents and what they did to each other. When she finished she hugged Louise and they went to bed. Then in the dark Carrie spoke across the room: "Louise? I just wanted to tell you. One night last week I woke up and smelled chocolate. You were eating chocolate, in your bed. I wish you'd eat it in front of me, Louise, whenever you feel like it."

Stiffened in her bed, Louise could think of nothing to say. In the silence she was afraid Carrie would think she was asleep and would tell her again in the morning or tomorrow night. Finally she said Okay. Then after a moment she told Carrie if she ever wanted any she could feel free to help herself; the candy was in the top drawer. Then she said thank you.

They were roommates for four years and in the summers they exchanged letters. Each fall they greeted with embraces, laughter, tears, and moved into their old room, which had been stripped and cleaned for them for the summer. Neither girl enjoyed summer. Carrie did not like being at home because her parents did not love each other. Louise lived in a small city in Louisiana. She did not like summer because she had lost touch with Joan and Marjorie; they saw each other, but it was not the same. She liked being with her father but with no one else. The flicker of disappointment in her mother's eyes at the airport was a vanguard of the army of relatives and acquaintances who awaited her: they would see her on the streets, in stores, at the country club, in her home, and in theirs; in the first moments of greeting, their eyes would tell her she was still fat Louise, who had been fat as long as they could remember, who had gone to college and returned as fat as ever. Then their eyes dismissed her, and she longed for school and Carrie, and she wrote letters to her friend. But that saddened her too. It wasn't simply that Carrie was her only friend, and when they finished college they might never see each other again. It was that her existence in the world was so divided; it had begun when she was a child creeping to the kitchen; now that division was much sharper, and her friendship with Carrie seemed disproportionate and perilous. The world she was destined to live in had nothing to do with the intimate nights in their room at school.

In the summer before their senior year, Carrie fell in love. She wrote to Louise about him, but she did not write much, and this hurt Louise more than if Carrie had shown the joy her writing tried to conceal. That fall they returned to their room; they were still close and warm, Carrie still needed Louise's ears and heart at night as she spoke of her parents and her recurring malaise whose source the two friends never discovered. But on most week-ends Carrie left, and caught a bus to Boston where her boyfriend studied music. During the week she often spoke hesitantly of sex; she was not sure if she liked it. But Louise, eating candy and listening, did not know whether Carrie was telling the truth or whether, as in her letters of the past summer, Carrie was keeping from her those delights she may never experience.

Then one Sunday night when Carrie had just returned from Boston and was unpacking her overnight bag, she looked at Louise and said: "I was thinking about you. On the bus coming home tonight." Looking at Carrie's concerned, determined face, Louise prepared herself for humiliation. "I was thinking about when we graduate. What you're going to do. What's to become of you. I want you to be loved the way I love you. Louise, if I help you, really help you, will you go on a diet?"

Louise entered a period of her life she would remember always, the way some people remember having endured poverty. Her diet did not begin the next day. Carrie told her to eat on Monday as though it were the last day of her life. So for the first time since grammar school Louise went into a school cafeteria and ate everything she wanted. At breakfast and lunch and dinner she glanced around the table to see if the other girls noticed the food on her tray. They did not. She felt there was a lesson in this, but it lay beyond her grasp. That night in their room she ate the four remaining candy bars. During the day Carrie rented a small refrigerator, bought an electric skillet, an electric broiler, and bathroom scales.

On Tuesday morning Louise stood on the scales, and Carrie wrote in her notebook: *October 14: 184 lbs.* Then she made Louise a cup of black coffee and scrambled one egg and sat with her while she ate. When Carrie went to the dining room for breakfast, Louise walked about the campus for thirty minutes. That was part of the plan. The campus was pretty, on its lawns grew at least one of every tree native to New England, and in the warm morning sun Louise felt a new hope. At noon they met in their room, and Carrie broiled her a piece of hamburger and served it with lettuce. Then while Carrie ate in the dining room Louise walked again. She was weak with hunger and she felt queasy. During her afternoon classes she was nervous and tense, and she chewed her pencil and tapped her heels on the floor and tightened her calves. When she returned to her room late that afternoon, she was so glad to see Carrie that she embraced her; she had felt she could not bear another minute of hunger, but now with Carrie she knew she could make it at least through tonight. Then she would sleep and face tomorrow when it came. Carrie broiled her a steak and served it with lettuce. Louise studied while Carrie ate dinner, then they went for a walk.

That was her ritual and her diet for the rest of the year, Carrie alternating fish and chicken breasts with the steaks for dinner, and every day was nearly as bad as the first. In the evenings she was irritable. In all her life she had never been afflicted by ill temper and she looked upon it now as a demon which, along with hunger, was taking possession of her soul. Often she spoke sharply to Carrie. One night during their after-dinner walk Carrie talked sadly of night, of how darkness made her more aware of herself, and at night she did not know why she was in college, why she studied, why she was walking the earth with other people. They were standing on a wooden foot bridge, looking down at a dark pond. Carrie kept talking; perhaps soon she would cry. Suddenly Louise said: "I'm sick of lettuce. I never want to see a piece of lettuce for the rest of my life. I hate it. We shouldn't even buy it, it's immoral."

Carrie was quiet. Louise glanced at her, and the pain and irritation in Carrie's face soothed her. Then she was ashamed. Before she could say she was sorry, Carrie turned to her and said gently: "I know. I know how terrible it is."

Carrie did all the shopping, telling Louise she knew how hard it was to go into a supermarket when you were hungry. And Louise was always hungry. She drank diet soft drinks and started smoking Carrie's cigarettes, learned to enjoy inhaling, thought of cancer and emphysema but they were as far away as those boys her mother had talked about when she was nine. By Thanksgiving she was smoking over a pack a day and her weight in Carrie's notebook was one hundred and sixty-two pounds. Carrie was afraid if Louise went home at Thanksgiving she would lapse from the diet, so Louise spent the vacation with Carrie, in Philadelphia. Carrie wrote her family about the diet, and told Louise that she had. On the plane to Philadelphia, Louise said: "I feel like a bedwetter. When I was a little girl I had a friend who used to come spend the night and Mother would put a rubber sheet on the bed and we all pretended there wasn't a rubber sheet and that she hadn't wet the bed. Even me, and I slept with her." At Thanksgiving dinner she lowered her eyes as Carrie's father put two slices of white meat on her plate and passed it to her over the bowls of steaming food.

When she went home at Christmas she weighed a hundred and fifty-five pounds; at the airport her mother marvelled. Her father laughed and hugged her and said: "But now there's less of you to love." He was troubled by her smoking but only mentioned it once; he told her she was beautiful and, as always, his eyes bathed her with love. During the long vacation her mother cooked for her as Carrie had, and Louise returned to school weighing a hundred and forty-six pounds.

Flying north on the plane she warmly recalled the surprised and congratulatory eyes of her relatives and acquaintances. She had not seen Joan or Marjorie. She thought of returning home in May, weighing the hundred and fifteen pounds which Carrie had in October set as their goal. Looking toward the stoic days ahead, she felt strong. She thought of those hungry days of fall and early winter (and now: she was hungry now: with almost a frown, almost a brusque shake of the head, she refused peanuts from the stewardess): those first weeks of the diet when she was the pawn of an irascibility which still, conditioned to her ritual as she was, could at any moment take command of her. She thought of the nights of trying to sleep while her stomach growled. She thought of her addiction to cigarettes. She thought of the people at school: not one teacher, not one girl, had spoken to her about her loss of weight, not even about her absence from meals. And without warning her spirit collapsed. She did not feel strong, she did not feel she was committed to and within reach of achieving a valuable goal. She felt that somehow she had lost more than pounds of fat; that some time during her dieting she had lost herself too. She tried to remember what it had felt like to be Louise before she had started living on meat and fish, as an unhappy adult may look sadly in the memory of childhood for lost virtues and hopes. She looked down at the earth far below, and it seemed to her that her soul, like her body aboard the plane, was in some rootless flight. She neither knew its destination nor where it had departed from; it was on some passage she could not even define.

During the next few weeks she lost weight more slowly and once for eight days Carrie's daily recording stayed at a hundred and thirty-six. Louise woke in the morning thinking of one hundred and thirty-six and then she stood on the scales and they echoed her. She became obsessed with that number, and there wasn't a day when she didn't say it aloud, and through the days and nights the number stayed in her mind, and if a teacher had spoken those digits in a classroom she would have opened her mouth to speak. What if that's me, she said to Carrie. I meant what if a hundred and thirty-six is my real weight and I just can't lose anymore. Walking hand-in-hand with her despair was a longing for this to be true, and that longing angered her and wearied her, and every day she was gloomy. On the ninth day she weighed a hundred and thirty-five and a half pounds. She was not relieved; she thought bitterly of the months ahead, the shedding of the last twenty and a half pounds.

On Easter Sunday, which she spent at Carrie's, she weighed one hundred and twenty pounds, and she ate one slice of glazed pineapple with her ham and lettuce. She did not enjoy it: she felt she was being friendly with a recalcitrant enemy who had once tried to destroy her. Carrie's parents were laudative. She liked them and she wished they would touch sometimes, and look at each other when they spoke. She guessed they would divorce when Carrie left home, and she vowed that her own marriage would be one of affection and tenderness. She could think about that now: marriage. At school she had read in a Boston paper that this summer the cicadas would come out of their seventeen year hibernation on Cape Cod, for a month they would mate and then die, leaving their young to burrow into the ground where they would stay for seventeen years. That's me, she had said to Carrie. Only my hibernation lasted twenty-one years.

Often her mother asked in letters and on the phone about the diet, but Louise answered vaguely. When she flew home in late May she weighed a hundred and thirteen pounds, and at the airport her mother cried and hugged her and said again and again: You're so *beautiful*. Her father blushed and bought her a martini. For days her relatives and acquaintances congratulated her, and the applause in their eyes lasted the entire summer, and she loved their eyes, and swam in the country club pool, the first time she had done this since she was a child.

She lived at home and ate the way her mother did and every morning she weighed herself on the scales in her bathroom. Her mother liked to take her shopping and buy her dresses and they put her old ones in the Goodwill box at the shopping center; Louise thought of them existing on the body of a poor woman whose cheap meals kept her fat. Louise's mother had a photographer come to the house, and Louise posed on the couch and standing beneath a live oak and sitting in a wicker lawn chair next to an azalea bush. The new clothes and the photographer made her feel she was going to another country or becoming a citizen of a new one. In the fall she took a job of no consequence, to give herself something to do.

Also in the fall a young lawyer joined her father's firm, he came one night to dinner, and they started seeing each other. He was the first man outside her family to kiss her since the barbecue when she was sixteen. Louise celebrated Thanksgiving not with rice dressing and candied sweet potatoes and mince meat and pumpkin pies, but by giving Richard her virginity which she realized, at the very last moment of its existence, she had embarked on giving him over thirteen months ago, on that Tuesday in October when Carrie had made her a cup of black coffee and scrambled one egg. She wrote this to Carrie, who replied happily by return mail. She also, through glance and smile and innuendo, tried to tell her mother too. But finally she controlled that impulse, because Richard felt guilty about making love with the daughter of his partner and friend. In the spring they married. The wedding was a large one, in the Episcopal church, and Carrie flew from Boston to be maid of honor. Her parents had recently separated and she was living with the musician and was still victim of her unpredictable malaise. It overcame her on the night before the wedding, so Louise was up with her until past three and woke next morning from sleep so heavy that she did not want to leave it.

Richard was a lean, tall, energetic man with the metabolism of a pencil sharpener. Louise fed him everything he wanted. He liked Italian food and she got recipes from her mother and watched him eating spaghetti with the sauce she had only tasted, and ravioli and lasagna, while she ate antipasto with her chianti. He made a lot of money and borrowed more and they bought a house whose lawn sloped down to the shore of a lake; they had a wharf and a boathouse, and Richard bought a boat and they took friends waterskiing. Richard bought her a car and they spent his vacations in Mexico, Canada, the Bahamas, and in the fifth year of their marriage they went to Europe and, according to their plan, she conceived a child in Paris. On the plane back, as she looked out the window and beyond the sparkling sea and saw her country, she felt that it was waiting for her, as her home by the lake was, and her parents, and her good friends who rode in the boat and waterskied; she thought of the accumulated warmth and pelf of her marriage, and how by slimming her body she had bought into the pleasures of the nation. She felt cunning, and she smiled to herself, and took Richard's hand.

But these moments of triumph were sparse. On most days she went about her routine of leisure with a sense of certainty about herself that came merely from not thinking. But there were times, with her friends, or with Richard, or alone in the house, when she was suddenly assaulted by the feeling that she had taken the wrong train and arrived at a place where no one knew her, and where she ought not to be. Often, in bed with Richard, she talked of being fat: "I was the one who started the friendship with Carrie, I chose her, I started the conversations. When I understood that she was my friend I understood something else: I had chosen her for the same reason I'd chosen Joan and Marjorie. They were all thin. I was always thinking about what people saw when they looked at me and I didn't want them to see two fat girls. When I was alone I didn't mind being fat but then I'd have to leave the house again and then I didn't want to look like me. But at home I didn't mind except when I was getting dressed to go out of the house and when Mother looked at me. But I stopped looking at her when she looked at me. And in college I felt good with Carrie; there weren't any boys and I didn't have any other friends and so when I wasn't with Carrie I thought about her and I tried to ignore the other people around me, I tried to make them not exist. A lot of the time I could do that. It was strange, and I felt like a spy."

If Richard was bored by her repetitions he pretended not to be. But she knew the story meant very little to him. She could have been telling him of a childhood illness, or wearing braces, or a broken heart at sixteen. He could not see her as she was when she was fat. She felt as though she were trying to tell a foreign lover about her life in the United States, and if only she could command the language he would know and love all of her and she would feel complete. Some of the acquaintances of her childhood were her friends now, and even they did not seem to remember her when she was fat.

Now her body was growing again, and when she put on a maternity dress for the first time she shivered with fear. Richard did not smoke and he asked her, in a voice just short of demand, to stop during her pregnancy. She did. She ate carrots and celery instead of smoking, and at cocktail parties she tried to eat nothing, but after her first drink she ate nuts and cheese and crackers and dips. Always at these parties Richard had talked with his friends and she had rarely spoken to him until they drove home. But now when he noticed her at the hors d' oeuvres table he crossed the room and, smiling, led her back to his group. His smile and his hand on her arm told her he was doing his clumsy, husbandly best to help her through a time of female mystery.

She was gaining weight but she told herself it was only the baby, and would leave with its birth. But at others times she knew quite clearly that she was losing the discipline she had fought so hard to gain during her last year with Carrie. She was hungry now as she had been in college, and she ate between meals and after dinner and tried to eat only carrots and celery, but she grew to hate them, and her desire for sweets was as vicious as it had been long ago. At home she ate bread and jam and when she shopped for groceries she bought a candy bar and ate it driving home and put the wrapper in her purse and then in the garbage can under the sink. Her cheeks had filled out, there was loose flesh under her chin, her arms and legs were plump, and her mother was concerned. So was Richard. One night when she brought pie and milk to the living room where they were watching television, he said: "You already had a piece. At dinner."

She did not look at him.

"You're gaining weight. It's not all water, either. It's fat. It'll be summer-time. You'll want to get into your bathing suit."

The pie was cherry. She looked at it as her fork cut through it; she speared the piece and rubbed it in the red juice on the plate before lifting it to her mouth.

"You never used to eat pie," he said. "I just think you ought to watch it a bit. It's going to be tough on you this summer."

In her seventh month, with a delight reminiscent of climbing the stairs to Richard's apartment before they were married, she returned to her world of secret gratification. She began hiding candy in her underwear drawer. She ate it during the day and at night while Richard slept, and at breakfast she was distracted, waiting for him to leave.

She gave birth to a son, brought him home, and nursed both him and her appetites. During this time of celibacy she enjoyed her body through her son's mouth; while he suckled she stroked his small head and back. She was hiding candy but she did not conceal her other indulgences; she was smoking again but still she ate between meals, and at dinner she ate what Richard did, and coldly he watched her, he grew petulant, and when the date marking the end of their celibacy came they let it pass. Often in the afternoons her mother visited and scolded her and Louise sat looking at the baby and said nothing until finally, to end it, she promised to diet. When her mother and father came for dinners, her father kissed her and held the baby and her mother said nothing about Louise's body, and her voice was tense. Returning from work in the evenings Richard looked at a soiled plate and glass on the table beside her chair as if detecting traces of infidelity, and at every dinner they fought.

"Look at you," he said. "Lasagna, for God's sake. When are you going to start? It's not simply that you haven't lost any weight. You're gaining. I can see it. I can feel it when you get in bed. Pretty soon you'll weigh more than I do and I'll be sleeping on a trampoline."

"You never touch me anymore."

"I don't want to touch you. Why should I? Have you looked at yourself?"

"You're cruel,' she said. "I never knew how cruel you were."

She ate, watching him. He did not look at her. Glaring at his plate, he worked with fork and knife like a hurried man at a lunch counter.

"I bet you didn't either," she said.

That night when he was asleep she took a Milky Way to the bathroom. For a while she stood eating in the dark, then she turned on the light. Chewing, she looked at herself in the mirror; she looked at her eyes and hair. Then she stood on the scales and looking at the numbers between her feet, one hundred and sixty-two; she remembered when she had weighed a hundred and thirty-six pounds for eight days. Her memory of those eight days was fond and amusing, as though she were recalling an Easter egg hunt when she was six. She stepped off the scales and pushed them under the lavatory and did not stand on them again.

It was summer and she bought loose dresses and when Richard took friends out on the boat she did not wear a bathing suit or shorts; her friends gave her mischievous glances, and Richard did not look at her. She stopped riding on the boat. She told them she wanted to stay with the baby, and she sat inside holding him until she heard the boat leave the wharf. Then she took him to the front lawn and walked with him in the shade of the trees and talked to him about the blue jays and mockingbirds and cardinals she saw on their branches. Sometimes she stopped and watched the boat out on the lake and the friend skiing behind it.

Every day Richard quarrelled, and because his rage went no further than her weight and shape, she felt excluded from it, and she remained calm within layers of flesh and spirit, and watched his frustration, his impotence. He truly believed they were arguing about her weight. She knew better: she knew that beneath the argument lay the question of who Richard was. She thought of him smiling at the wheel of his boat, and long ago courting his slender girl, the daughter of his partner and friend. She thought of Carrie telling her of smelling chocolate in the dark and, after that, watching her eat it night after night. She smiled at Richard, teasing his anger.

He is angry now. He stands in the center of the living room, raging at her, and he wakes the baby. Beneath Richard's voice she hears the soft crying, feels it in her heart, and quietly she rises from her chair and goes upstairs to the child's room and takes him from the crib. She brings him to the living room and sits holding him in her lap, pressing him gently against the folds of fat at her waist. Now Richard is pleading with her. Louise thinks tenderly of Carrie broiling meat and fish in their room, and walking with her in the evenings. She wonders if Carrie still has the malaise. Perhaps she will come for a visit. In Louise's arms now the boy sleeps.

"I'll help you," Richard says. "I'll eat the same things you eat."

But his face does not approach the compassion and determination and love she had seen in Carrie's during what she now recognizes as the worst year of her life. She can remember nothing about that year except hunger, and the meals in her room. She is hungry now. When she puts the boy to bed she will get a candy bar from her room. She will eat it here, in front of Richard. This room will be hers soon. She considers the possibilities: all these rooms and the lawn where she can do whatever she wishes. She knows he will leave soon. It has been in his eyes all summer. She stands, using one hand to pull herself out of the chair. She carries the boy to his crib, feels him against her large breasts, feels that his sleeping body touches her soul. With a surge of vindication and relief she holds him. Then she kisses his forehead and places him in the crib. She goes to the bedroom and in the dark takes a bar of candy from her drawer. Slowly she descends the stairs. She knows Richard is waiting but she feels his departure so happily that, when she enters the living room, unwrapping the candy, she is surprised to see him standing there.

DISCUSSION QUESTIONS

1. What do you think Dubus means when he writes: "He truly believed they were arguing about her weight. She knew better: she knew that beneath the argument lay the question of who Richard was"?

2. If Louise were a classmate, would you befriend her? Why or why not?

3. When children were shown pictures of other children with a variety of physical attributes—including excess weight, facial disfigurement, and missing limbs—they picked their overweight peers last when asked whom they would like to play with. Why do you think this occurs?

4. It has been found that the fear of becoming fat can lead to eating disorders in both sexes. What can be done to teach more size and weight tolerance in our schools?

SUGGESTIONS FOR JOURNAL ENTRIES

1. Write about a time when you were made fun of because of something over which you had no control (gender, race, height, weight, looks, age, ethnicity, religion, etc.).

2. If you have ever dieted, write about what it was like. If not, interview someone who has.

If I Had My Life to Live Over

Nadine Stairs

*This free verse poem written by an eighty-five-year-old woman cautions
young people not to grow up too quickly and neglect the "free child" that is
within all of us.*

I'd dare to make more mistakes next time.
I'd relax. I would limber up. I would be sillier than
I have been this trip. I would take few things
seriously. I
would climb more
mountains and swim more rivers. I would eat
more ice cream and less beans. I would perhaps
have more actual troubles, but I'd have few
imaginary ones.
You see, I'm one of those people who lives
sensibly and sanely hour after hour, day after
day. Oh, I've had my moments and if I had it
to do over again, I'd have more of them. In
fact, I'd try to have
nothing else. Just moments,
one after another, instead of living so many
years ahead of each. I've been one of those
persons who never goes anywhere without a
thermometer, a hot water bottle, a raincoat,
and a parachute. If I had to do it again, I would
travel lighter than I have.
If I had my life to live over, I would start
barefoot earlier in the spring and stay that way
later in the fall. I would go to more dances.
I would ride more merry-go-rounds. I would
pick more daisies.

Risks

Anonymous

This short free verse poem by an unknown author heralds risk-taking as the only alternative to slavery.

To laugh is to risk appearing foolish.
To weep is to risk appearing sentimental.
To reach out for another is to risk involvement.
To expose feelings is to risk exposing your true self.
To hope is to risk despair.
To try is to risk failure.
To live is to risk dying.

But risks must be taken
because the greatest hazard in life is to risk nothing.
The person who risks nothing,
does nothing, has nothing and is nothing.
He may avoid suffering and sorrow
but he simply cannot learn, feel, change, grow, love, or live.
Chained by his opinions, he is a slave,
he has forfeited freedom.
Only a person who risks is free.

DISCUSSION QUESTIONS

1. Both of these poems talk about the importance of taking risks and making mistakes for living and growing. Can you think of an example from your own life?
2. One of the themes of Stairs' poem is the lost innocence of childhood. Do you think your generation has been forced to grow up more quickly than your grandparents' generation. Why or why not?
3. What "risks" have you taken since coming to college?
4. Which poem do you like better and why?

SUGGESTIONS FOR JOURNAL ENTRIES

1. Select one of the first seven lines from "Risks" and write about what it means to you.
2. The very decision to go to college is a form of risk-taking. Write about the various stages you went through in making this decision and what helped you to choose to come.

SPIRITUAL QUEST

This is one of the last sections, but not an unimportant one. Since more and more educators are recognizing the importance of a holistic approach to college students, the spiritual domain is being recognized as an integral component of a college student's life.

This is not an easy thing to teach or even talk about in many university settings. Nevertheless, my own experience is that many students today are searching for their own answers to the perennial questions about the meaning of life. Indeed, it has been said that spirituality is about questions, as opposed to religion, which is about answers. If pressed to explain what I mean by the word, "spirituality" I usually reply that it is that "yes" in me that pushes me to become who I am. It is what connects me to the earth and all of life: plants, animals, humans, and especially the beyond. Therefore, for me as a believer, it means cultivating a lifestyle that helps me to get closer to (love) all forms of life, including my neighbor and my Self (the Higher Self, not the ego) and therefore closer to God/Goddess (or the Force, or the Great Mysterious Presence or the Cosmic Person or whatever name you wish to give). It is my hope that the following four essays will assist you as you begin your own spiritual quest.

The first essay is by the famous poet, Robert Bly, who describes the Jungian notion of the "shadow," and how we must confront the fact that some of our best parts have been repressed and stuffed into a "long bag that we drag behind us." To do so, according to Jung, is to discover 90 percent pure gold.

The second essay by John White tries to answer the difficult question, "What is meditation?" Many college students are asking the same question and taking courses on meditation to find out. Having discovered meditation myself about ten years ago, I believe that White's answer is the best available in the literature.

The third essay is an excerpt from Gerard Jampolsky's book, *Teach Only Love*. It describes the phenomenal faith and courage of a blind young woman who had what seems like a miraculous healing, proving "nothing real is impossible."

The fourth and final essay is a famous letter of the great German poet Rainer Maria Rilke with advice "to a young poet" in 1903 to "Go into yourself," the message of all of these essays more or less and one that desperately needs to be heard today.

READING 42

The Long Bag We Drag behind Us

Robert Bly

Robert Bly, Harvard '50, poet, writer, and translator, writes graphically about the Jungian concept of the "shadow" and how we must make friends with it in order to achieve wholeness. The following is an excerpt from A Little Book on the Human Shadow *(1988).*

It's an old Gnostic tradition that we don't invent things, we just remember. The Europeans I know of who remember the dark side best are Robert Louis Stevenson, Joseph Conrad, and Carl Jung. I'll call up a few of their ideas and add a few thoughts of my own.

Let's talk about the personal shadow first. When we were one or two years old we had what we might visualize as a 360-degree personality. Energy radiated out from all parts of our body and all parts of our psyche. A child running is a living globe of energy. We had a ball of energy, all right; but one day we noticed that our parents didn't like certain parts of that ball. They said things like: "Can't you be still?" or "It isn't nice to try and kill your brother." Behind us we have an invisible bag, and the part of us our parents don't like, we, to keep our parents' love, put in the bag. By the time we go to school our bag is quite large. Then our teachers have their say: "Good children don't get angry over such little things." So we take our anger and put it in the bag. By the time my brother and I were twelve in Madison, Minnesota, we were known as "the nice Bly boys." Our bags were already a mile long.

Then we do a lot of bag-stuffing in high school. This time it's no longer the evil grownups that pressure us, but people our own age. So the student's paranoia about grownups can be misplaced. I lied all through high school automatically to try to be more like the basketball players. Any part of myself that was a little slow went into the bag. My sons are going through the process now; I watched my daughters, who were older, experience it. I noticed with dismay how much they put into the bag, but there was nothing their mother or I could do about it. Often my daughters seemed to make their decision on the issue of fashion and collective ideas of beauty, and they suffered as much damage from other girls as they did from men.

So I maintain that out of a round globe of energy the twenty-year-old ends up with a slice. We'll imagine a man who has a thin slice left—the rest is in the bag—and we'll imagine that he meets a woman; let's say they are both twenty-four. She has a thin, elegant slice left. They join each other in a ceremony, and this union of two slices is called marriage. Even together the two do not make up one person! Marriage when the bag is large entails loneliness during the honeymoon for that very reason. Of course we all lie about it. "How is your honeymoon?" "Wonderful, how's yours?"

Different cultures fill the bag with different contents. In Christian culture sexuality usually goes into the bag. With it goes much spontaneity.

Marie-Louise von Franz warns us, on the other hand, not to sentimentalize primitive cultures by assuming that they have no bag at all. She says in effect that they have a different but sometimes even larger bag. They may put individuality into the bag, or inventiveness. What anthropologists know as "participation mystique," or "a mysterious communal mind," sounds lovely, but it can mean that tribal members all know exactly the same thing and no one knows anything else. It's possible that bags for all human beings are about the same size.

We spend our life until we're twenty deciding what parts of ourself to put into the bag, and we spend the rest of our lives trying to get them out again. Sometimes retrieving them feels impossible, as if the bag were sealed. Suppose the bag remains sealed—what happens then? A great nineteenth-century story has an idea about that. One night Robert Louis Stevenson woke up and told his wife a bit of a dream he'd just had. She urged him to write it down; he did, and it became "Dr. Jekyll and Mr. Hyde." The nice side of the personality becomes, in our idealistic culture, nicer and nicer. The Western man may be a liberal doctor, for example, always thinking about the good of others. Morally and ethically he is wonderful. But the substance in the bag takes on a personality of its own; it can't be ignored. The story says that the substance locked in the bag appears one day *somewhere else* in the city. The substance in the bag feels angry, and when you see it, it is shaped like an ape, and moves like an ape.

The story says then that when we put a part of ourselves in the bag it regresses. It de-evolves toward barbarism. Suppose a young man seals a bag at twenty and then waits fifteen or twenty years before he opens it again. What will he find? Sadly, the sexuality, the wildness, the impulsiveness, the anger, the freedom he put in have all regressed; they are not only primitive in mood, they are hostile to the person who opens the bag. The man who opens his bag at forty-five or the woman who opens her bag rightly feels fear. She glances up and sees the shadow of an ape passing along the alley wall; anyone seeing that would be frightened.

I think we could say that most males in our culture put their feminine side or interior woman into the bag. When they begin, perhaps around thirty-five or forty, trying to get in touch with their feminine side again, she may be by then truly hostile to them. The same man may experience in the meantime much hostility from women in the outer world. The rule seems to be: the outside has to be like the inside. That's the way it is on this globe. If a woman, wanting to be approved for her femininity, has put her masculine side or her internal male into the bag, she may find that twenty years later he will be hostile to her. Moreover he may be unfeeling and brutal in his criticism. She's in a spot. Finding a hostile man to live with would give her someone to blame, and take away the pressure, but that wouldn't help the problem of the closed bag. In the meantime, she is liable to sense a double rejection, from the male inside and the male outside. There's a lot of grief in this whole thing.

Every part of our personality that we do not love will become hostile to us. We could add that it may move to a distant place and begin a revolt against us as well. A lot of the trouble Shakespeare's kings experience blossoms in that sentence. Hotspur "in Wales" rebels against the King. Shakespeare's poetry is marvelously sensitive to the danger of these inner revolts. Always the king at the center is endangered.

When I visited Bali a few years ago, it became clear that their ancient Hindu culture works through mythology to bring shadow elements up into daily view. The temples put on plays virtually every day from the *Ramayana*. I saw some terrifying plays performed as a part of religious life, in a day by day way. Almost every Balinese house has standing outside it a fierce, toothy, aggressive, hostile figure carved in stone. This being doesn't plan to do good. I visited a mask maker, and noticed his nine- or ten-year-old son sitting outside the house, making with his chisel a hostile, angry figure. The person does not aim to act out the aggressive energies as we do in football or the Spanish in bull-fighting, but each person aims to bring them upward into art: that is the ideal. The Balinese can be violent and brutal in war, but in daily life they seem much less violent than we are. What can this mean? Southerners in the United States put figures of helpful little black men on the lawn, cast in iron, and we in the North do the same with serene deer. We ask for roses in the wallpaper. Renoir above the sofa, and John Denver on the stereo. Then the aggression escapes from the bag and attacks everyone.

We'll have to let this contrast between Balinese and American cultures lie there and go on. I want to talk about the connection between shadow energies and the moving picture projector. Let's suppose that we have miniaturized certain parts of ourselves, flattened them out, and put them inside a can, where it will be dark. Then one night—always at night—the shapes reappear, huge, and we can't take our eyes away from them. We drive at night in the country and see a man and woman on an enormous outdoor movie screen; we shut off the car and watch. Certain figures who have been rolled up inside a can, doubly invisible by being partially "developed" and by being kept always in the dark, exist during the day only as pale images on a thin gray strip of film. When a certain light is ignited in the back of our heads, ghostly pictures appear on a wall in front of us. They light cigarettes; they threaten others with guns. Our psyches then are natural projection machines—images that we stored in a can we can bring out while still rolled up, and run them for others, or on others. A man's anger, rolled up inside the can for twenty years, he may see one night on his wife's face. A wife might see a hero every night on her husband's face and then one night see a tyrant. Nora in *A Doll's House* saw the two images in turn.

The other day I found some of my old diaries, and picked out one at random, from 1956, I had been struggling that year to write a poem describing the nature of advertising men. I remember that, and I recall that at that time the story of Midas was important in my mood. Everything that Midas touched turned to gold. I declared in my poem that every living thing an advertising man touches turns into some form of money, and that's why ad men have such starved souls. I kept in mind the ad men I'd known and was having a good time attacking them from my concealed position. As I read the old passages I felt a shock seeing the movie I was running. Between the time I wrote them and now I'd discovered that I had known for years how to eat in such a way as to keep me from taking in any kind of nourishment. Whatever food a friend offered me, or a woman, or a child, turned into metal on the way to my mouth. Is the image clear? No one can eat or drink metal. So Midas was a good image for me. But the film showing my interior Midas was rolled up in the can. Advertising men, evil, and foolish, tended to appear at night on a large screen, and I was naturally fascinated. A year or two later I composed a book called *Poems for the Ascension of J. P. Morgan,* in which each poem I had written about business alternated with a culpable advertisement reproduced from magazines or newspapers. It is a lively book in its way. No one would publish it, but that was all right. It was mostly projection anyway. I'm going to read you a poem I wrote around that time. It's called "Unrest."

> A strange unrest hovers over the nation:
> This is the last dance, the wild tossing of Morgan's seas,
> The division of spoils. A lassitude
> Enters into the diamonds of the body.
> In high school the explosion begins, the child is partly killed;
> When the fight is over, and the land and the sea ruined,
> Two shapes inside us rise, and move away.
>
> But the baboon whistles on the shores of death—
> Climbing and falling, tossing nuts and stones,
> He gambols by the tree
> Whose branches hold the expanses of cold,
> The planets whirling and the black sun,
> The cries of insects, and the tiny slaves
> In the prisons of bark.
> Charlemagne, we are approaching your islands!
>
> We are returning now to the snowy trees,
> And the depth of the darkness buried in snow, through
>   which you rode all night
> With stiff hands; now the darkness is falling
> In which we sleep and awake—a darkness in which
> Thieves shudder, and the insane have a hunger for snow,
> In which bankers dream of being buried by black stones,
> And businessmen fall on their knees in the dungeons of sleep.

About five years ago I began to be suspicious of this poem. Why are bankers and businessmen being singled out? If I had to rephrase "banker" what would I say? "Someone who plans very well." I plan very well. How would I rephrase "businessman"? "Someone with a stiff face." I looked in the mirror then. I'll read you the way the passage goes now, after I've rewritten it:

> . . . a darkness in which
> Thieves shudder, and the insane have a hunger for snow,
> In which good planners dream of being buried by black stones,
> And men with stiff faces like me fall on their knees in the
>   dungeons of sleep.

Now when I go to a party I feel different from the way that I used to when I meet a businessman. I say to a man, "What do you do?" He says, "I'm a stockbroker." And he says it in a faintly apologetic way. I say to myself, "Look at this: something of me that was deep inside me is standing right next to me." I have a funny longing to hug him. Not all of them, of course.

But projection is a wonderful thing too. Marie-Louise von Franz remarked somewhere, "Why do we always assume projection is bad? 'You are project-ing' becomes among Jungians an accusation. Sometimes projection is helpful and the right thing." Her remark is very wise. I know that I was starving my-self to death, but the knowledge couldn't move directly from the bag to the conscious mind. It has to go out onto the world first. "How wicked advertis-ing men are," I said to myself. Marie-Louise von Franz reminds us that if we didn't project, we might never connect with the world at all. Women some-times complain that a man often takes his ideal feminine side and projects it onto a woman. But if he didn't, how could he get out of his mother's house or his bachelor room? The issue is not so much that we do project but how long we keep the projections out there. Projection without personal contact is dan-gerous. Thousands, even millions of American men projected their internal feminine onto Marilyn Monroe. If a million men do that, and leave it there, it's likely she will die. She died. Projections without personal contact can damage the person receiving them.

We have to also say that Marilyn Monroe called for these projections as a part of her power longing, and her disturbance must have gone back to vic-timization in childhood. But the process of projection and recall, done so deli-cately in tribal culture, face to face, goes out of whack when the mass media arrives. In the economy of the psyche her death was inevitable and even right. No single human being can carry so many projections—that is, so much un-consciousness—and survive. So it's infinitely important that each person bring back his or her own.

But why would we give away, or put into the bag, so much of ourselves? Why would we do it so young? And if we have put away so many of our angers, spontaneities, hungers, enthusiasms, our rowdy and unattractive parts, then how can we live? What holds us together? Alice Miller spoke to this point in her book *Prisoners of Childhood*, which in paperback form is called *The Drama of the Gifted Child.*

The drama is this. We came as infants "trailing clouds of glory," arriving from the farthest reaches of the universe, bringing with us appetites well pre-served from our mammal inheritance, spontaneities wonderfully preserved from our 150,000 years of tree life, angers well preserved from our 5,000 years of tribal life—in short, with our 360-degree radiance—and we offered this gift to our parents. They didn't want it. They wanted a nice girl or a nice boy. That's the first act of the drama. It doesn't mean our parents were wicked; they needed us for something. My mother, as a second generation immigrant, needed my brother and me to help the family look more classy. We do the same thing to our children; it's part of life on this planet. Our parents rejected who we were before we could talk, so the pain of rejection is probably stored in some pre-verbal place.

When I read her book I fell into depression for three weeks. With so much gone, what can we do? We can construct a personality more acceptable to our parents. Alice Miller agrees that we have betrayed ourselves, but she says, "Don't blame yourself for that. There's nothing else you could have done." Children in ancient times who opposed their parents probably were set out to die. We did, as children, the only sensible thing under the circumstances. The proper attitude toward that, she says, is mourning.

Let's talk now about the different sorts of bags. When we have put a lot in our private bag, we often have as a result little energy. The bigger the bag, the less the energy. Some people have by nature more energy than others, but we all have more than we can possibly use. Where did it go? If we put our sexuality into the bag as a child, obviously we lose a lot of energy. When a woman puts her masculinity into the bag, or rolls it up and puts it into the can, she loses energy with it. So we can think of our personal bag as containing energy now unavailable to us. If we identify ourselves as uncreative, it means we took our creativity and put it into the bag. What do you mean, "I am not creative"? "Let experts do it"—isn't that what such a person is saying? That's damn well what such people are saying. The audience wants a poet, a hired gun, to come in from out of town. Everybody in this audience should be writing their own poems.

We talked of our personal bag, but each town or community also seems to have a bag. I lived for years near a small Minnesota farm town. Everyone in the town was expected to have the same objects in the bag; a small Greek town clearly would have different objects in the bag. It's as if the town, by collective psychic decision, puts certain energies in the bag, and tries to prevent anyone from getting them out. Towns interfere with our private process in this matter, so it's more dangerous to live in them than in nature. On the other hand, certain ferocious hatreds that one feels in a small town help one sometimes to see where the projections have gone. And the Jungian community, like the town, has its bag, and usually recommends that Jungians keep their vulgarity and love of money in the bag; and the Freudian community usually demands that Freudians keep their religious life in the bag.

There is also a national bag, and ours is quite long. Russia and China have noticeable faults, but if an American citizen is curious to know what is in our national bag at the moment, he can listen closely when a State Department official criticizes Russia. As Reagan says, we are noble; other nations have empires. Other nations endure stagnated leadership, treat minorities brutally, brainwash their youth, and break treaties. A Russian can find out about his bag by reading a *Pravda* article on the United States. We're dealing with a network of shadows, a pattern of shadows projected by both sides, all meeting somewhere out in the air. I'm not saying anything new with this metaphor, but I do want to make the distinction clear between the personal shadow, the town shadow, and the national shadow.

I have used three metaphors here: the bag, the film can, and projection. Since the can or bag is closed and its images remain in the dark, we can only see the contents of our own bag by throwing them innocently, as we say, out into the world. Spiders then become evil, snakes cunning, goats oversexed; men become linear, women become weak, the Russians become unprincipled, and Chinese all look alike. Yet it is precisely through this expensive, damaging, wasteful, inaccurate form of mud-slinging that we eventually come in touch with the mud that the crow found on the bottom of its feet.

DISCUSSION QUESTIONS

1. Why is Bly so insistent on opening the bag? Do you agree that this is a good idea?
2. Bly contends that we start to open the bag around the age of 20 and spend the rest of our lives trying to get those repressed parts of ourselves out. Can you think of evidence to support Bly's claim?
3. What do you think American culture favors putting into the bag?
4. Do you think your parents' generation favored putting different things into the bag than your generation does?

SUGGESTIONS FOR JOURNAL ENTRIES

1. Ask your best friend for three things he or she feels you have put into your bag and write about what they tell you.
2. Write a poem about what you think your shadow looks like.
3. Write about a time when someone was obviously projecting his or her shadow onto you.

What Is Meditation?

John W. White

John White's essay demythologizes meditation, summarizes the research on its effects, and introduces the major schools. He concludes with the observation that "the highest development in meditation regardless of the school or path, brings technique and daily life together." White, University of Manchester (England) '52, is an internationally recognized author and lecturer in the fields of parascience and consciousness research and this article appeared in 1984 in New Realities *magazine for which he is a contributing editor.*

Meditation is a time-honored technique—probably humanity's oldest spiritual discipline—for helping people to release their potential for expanded consciousness and fuller living. As a technique for assisting in the enlightenment process of knowing self, ultimate reality, or God, it appears in some form in nearly every major religious tradition. The entranced yogi in a lotus posture, the Zen Buddhist sitting in zazen, the Christian contemplative kneeling in adoration of Jesus, the Sufi dervish whirling in an ecstasy-inducing trance: all can be properly described as practicing meditation. Meditation's core experience is an altered state of consciousness in which our ordinary sense of "I"— the ego—is diminished, while a larger sense of self-existence-merged-with-the cosmos comes into awareness.

Meditation works on all levels, however—physical, psychological, social. It improves general health and stamina, it decreases tension, anxiety and aggressiveness, it increases self-control and self-knowledge. Drug use and abuse are usually curbed, and sometimes even stopped. Psychotherapy progresses faster than usual. Personal and family relations seem to improve. Meditators say that it changes their lives. And except for borderline psychotics (who may be precipitated into full psychosis), it is safe, harmless, easy to learn, beautifully portable, available in endless supply, and legal. Edgar Cayce described meditation as an emptying "of all that hinders the creative forces from rising along the natural channels of the physical man to be disseminated through those centers and sources that create the activities of the physical, the mental, the spiritual man; properly done [this] must make one stronger mentally, physically . . ."

In the more advanced stages of meditation, mental and physical stillness is complete. The meditator is totally absorbed in a blissful state of awareness having no particular object. His consciousness is without any thoughts or other contents; he is simply conscious of consciousness. In yoga, this emptiness of consciousness without loss of consciousness is called *samadhi*. In Zen, it is called *satori*. In the West it is best known as cosmic consciousness or enlightenment. And there is a paradox in this. In this emptiness comes a fullness— unity with divinity, knowledge of man's true nature and, to use a phrase from St. Paul, "the peace that passeth understanding."

Anagarika Govinda, a German who became a Tibetan Buddhist Lama, says that meditation is "the means to reconnect the individual with the whole—i.e., to make the individual conscious of his universal origin. This is the only positive way to overcome the ego-complex, the illusion of separateness, which no amount of preaching and moral exhortation will achieve. To give up the smaller for the bigger is not felt as a sacrifice but as a joyous release from oppression and narrowness. The 'selflessness' resulting from this experience is not due to moral considerations or pressures, but a natural attitude, free from the feeling of moral superiority; and the compassion which flows from it is the natural expression of solidarity with all forms of sentient life."

Definitions and Techniques   That experience of peace and unity is difficult to attain, however, because the mind is always wandering. Meditation might be described as a technique for developing attention control so that worry, fear, anger, and all the other thoughts and feelings and concerns that seem constantly to hassle people are dealt with in a firm but calm matter. The dictionary definition of meditation, based on Western psychology, is inadequate to describe this experience. "To contemplate" or "to ponder" is not synonymous with meditation as a spiritual practice. And even a "a form of private devotion consisting of deep, continued reflection on some religious theme" is not completely adequate to explain meditation.

In physiological terms, meditation appears to induce a fourth major state of consciousness. It is neither waking, sleeping, nor dreaming, but rather what has been described as a "wakeful hypo-metabolic condition." Brainwaves, heartbeat rate, blood pressure, respiration, galvanic skin resistance and many other body functions are altered in meditation. They slow to the point achieved in deep sleep, and sometimes beyond, yet the meditator remains awake and emerges from meditation with a feeling of rest and loss of stress or tension. All this certainly is not included in the dictionary definition of meditation.

The common core of all meditation experiences is an altered state of consciousness that leads to a diminishing (and hopefully to a total abolition) of ego, the self-centered sense of "I." This core-experience has been called "relaxed attention," "non-anxious attention," "detached alertness," "passive volition."

To attain this state, many forms and techniques of meditation have been developed. Some are passive, for example, when a yogi sits cross-legged in a lotus asana with so little motion that even his breathing is hard to detect. Other forms of meditation, such as *t'ai chi*, involved graceful body movements. Sometimes the eyes are open; sometimes they are closed. Sometimes other sense organs than the eyes are emphasized, as when beginners in Zen pay attention to their nasal breathing. In other traditions, however, sensory withdrawal is dominant; attention is taken away from the senses. Some meditative techniques are silent; some are vocal. Transcendental Meditation is an example of the silent form while the Krishna Consciousness Society uses the "Hare Krishna" chant (which means "Hail, Lord Krishna"). They chant that together with music and dancing. Some meditations are private and some—such as a Quaker meeting—

are public. And although most forms of meditation are self-directed, sometimes they are guided by a group leader.

Silent Forms of Meditation   So there is a wide range of approaches. The silent forms center on three techniques: concentration, contemplation and the mental repetition of a sound. The sound may be a single syllable such as "Om." It may be a word, phrase or verse from a holy text. The Tibetan Buddhist "Om mani padme hum" is an example. So is the simple prayer in the book called *The Way of A Pilgrim* which goes, "Lord Jesus Christ, have mercy on me." Many Christians use the Lord's Prayer as a basis for meditation. The Indian sage Darshan Singh teaches his followers to silently repeat five names of God that he gives them in a formal initiation. In a similar fashion, Maharishi Mahesh Yogi, head of the Transcendental Meditation movement, initiates people into TM with various Sanskrit sounds called *mantras,* which are said to be appropriate for their mental characteristics; the meditator silently repeats the mantra during his meditations. Zen Buddhism has a variety of meditative techniques, some of which involve use of a *koan,* that is, an apparently insoluble riddle which the meditator mentally examines. A widely-known koan asks, "What is the sound of one hand clapping?" Another inquires more directly about the basic nature of self-identity: "Who am I?"

In contemplative forms of meditation, the eyes are open so that the meditator sees what is called a *yantra,* a form on which he centers his attention. The focus of attention may be a religious object such as a crucifix, statue or picture. It might be an inscription, a candle flame, a flower. They all serve the purpose. Or the meditator may use a *mandala,* a painting or a drawing, typically a square-in-a-circle design of many colors, which symbolizes the unity of microcosm and macrocosm.

Concentration is generally considered the most difficult form of meditation. In concentration techniques, an image is visualized steadily in the mind. It could be the thousand-petal lotus of the Hindu and Buddhist traditions or it could be the crescent moon of Islam; it could be Judaism's Star of David or it could be the Christian mystic rose. Alternatively, the mind may be held free of all imagery and "mental chatter"—a clearing away of all thought. Or the attention might be focused at some part of the body. For example, the mystical "third eye" at a point midway between the eyebrows is often used. This is said to coincide with the pineal gland. Also common is the so-called concentration on your navel. This phrase is actually a misunderstanding of the process of directing attention to the abdominal area about two inches below the navel and simply becoming one with your breathing. The meditator flows into awareness of the rhythmical, cyclical body process by which life is sustained and united with the universe.

Some disciplines combine different aspects of several meditative techniques. For example, in its advanced stages karate and other martial arts such as akido use meditation in their training regimen. The Russian mystic Gurdjieff taught his students to combine movements and meditation. Dr. Ira Progoff of Dialogue House in New York City guides people through therapeutic sessions using a technique he developed called *process meditation*. It is usually performed in a group, and he speaks in order to guide the meditators into exploration of whatever imagery appears in their minds.

So meditation cannot be defined in a sentence or two. The term means many things to many people, varying in this or that aspect, depending upon culture, religious traditions, psychological orientation, the individual's purpose, and other factors.

Meditation Research   In meditation, it is not really the definition but the experience that matters. Toward that end, it has become the object of scientific study. Why should science examine a spiritual phenomenon? Because of the traditions associated with meditation: the development of incredible self-control over physiological functions, spontaneous and willed productions of psychic phenomena, and the ability to enter unusual states of consciousness in a voluntary manner.

In the 1950s, researchers in India began to bring yogis into the laboratory to record their brainwaves, heartbeat, and respiration. Likewise, in Japan, Zen monks were allowing themselves to be instrumentally monitored. As science and religion converged, a growing body of literature began to attract attention among physiological psychologists and biofeedback researchers.

In the 1960s, Maharishi Mahesh Yogi brought Transcendental Meditation to the West in a secular manner and encouraged scientific examination of his claims. A graduate student named R. Keith Wallace earned his Ph.D. in psychology by studying the physiological effects of Transcendental Meditation and proposing that the meditative state was a fourth major state of consciousness—neither sleeping, dreaming, nor waking. Wallace's startling results were published in prestigious scientific journals, including *Science* (March 27, 1970) and *Scientific American* (February 1972), the latter article being co-authored by Dr. Herbert Benson of Harvard Medical School.

With these publications the topic burst upon the scientific community. Sophisticated instruments such as strain gauges for measuring breathing, the electroencephalograph (EEG) for measuring brainwaves, the electrocardiograph (EKG) for measuring heart activity, and the electromyograph (EMG) for measuring muscle tension were used to produce reams of data—data that promised new approaches to physical and mental health. In addition, the American Psychiatric Association established a task force on meditation research.

Suddenly, ancient wisdom became respectable. Three meditative traditions received most of the attention: yoga, Zen, and Transcendental Meditation. TM is derived from the yogic tradition, but has been widely enough researched in its own right to give it separate treatment here.

Yoga   The data on yogic meditation began when scientists investigated claims that yogis acquired remarkable physical powers, such as the ability to suspend breathing or stop the heart. However, these are matters outside the scientific study of meditation per se.

The physiological data on yogic meditation is somewhat confusing, taken as a whole. For instance, in the 1950s the French researchers N. Das and H. Gastaut studied seven subjects, who were fully concentrated in meditation, and reported "definite acceleration" of heart and brain rhythms. Other investigators, however, have recorded more alpha brainwave activity (a slower brainwave than the beta brainwave characteristic of normal waking consciousness) in subjects during yogic meditation than during control resting periods. Possibly Das and Gastaut's subjects were practicing a form of meditation qualitatively different from other yoga meditators.

Other physiological changes that have been noted during yogic meditation include slower heart rate, slower respiration and lower skin conductance of an electrical current. All these changes indicate that the subjects were more relaxed while meditating than while resting normally. In addition, the alpha blocking response is not observed in yoga meditators. In normal subjects, any startling stimulus will change a relaxed alpha brainwave pattern into more aroused beta activity, blocking alpha activity. However, a variety of stimuli failed to produce such a response in yoga meditators, and they later reported no awareness of the stimuli presented, which included flashes of light, loud noises and even the touch of a hot glass tube.

The effect of yogic meditation on ESP scoring was explored by Hamlyn Dukhan and K. Ramakrishna Rao of Andhra University in India, using Western students of yoga at various ashrams in that country. Their pilot study and two confirming studies support the hypothesis that meditation facilitates high ESP scoring. This is to be expected if one accepts the traditional viewpoint of yoga training, which says that psychic development is likely in the course of one's practice. The high scoring subjects were people "who had already attained some experience in yoga and a fair level of yogic development." (It should be noted, however, that yogic tradition—in fact, all major spiritual traditions—lays a strong injunction against deliberate pursuit of psychic powers because they are said to be obstacles or byroads from the main avenue—namely, attaining yoga or union with the divine.)

Zen   The physiological data on Zen is generally similar to that on yoga. The Japanese researchers Akira Kasamatsu and Tomio Hirai reported that EEG recordings of subjects doing zazen show the rapid appearance of alpha waves, which may slow into trains of theta waves (normally seen only in sleeping subjects). Other physiological changes recorded in Zen meditators paralleling those in yoga meditators include slowed heart rate and respiration, and decreased oxygen consumption. However, unlike yoga meditators, who show no alpha blocking, practitioners of zazen showed consistent alpha blocking to stimuli presented twenty times; no habituation was observed.

As Charles Tart has pointed out in his anthology *Altered States of Consciousness,* this difference is consistent with the essential philosophic differences between yoga and Zen. Yogic meditators try to attend to one focus until all outer and inner distractions fall away; this sensory withdrawal is in keeping with their renunciation of worldly attachments. Zen meditators seek to remain aware of each "here and now" moment without getting carried away into intellectual thoughts or conceptualizations about it. Thus the experienced Zen meditator consistently shows alpha blocking for three to five seconds after a stimulus is presented and then returns to predominant alpha production, as if each stimulus presented were new, while the yoga meditator shows no awareness of the stimulus at all.

In addition to the physiological testing, a few psychological studies have been done on Zen meditators. Kasamatsu and Hirai noted no remarkable differences in Rorschach test scores between Zen practitioners and ordinary people. On the other hand, Edward Maupin, formerly in charge of the resident program at Esalen Institute reported interesting psychological effects on twenty-eight subjects who were taught a Zen breath-concentration technique; their subjective response to the exercise was compared with test results related to attention, tolerance for unrealistic experience, and capacity for what psychoanalysts call "regression in the service of the ego." Capacity for regression and tolerance for unrealistic experience turned out to be significant for predicting a person's response to meditation, while attention measurements were not. A third study, done by Terry V. Lesh at University of Lethbridge in Canada, supported these results from Maupin's work and also showed that the practice of zazen helped counselors develop their empathy so that they could relate to patients better.

Transcendental Meditation   What does meditation research tell us about TM? Wallace's study, done at UCLA used twenty-seven adult subjects who had been practicing TM from one week to nine years, with an average of about two-and-a-half years. Wallace found that "During meditation oxygen consumption, carbon dioxide elimination, cardiac output, heart rate and respiration rate significantly decreased, and skin resistance significantly increased . . ." His major finding, moreover, was a marked decrease in blood lactate, which indicates rest, relaxation, and rejuvenation.

Other studies have confirmed these results. Typical EEG changes during TM include predominant alpha production alternating with low voltage theta waves. In addition, Wallace noted that in most of his subjects, alpha blocking caused by repeated sound or light stimuli showed no habituation.

Several psychological studies have been carried out with practitioners of TM. Robert Shaw and David Kolb at the University of Texas found that twenty minutes of TM improved reaction times of meditators over their premeditation times; nonmeditators did worse after twenty minutes of rest. This suggests that the restful meditation state may improve alertness as well as some motor abilities, while ordinary rest may leave one unalert for some time.

Other investigators have been studying long-term behavioral and personality changes in groups of meditators and control groups. These also indicate that TM seems beneficial. David W. Orme-Johnson of Maharishi International University in Fairfield, Iowa, found that regular practice of TM produces rapid galvanic skin response (GSR) habituation and low levels of spontaneous GSR. These measurements are often found to be correlated with physiological and behavioral characteristics associated with good mental health. William Seeman, Sanford Nidich, and Thomas Banta found that TM practitioners scored significantly higher in six of twelve indices on a test of "self-actualiza-tion" than they had before learning TM, whereas the nonmeditator control group scored about the same as they had before.

Another investigation, done by Maynard Shelley at University of Kansas indicated that TM practitioners are generally happier and more relaxed than nonmeditators. In addition to behavioral changes, several recent studies claim that students practicing TM increase their grades significantly over nonmedi-tating students, and perhaps even increase their IQ.

However, not all claims about TM are positive. A study once done at Stan-ford Research Institute International by Leon Otis warned about the possible dangers of TM. Otis feels that TM is a self-paced form of psychological desen-sitization that may be inappropriate for some people—specifically, for those who aren't able to sufficiently control the release of massive anxiety without supervision. Three people practicing TM in his experiment dropped out be-cause "of the recurrence of serious psychosomatic symptoms previously under control." He cautioned that meditation teachers ought to screen out such people from instruction.

An even more far-reaching criticism of TM came from Jonathan Smith of the Illinois State Psychiatric Institute in Chicago. His doctoral work involved a year-long study of 170 people either practicing TM or acting as a control by fol-lowing a placebo-like treatment involving sitting down twice daily with eyes closed in simulation of TM while actively generating as much thought activity as possible. Smith found that TM is psychotherapeutic for highly anxious peo-ple, but no more so than the control treatment. He concludes that TM's thera-peutic value is not due to the meditation but rather to the daily sitting and to the expectation of relief.

The Goal of Meditation   Smith observes in a private correspondence that rel-atively healthy and non-anxious people might find TM more rewarding than simply sitting or thinking positive thoughts. This is highly probable. Histori-cally, the goal of meditation has been a transformation of the whole person. Research data dramatically validates many of the claims that meditators make. Traditionally, these behavioral changes are reinforced through voluntary con-formity with the meditative ethos and lifestyle—an aspect still unresearched by science. Throughout history, teachers of meditation, and spiritual masters have emphasized "right living" to support one's meditation. By that they mean a healthy diet; an honest means of income; association with virtuous and sympathetic people; truthful speech; kindness and humility in relations with others; a social conscience; giving up egotistical desire for power, fame, prestige, wealth, and so forth.

As psychiatrist Arthur Deikman points out, "Probably the importance of meditation lies in its changing a person's orientation towards living, not in its ability to produce dramatic changes in states of consciousness. It's fairly easy for a normal person to have 'unnormal' experiences, but people meditating without the supporting philosophy are less likely to be involved long enough for some of the subtle changes to occur or to change their orientation from doing to allowing things to happen spontaneously."

This does not mean, however, that successful meditation requires extreme asceticism and withdrawal from society. The true aim of meditation is to bring the meditator more fully into the world, not retreat from it. A religious retreat may be appropriate for some in the course of their meditative training and discipline. This is an honorable tradition—the way of the anchorite, monk, and religious devotee.

Here it is important to note that meditation does not require sacrifice or abandonment of the intellect. It is true that in meditation the intellect's limitations become apparent, and other (usually unsuspected) modes of creative problem-solving and insight emerge. However, enlightened teachers have always been recognized as brilliant people with finely-honed intellectual powers who have enhanced their meditation "research" through scholarly studies that cultivate the mind. Their writings and discourses display clear logic, a keen analytical discrimination and a knowledge of tradition. It is no accident, then, that students frequently report improvement in their grades and ability to study after beginning meditation.

The best that can happen through meditation is enlightenment. Spiritual masters of all ages have been unanimous in declaring that through meditation, people can come to know God.

Through direct experience—not through bookish learning or intellectual conceptualization—people can reach a state of conscious union with ultimate reality and the divine dimension of the universe. In that state, all the long-sought answers to life's basic questions are given, along with peace of mind and heart. There are other paths to God-knowledge, of course, but this is one path easily available to many and the chief reason for the worldwide interest and enduring value placed on meditation. It is a tool for learning spiritual psychology, a technique for expanding consciousness.

The highest development in meditation, regardless of the "school" or "path," brings technique and daily life together. When learning and living are integrated in spontaneous practice, the meditator becomes what has been called "meditation in action." Meditation is no longer just a tool or device, no longer just a "visit" to the fourth major state of consciousness. All four states are integrated in a manner of living that is best described as the fifth major state of consciousness. The meditator has so completely mastered the lessons of meditation that his entire life is a demonstration of the higher consciousness which can be experienced if sincerely sought.

People such as this have always been recognized through the ages as special persons for whom attention and reverence is proper. In them the alteration of consciousness called meditation had led to a transformation of consciousness. Changing consciousness changes thought, changing thought changes behavior, and changing behavior changes society. Thus the changed ones live as examples to others who are on their way to transformation of self and world.

DISCUSSION QUESTIONS

1. Have you ever tried meditation? What has been your experience?
2. As a result of reading White's essay, are you persuaded to try meditation? Why or why not?
3. Why do you think that meditation seems to transform the whole person including even improvement in school grades and the ability to study?
4. If meditation produces all of the benefits that White describes, why do you think it is not being taught more in the schools in the United States?

SUGGESTIONS FOR JOURNAL ENTRIES

1. Try the following meditation exercise for a minimum of fifteen minutes twice a day for a couple of days and write about your experience. Find a comfortable sitting position (preferably sitting with the back straight) in a quiet place; select an object to concentrate on, like a word (mantra) or symbol or image but keep your eyes closed; empty your mind of all thoughts.
2. Interview someone (preferably someone you know) who meditates and write a report of how meditation has affected their life.

READING 44

Nothing Real Is Impossible

Gerald Jampolsky

This excerpt from Teach Only Love *(1984) describes a college senior's struggle with congenital blindness and the eventual regaining of her eyesight through beginning to think of herself as a seeing person. Jampolsky, Stanford University '47, is a California psychiatrist who specializes in working with children and adolescents with catastrophic illness.*

This concept was life changing for Colleen Mulvihill, a twenty-three-year-old woman who was a senior working toward a Movement Education degree at a liberal arts college in northern California. Colleen was pretty enough to model, and she sometimes did. When I first met her, she also had two, year-round, part-time jobs, one as a sports medicine coordinator in her college athletic department and the other as a tutor in the school's developmental movement laboratory where children with neurological and academic handicaps are helped to develop motor skills. During the summer months, she had assumed an additional job of teaching swimming and crafts at a nearby day camp. Colleen lived in a small apartment five hundred miles away from her family, and her best friend was a German shepherd named Sasha, a Seeing Eye dog.

When she first came to me, Colleen was legally blind. (The term applies to those whose sight is so limited that they cannot function as sighted, although they might have a small amount of close vision.) From birth, she has had a condition known as rentrolental fibroplasia, which is a progressive accumulation of scar tissue behind the retina which may eventually cause blindness or at least severely limited vision.

When she was born, it was standard medical practice to put premature infants into high-pressure oxygen tanks. Later in life she was told that it was such a procedure that had caused her blindness. Possibly you can imagine the rage and resentment a person with this condition might have against the world. Colleen indeed had such feelings as well as a great deal of pain that is often associated with this type of disease.

She was born and raised in the Los Angeles area by parents who saw value in her attending regular public school instead of special schools for the handicapped. They reasoned that this would better prepare her for the real world. It was obviously a good decision for Colleen, although there is, of course, no right or wrong procedure that can be applied to all cases involving handicapped children. With the understanding assistance of teachers who always seated her in the front of the room and gave her additional auditory and visual cues, she graduated from both elementary and high school and then decided on a small college away from home.

This intelligent and highly spirited girl found her situation more difficult as her limited vision continued to fade. In 1975, Sasha, a two-year-old Seeing

Eye dog, came into Colleen's life. She and Sasha trained together in North Hollywood and have been inseparable companions ever since. Sasha accompanied her to college classes and even to the State Capitol in Sacramento where Colleen was an active lobbyist for the National Federation of the Blind.

Several years ago, Colleen became aware that many people were discussing supplements to traditional medical procedures and she began to hear evidence that the mind can affect the body. It was shortly after this that she began to visit me. I introduced her to *A Course in Miracles.*

Later, I referred her to the adult attitudinal healing group at our Center. I emphasized to her that the mind knows no boundaries and that nothing is impossible. I told her to let go of every negative value she ever had, and not to limit herself to her past beliefs or confine herself to a reality that came to her only through her physical senses.

We talked about the very important concept from *A Course in Miracles:*

There is no order of difficulty in miracles.

Miracles can be defined as shifts in perception which remove the blocks to our awareness of love's presence. Therefore, they can be seen as a natural occurrence. Although miracles are not physical phenomena, changes at the physical level may sometimes accompany them. I shared with Colleen my conviction that anyone can learn to shift his perception and see the presence of love and that is true sight.

One day, Colleen asked a question that was very important to her. "Is it possible for me to regain my sight?" I replied, "Anything is possible. You do not *have* to be a negative statistic on a probability curve of people with retrolental fibroplasia."

She began to grasp the idea that the thoughts we put into our minds determine our perceptions. She began to work on "positive mental pictures," and to activate the principles in *A Course in Miracles.* Practicing peace of mind, peace of God, became her single goal; practicing forgiveness her single function; and listening to, and being directed by, her inner voice became her way of experiencing a sense of completion and oneness. She began to forgive God and the universe for her blindness. Her bitterness dissolved and was replaced by an increasing sense of peace. As this happened, her head and neck pains began to ease.

Gradually, a subtle but quite real change began to take place in the way Colleen pictured herself. She told me later, "It was as though my attitude about myself began to shift. Where I had always treated myself as a blind person, I now began to think of myself as normal." Even so, Colleen was totally unprepared for the partial recovery that happened in March 1978. Her daytime vision improved enough so that she could see where she was going, and her ophthalmologist informed her that she was now legally sighted during the daytime although she remained legally blind at night. When I talked to him on the phone, he stated that he had never seen a person with Colleen's condition make this kind of visual improvement.

Her increasing ability to see brought a new set of problems involving Sasha. "It is very traumatic," Colleen explained, "for a guide dog to find she is not essential for the totality of her master's mobility." But that problem, too, was gradually solved as she and Sasha worked together for a new understanding of each other's needs.

Colleen continued in school to prepare herself to be of service to others who are ill. She is primarily interested in the holistic health approach in which one attempts to assist the whole person rather than to treat only sick organs. She has helped many people at our Center and in other cities and has been active in our telephone network, working with blind people on the phone throughout the United States.

Recently, Colleen called me. "Jerry," she said. "I want to take you for a drive." "What do you mean?" I said. "I am now licensed to drive a car in two different states and legally sighted for both day and night." I want you to know, my drive with Colleen Mulvihill was the happiest time I have ever had in a car, even though I cried.

There are many times I forget some of the principles I have mentioned in this book and I end up depressed. When I see Colleen and experience her unconditional love, I am aware that she also sees the light in me, and this helps me let go of feelings of darkness by reminding me of my true reality. To me, Colleen brings to life Jesus' statement as it appears in a modern translation: "I have come into the world to give sight to those who are spiritually blind, and to show those who think that they see that they are blind."

Judgment is blind. Only love sees.

DISCUSSION QUESTIONS

1. What do you think of the idea that "the mind can affect the body"?
2. Would you describe what happened to Colleen as a "miracle"? Why or why not?
3. Have you ever had an experience like Colleen's or know someone who did?
4. How do you feel about children like Colleen attending regular schools rather than special schools for the handicapped? What is the attitude toward handicapped persons on your campus?

SUGGESTIONS FOR JOURNAL ENTRIES

1. Write about what you consider a "miracle" in your own life or the life of someone close to you.
2. Interview a handicapped person on their experience of being handicapped in this culture and write a report on what you discover.

READING 45

Letter to a Young Poet

Rainer Maria Rilke

Rainer Marie Rilke (1875–1926) was a German lyric poet who deserted the military for art and became involved in mysticism. Seeing the poet as the mediator between God and man, the following is a letter written to a "young poet" in 1903 on the critical importance of inner reflection for the writing of poetry and a rich life.

Paris, February 17th, 1903

My Dear Sir,

Your letter only reached me a few days ago. I want to thank you for its great and kind confidence. I can hardly do more. I cannot go into the nature of your verses; for all critical intention is too far from me. With nothing can one touch a work of art so little as with critical words: they always come down to more or less lucky misunderstandings. Things are not all so comprehensible and expressible as one would mostly have us believe; most events are inexpressible, take place in a realm which no word has ever entered, and most inexpressible than all else are works of art, mysterious existences, the life of which, while ours passes away, endures.

After these prefatory remarks, let me only tell you further that your verses have no individual style, although they do show a quiet and hidden incipience of the personal. I feel this most clearly in the last poem "My Soul." There something of your own wants to come through to expression. And in the lovely poem "To Leopardi" there does perhaps grow up a sort of kinship with that great solitary man. Nevertheless the poems are not yet anything on their own account, nothing independent, even the last and the one to Leopardi. Your kind letter, which accompanied them, does not fail to make clear to me various shortcomings which I felt in reading your verses without at the time being able particularly to name them.

You ask whether your verses are good. You ask me. You have asked others before. You send them to magazines. You compare them with other poems, and you are disturbed when certain editors reject your efforts. Now (since you have allowed me to advise you) I beg you to give up all that. You are looking outward, and that above all you should not now do. Nobody can counsel and help you, nobody. There is only one single way. Go into yourself. Investigate the reason that bids you write; find out whether it is spreading out its roots in the deepest places of your heart, acknowledge to yourself whether you would have to die if it were denied you to write. This above all: ask yourself in the stillest hour of your night: *must* I write? Delve into yourself for a deep answer. And if this should be affirmative, if you may meet this earnest question with a strong and simple *"I must,"* then build your life according to this necessity; your life even into its most indifferent and slightest hour must be a sign of this urge and a testimony to it. Then draw near to Nature. Then try, as a first human being, to say what you see and experience and love and lose. Do not write love-poems; avoid at first those forms that are too hackneyed and commonplace: they are the most difficult, for it takes a great, fully matured power to give something of your own where good and even excellent traditions come to mind in quantity. Therefore save yourself from these general themes and seek those which your own everyday life offers you; describe your sorrows and desires, passing thoughts and the belief in some sort of beauty—describe all these with loving, quiet, humble sincerity and use, to express yourself, the things in your environment, the pictures from your dreams, and the subjects of your memory. If your daily life seems poor, do not blame it; blame yourself, tell yourself that you are not poet enough to call forth its riches; for to the creator there is no poverty and no poor indifferent place. And even if you were in some prison the walls of which let none of the sounds of the world come to your senses—would you not then still have your childhood, that precious, kingly possession, that treasure-house of memories? Turn your attention thither. Try to bring up the sunken sensations of that far past; your personality will grow more firm, your solitude will widen and will become a dusky dwelling by which the noise of others passes far away. And if out of this turning inward, out of this sinking into your own world verses come, then it will not occur to you to ask any one whether they are good verses. Nor will you try to interest magazines in your poems: for you will see in them your fond natural possession, a fragment and a voice of your life. A work of art is good if it has sprung from necessity. In this nature of its origin lies its judgment: there is no other. Therefore, my dear sir, I have known no advice for you save this: to go into yourself and test the deeps in which your life takes rise; at its source you will find the answer to the question whether you *must* create. Accept it, just as it sounds, without trying to interpret it. Perhaps it will turn out that you are called to be an artist. Then take that destiny upon yourself and bear it, its burden and its greatness, without ever asking what recompense might come from outside. For the creator must be a world for himself and find everything in himself and in Nature with whom he has allied himself.

But perhaps after this descent into yourself and into your inner solitude you will have to give up becoming a poet (it is enough, as I have said, to feel that one could live without writing: then one should not be allowed to do it at all). But even then this inward searching which I ask of you will not have been in vain. Your life will in any case find its own ways thence, and that they may be good, rich and wide I wish you more than I can say.

What more shall I say to you? Everything seems to me to have its just emphasis; and after all I do only want to advise you to keep growing quietly and seriously throughout your development; you cannot disturb it more rudely than by looking outward and expecting from outside replies to questions that only your inmost feeling in your quietest hours can perhaps answer.

It was a pleasure to me to find in your letter the name of Professor Horaček; I keep for that lovable and learned man a great veneration and a gratitude that endures through the years. Will you, please, tell him how I feel; it is very good of him still to think of me, and I know how to appreciate it.

The verses which you kindly entrusted to me I am returning at the same time. And I thank you once more for your great and sincere confidence, of which I have tried, through this honest answer given to the best of my knowledge, to make myself a little worthier than, as a stranger, I really am.

Yours faithfully and with all sympathy:

Rainer Maria Rilke

DISCUSSION QUESTIONS

1. What does Rilke mean when he says that "most events are inexpressible"? Do you agree or disagree?
2. Do you agree that "a work of art is good if it has sprung from necessity"? What does that mean?
3. Rilke says that if our "daily life seems poor, do not blame it; blame yourself, tell yourself that you are not poet enough to call forth its riches." What is the implication of this statement? Do you agree?
4. What does it mean to be "called" to be an artist.

SUGGESTIONS FOR JOURNAL ENTRIES

1. Write a poem in which you "say what you see and experience and love and lose."
2. Write how you would feel if this letter had been sent to you.

Closure

Closure is a concept in Gestalt psychology referring to the release of tension experienced when a problem or task is completed or "closed," and wholeness is established. Hopefully that is what you will experience at the end of your first year of college. Chances are you are reading this text in the first semester of your first year of college and therefore this section will be a bit premature. Thus, you will have to take the ideas and sentiments expressed in these last two readings on faith. For example, the last reading is a letter that I sent to my daughter at the end of her freshman year, in which I wrote, "You may not believe it, Sweetheart, but you have just finished the most difficult year of college."

The first reading is a student's essay, "Exile and Return," in which James Keller describes his poignant experience of visiting his old high school during the summer after his first year of college and discovering that "the life and laughter (had) died." The message here is that you are undergoing radical change and you probably won't realize it until someone like a parent tells you or you have an experience like Keller, reaffirming the truth of the title of Thomas Wolfe's novel, *You Can't Go Home Again.*

READING 46

Exile and Return

James Keller

James Keller was managing editor of the student newspaper at Middlesex County College when he wrote this essay about revisiting his high school during the summer after his first year of college in 1994.

It's all different, quiet and grey now, like the sun reflecting on the previous night's darkness or predicting the afternoon's storm. On this stifling summer morning, I scarcely recognize the school I had attended for four years. The life and laughter have died. It is another world.

I walk down the vacant halls, and what light there is shines a path on the mirrored beige floors, leading me past imposing grey lockers that stand erect in columns. At one time, they woke the dead in closing but now remain closed in silence. I remember the faces of people who stood and sometimes slumped before them at day's end. They were friendly faces that looked up and nodded or said "Hello" as I galloped past. Now there are other faces, faces of people I never got to know.

The lockers soon give way to the classrooms, cement cells we once lived in, learned in, and often slept in. Steel I-beams I had once hardly noticed now hang like doom over cracked and peeling walls. The architect left them exposed, for want of talent, I assume. From the color scheme of putrid green to the neutral asbestos ceiling and steel rafters, the banality of the classrooms overwhelms me.

The rooms are empty now save the ancient desks. They are yellow clay and steel and much smaller than I remember. I can still read arcane graffiti, its meaning forgotten, on their dull surfaces. The handwriting is my own. I recognize the doodles drawn as every minute ran past like a turtle climbing up a glass wall. Back then, they killed the time. They didn't do much for the furniture either.

Eventually my eyes come to rest on the chalkboards. Old habits die hard. I remember staring at them through teachers whose words "had forked no lightning." My teachers and classmates are gone, but many faces remain. From seats in front and to my side, they turn and stare. They are shadows of the past, bloodless visions, returned from long exile to mock my exile and return. They're looking for me and through me. But they're only memories. They've left, you know—some gone to school, some gone to the world, others gone to their own private hells. Faces that laughed, young and innocent, now cry, worn and haggard. Their expressions hide lives that were true and alive but now are neither.

Out of the building, I walked on grassy playing fields where so many of us found brief insignificant glory. They were greener in another spring. The empty stands play sentinel to the lonely track and football field, and a thousand ghosts applaud a hundred athletes only I can see. I no longer remember who won and lost, only that somehow we all walked away winners and losers to the same heart, veterans of so much happiness and so much pain. It is more than I can bear.

7   I leave now, maybe forever. I wonder if I ever existed and was ever here at all. To say good-by is to die a little. And so I do.

DISCUSSION QUESTIONS

1. Do you think Keller's experience would have been different had the school still been in session? If so, what does that tell you about school?
2. Do you think Keller will feel the same way about his college a year or more after graduation? Why or why not?
3. How would you characterize your high school experience in contrast to Keller's?
4. What do you think Keller means by his image of "teachers whose words 'had forked no lightning'"? Do you recognize the quote?

SUGGESTIONS FOR JOURNAL ENTRIES

1. Visit your high school alma mater and write about your visit.
2. Write about the differences you have perceived so far between your high school teachers and your college professors.

READING 47

The First Year's the Hardest

John D. Lawry

This letter written to my daughter in 1986 and excerpted from May You Never Stop Dancing *(1998) describes a father/professor's congratulations to his daughter on her successful navigation of the perils of the first year away from home at college.*

Dear Lili,

I can't believe the year is almost over. In a few short weeks you will no longer be a freshman but a veteran sophomore. During the remaining three years, it will never be the same as your freshman year. As you yourself said on the phone the other night with a tinge of anxiety, "Dad, I won't be one of the 'new girls' on campus next year." Yes, by now you have learned the ropes, and you are a familiar face on campus. You have become a bona fide member of the student community. You have "paid your dues." Thank God that doesn't include hazing anymore. (In case you are not familiar with the term, "hazing" refers to a practice popular in the 50s and early 60s that *Webster's* dictionary defines as, "to harass with abusive or ridiculous tricks, usually directed toward freshmen as a kind of initiation rite." It has been largely stamped out because of its tendency toward violent and inflammatory behavior and speech.)

Though you may not feel it, you have grown up quite a bit during this academic year. I know this growth has not always been easy. But the scars should disappear with time. You haven't made straight As, but your grades are more than respectable. You definitely belong where you are, in a so-called competitive school. You have shown that you can compete with your classmates and that the admissions office did not make a mistake when it accepted your application.

You may not believe it, Sweetheart, but you have just finished the most difficult year of college. I repeat what I said to you on the phone the other night. I am very proud of you.

Love,
Dad

DISCUSSION QUESTIONS

1. Have the adjustments required of your first year of college so far been more or less difficult than you expected? Explain.
2. From your vantage point, do you think that the first year will be the hardest?
3. Have you experienced any discrimination at all as a first-year student since coming to campus?

QUESTIONS FOR JOURNAL ENTRIES

1. Write about what the transition is like from being a high school senior to first-year college student.
2. Since this letter was originally written in 1986, the word "freshman" was current rather than "first-year student." Write about the different connotations the two words have for you and how you feel about which word is more common on your campus.

Acknowledgments

Bly, Robert. Text excerpt from *A Little Book on the Human Shadow* by Robert Bly. Copyright © 1988 by Robert Bly. Reprinted by permission of HarperCollins Publishers, Inc.

Darling, Lynn. "Sleeping with the Enemy" by Lynn Darling. Copyright © 1992 by Lynn Darling. Reprinted by permission of Sterling Lord Literistic, Inc.

Daum, Meghan. "Virtual Love" by Meghan Daum as appeared in *The New Yorker*, Aug 25 & Sept 1, 1997. Copyright © 1997 by Meghan Daum. Permission granted by International Creative Management.

Didion, Joan. "Why I Write" by Joan Didion first appeared in the *New York Times Book Review*. Copyright 1976 by Joan Didion. Reprinted by permission of Janklow and Nesbitt Associates.

Dubus, Andre. From *Adultery & Other Choices* by Andre Dubus. Reprinted by permission of David R. Godine Publishers Inc. Copyright © 1977 by Andre Dubus.

Franco Elvira M. "A Magic Circle of Adult Students" by Elvira M. Franco from *The New York Times*, January 28, 1990. Reprinted by permission of the author.

Gibbs, Nancy. "When Is It Rape?" by Nancy Gibbs from *Time*, June 3, 1991. © 1991 Time Inc. Reprinted by permission.

Goodman, Ellen. "Training for Real Life" by Ellen Goodman. Copyright 1987 The Boston Globe Newspaper Company/Washington Post Writers Group. Reprinted by permission.

Gregory, Dick. "Shame" Copyright © 1964 by Dick Gregory Enterprises, Inc., from *Nigger: An Autobiography* by Dick Gregory. Used by permission of Dutton Signet, a division of Penguin Books USA Inc.

Houston, Jean. Reprinted by permission of Jeremy P. Tarcher, Inc. a division of The Putnam Publishing Group from *The Possible Human* by Jean Houston. Copyright © 1982 by Jean Houston.

Hughes, Langston. From *Collected Poems* by Langston Hughes. Copyright © 1994 by the Estate of Langston Hughes. Reprinted by permission of Alfred A. Knopf Inc.

Jampolsky M.D., Gerald G., and Claire Huff. From *Teach Only Love* by Gerald G. Jampolsky, M.D. and Claire Huff. Copyright © 1983 by Gerald G. Jampolsky, M.D. Used by permission of Bantam Books, a division of Bantam Doubleday Dell Publishing Group, Inc.

Kantor, Michael. "Confessions of a Lonely TA" by Michael Kantor. Reprinted with permission from Michael Kantor. First published by *In View*, a Whittle Communications publication, 1990.

Keating, Kathleen. From *The Hug Therapy Book* by Kathleen Keating, illustrated by Mimi Noland. Copyright 1983 by Kathleen Keating. Published by The Hazelden Foundation, Minneapolis, Minnesota. Excerpted by permission only. Book is available from your bookseller or directly from The Hazelden Foundation.

Keegan, Paul. "Inhuman Architecture, Bad Food, Boredom, Death by Fun and Games" by Paul Keegan as appeared in *Esquire*, April 1992. Reprinted by permission of the author.

Lawry, John D. "Daughters, Fathers, & Dancing" by John D. Lawry from *The New York Times*, November 19, 1989. Reprinted by permission of the author.

Lawry, John D. From "May You Never Stop Dancing" by John D. Lawry. Saint Mary's Press: Winona, MN 1998. Used with permission of the publisher. All rights reserved.

Lee, Rebecca. "The Banks of the Vistula" by Rebecca Lee as appeared in *The Atlantic Monthly*, September 1997. Reprinted by permission of the author.

Malcolm X. From *The Autobiography of Malcolm X* by Malcolm X, with the assistance of Alex Haley. Copyright © 1964 by Alex Haley and Malcolm X. Copyright © 1965 by Alex Haley and Betty Shabazz. Reprinted by permission of Random House, Inc.

McCarroll, Tolbert. From *Exploring the Inner World* by Tolbert McCarroll. Copyright © 1974 by Tolbert McCarroll. Reprinted by permission of Julian Press, a division of Crown Publishers, Inc.

Merton, Andrew. "Father Hunger" by Andrew Merton from *New Age Journal*, September/October 1986. Copyright by Andrew Merton. Reprinted by permission.

Miller, Sylva. "Untitled Student Production" by Sylva Miller. Reprinted by permission of author.

Moon, Susan. "Sons and Mothers" by Susan Moon from *Ms.* Magazine, October, 1988. Reprinted by permission.

Oliphant, Robert. "Letter to a B Student" by Robert Oliphant. Copyright 1986 by the Association of American Colleges. Reprinted with permission from *Liberal Education* 72, 2 (Summer 1986), 183–187.

Oliver, Mary. "The Journey" from *Dream Work* by Mary Oliver. Copyright © 1986 by Mary Oliver. Used with permission of Grove/Atlantic, Inc.

Olsen, Tillie. "I Stand Here Ironing" by Tillie Olsen. Copyright © 1956, 1957, 1960, 1961 by Tillie Olsen. From *Tell Me A Riddle* by Tillie Olsen. Introduction by John Leonard. Used by permission of Delacorte Press/Seymour Lawrence, a division of Bantam Doubleday Dell Publishing Group, Inc.

Rheingold, Howard. Excerpted from *The Virtual Community* by Howard Rheingold. Copyright © 1993 by Howard Rheingold. Reprinted by permission of Addison Wesley Longman.

Rodriguez, Richard. From *Hunger of Memory* by Richard Rodriguez. Reprinted by permission of David R. Godine Publisher, Inc. Copyright © 1982 by Richard Rodriguez.

Romano, Rosalee. "Touching Lives" by Rosalee Romano from *About Campus*, 1996. Reprinted by permission of Jossey-Bass Publishers Inc.

Schmier, Louis. "The Power of Caring" by Louis Schmier from *Random Thoughts II: Teaching From the Heart.* © Atwood Publishing, Madison, WI. Reprinted by permission.

Schuster, Donna Farhi. "On Becoming a Better Student" by Donna Farhi Schuster. Reprinted with permission from *Yoga Journal*, September/October 1987. Copyright © 1987 by Yoga Journal. All rights reserved.

Shorris, Earl. "On the Uses of a Liberal Education as a Weapon in the Hands of the Restless Poor," by Earl Shorris. Copyright © 1997 by *Harper's Magazine*. All rights reserved. Reproduced from the September issue by special permission.

Sifton, Sam. "John of Arc" by Sam Sifton from *In View*, September/October 1990. Reprinted with permission from *In View*. Copyright 1991 Whittle Communications L.P.

Watters, Ethan. From "Claude Steele Has Scores to Settle" by Ethan Watters, *The New York Times*, September 17, 1995. Copyright © 1995 by The New York Times Company. Reprinted by permission.

White, John W. "What Is Meditation?" by John W. White from *New Realities*, September/October 1984. Copyright © 1984 by New Realities, L.P. Reprinted by permission of the publisher.

Wong, Elizabeth. "The Struggle to Be an All-American Girl" by Elizabeth Wong, originally published in *Los Angeles Times*, February 1981. Copyright by Elizabeth Wong. Reprinted by permission of the Writers & Artists Agency.

Zimbardo, Philip G. From *Psychology and Life 10th Edition* by Phillip Zimbardo. Copyright © 1979, 1977, 1975, 1971 by Scott, Foresman and Company. Reprinted by permission of Addison Wesley Educational Publishers, Inc.

Zinsser, William K. "College Pressures" by William Zinsser from *Blair and Ketchum's Country Journal*, Vol. VI, No. 4, April 1979. Copyright © 1979 by William K. Zinsser. Reprinted by permission of the author.

Index of Authors and Titles